27

twenty-seven
second set

TWENTY SEVEN: SECOND SET, First Printing. Published by Image Comics, Inc. Office of publication: 2134 Allston Way, Second Floor, Berkeley, California 94704. Copyright © 2012 CHARLES SOULE. Originally published in single magazine form as TWENTY SEVEN: SECOND SET #1-4. All rights reserved. TWENTY SEVEN™ (including all prominent characters featured herein), its logo and all character likenesses are trademarks of CHARLES SOULE, unless otherwise noted. Image Comics® and its logos are registered trademarks of Image Comics, Inc. Shadowline and its logos are ™ and © 2012 Jim Valentino. No part of this publication may be reproduced or transmitted, in any form or by any means (except for short excerpts for review purposes) without the express written permission of Image Comics, Inc. All names, characters, events and locales in this publication are entirely fictional. Any resemblance to actual persons (living or dead), events or places, without satiric intent, is coincidental.

PRINTED IN KOREA. 978-1-60706-521-0

Fame is a funny thing.

Or so I imagine.

I'm not under any illusions that "Comic Book Famous" is anything approaching "Rock Star Famous", and I'm not even terribly "Comic Book Famous", by any reasonable index; I've only been recognized on the street a couple times and that's only been in my hometown of NYC, which is a much smaller community than you may have been led to believe. When that sort of thing does happen, though, or when I meet a very complimentary fan at a con or a signing, or receive a fan letter via email or Tweet, the same thought always crosses my mind:

That's nothing like I imagined it would be.

I got into writing like most people got into writing, I imagine, or stand-up comedy, or acting, or directing, or painting, or, in Will Garland's case, music; because I was blown away by what I was reading and I thought, "I wanna make people feel like THIS." All writers, to some extent, want to experience the same thrill they get reading others' words through their own.

Except this is, of course, impossible.

By writing something, you have demolished the possibility of ever appreciating it like a reader. No matter how much it may please you in the abstract, when you look at your own work you see not just the words on the page in front of you but all the words that came before it, the words that were discarded in favor of the ones that finally made it to print, the possibilities that were considered and rejected, the scene you were convinced was the S-H-I-T until you realized oh, wait, no, actually it's just shit.

intro

My unavoidable alienation from my work as a reader is, I think, mirrored in alienation from my readers themselves. I am as gracious as I can be when strangers tell me they love my work; even though, when they describe it half the time, I can't believe they read the same thing I actually wrote.

I can't help but think: Who really isn't understanding my work here? Them?

Or me?

As baffling as I find quote-unquote fame at times, that's nothing compared to the confusion of my mother. Like a lot of good parents, she was skeptical of my decision to write for a living (and for nearly a decade, my lack of success gave her ample confirmation for it), but once my name began appearing on the covers of books and comics and, O-M-G, talk about validation, they made a movie out of one of my comics, she stopped treating my vocation as a hobby, but didn't quite know how to treat it instead. She didn't seem to understand why I wasn't a) rich b) mobbed by fans or c) any different than I was before. Mid-sized successes didn't register in the popular worldview of fame; you're either a god or you're crap. There's no room for anything other than deities or phantoms; or, perhaps more accurately, who the hell wants to be anything other than an extreme?

It's the haze between expectation and reality in which mythology exists; and that's the netherworld Charles Soule and Renzo Podesta have created in the excellent volume you hold in your hands. Valerie Hayes, Garland's nemesis, reminds me of my mother, caught up between two extremes; though, our one-hit wonder is cursed (or blessed) to exist in the beautiful and terrible world of 27, of metaphor and longing, where she has the opportunity to enter the myth, manipulate it, and become it.

I envy you who are experiencing this world for the first time.

I guarantee it will be nothing like you imagine it will be.

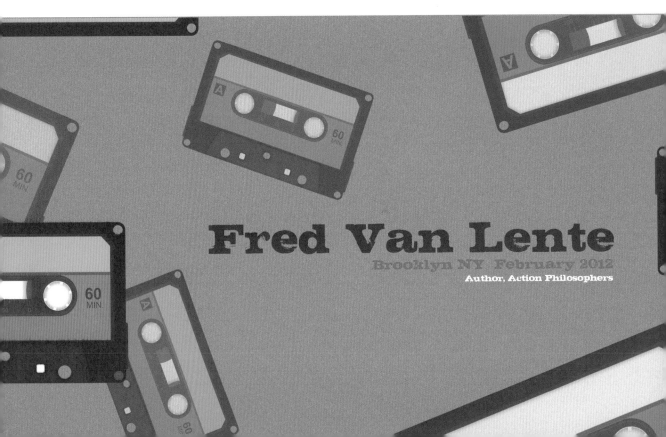

Fred Van Lente

Brooklyn NY February 2012
Author, Action Philosophers

charles soule
WORDS

renzo podesta
ART

w. scott forbes
COVER//SERIES COVERS

LETTERS shawn depasquale

DESIGN tim daniel

EDITS jade dodge

PUBLISHER jim valentino

Robert Kirkman - chief operating officer
Erik Larsen - chief financial officer
Todd McFarlane - president
Marc Silvestri - chief executive officer
Jim Valentino - vice-president

Eric Stephenson - publisher
Todd Martinez - sales & licensing coordinator
Jennifer de Guzman - pr & marketing director
Branwyn Bigglestone - accounts manager
Emily Miller - administrative assistant
Jamie Parreno - marketing assistant
Sarah deLaine - events coordinator
Kevin Yuen - digital rights coordinator
Tyler Shainline - production manager
Drew Gill - art director
Jonathan Chan - senior production artist
Monica Garcia - production artist
Vincent Kukua - production artist
Jana Cook - production artist

image

image comics, inc.//www.imagecomics.com

shadowlineonline.com ShadowlineComics @ShadowlineComic

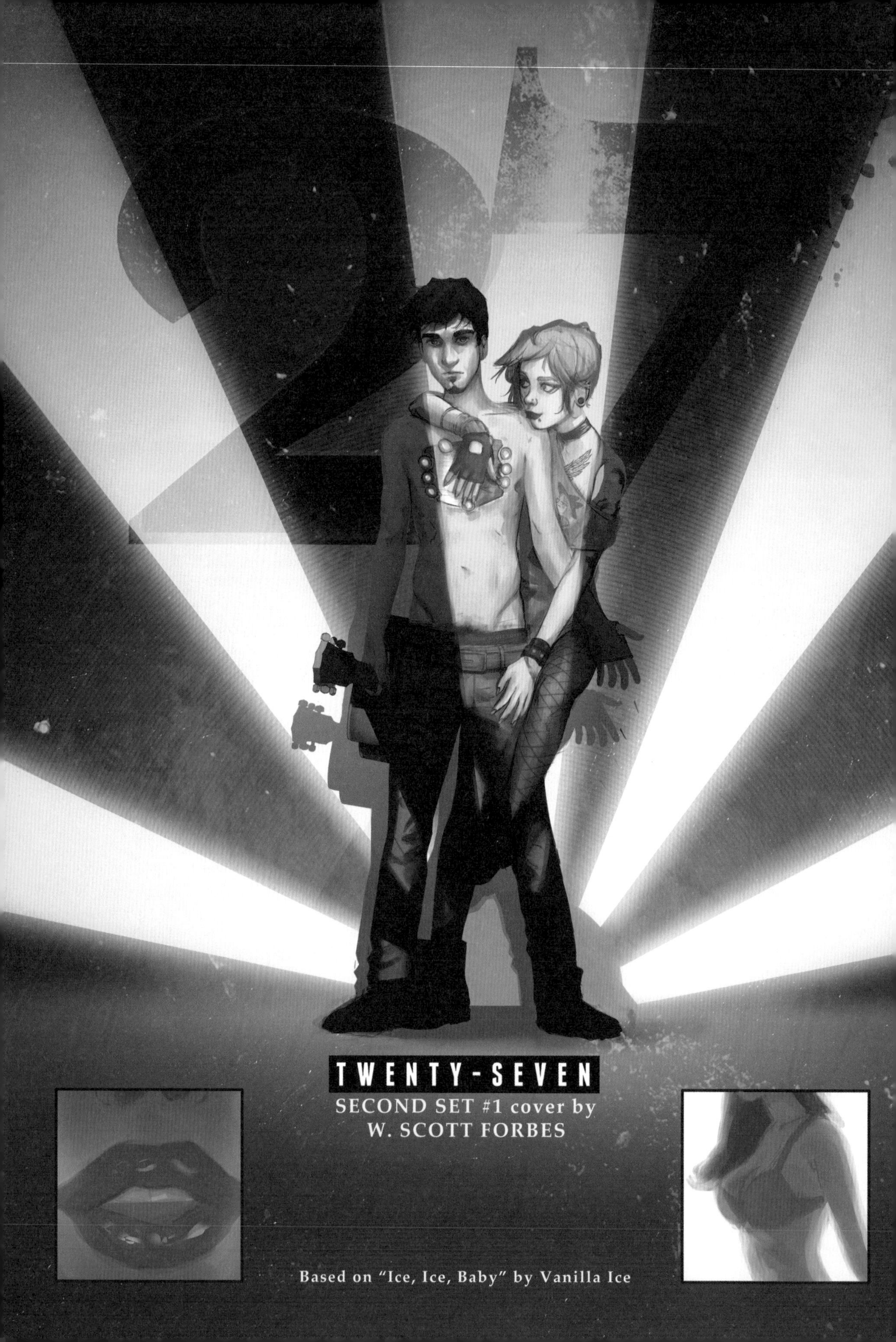

TWENTY-SEVEN

SECOND SET #1 cover by
W. SCOTT FORBES

Based on "Ice, Ice, Baby" by Vanilla Ice

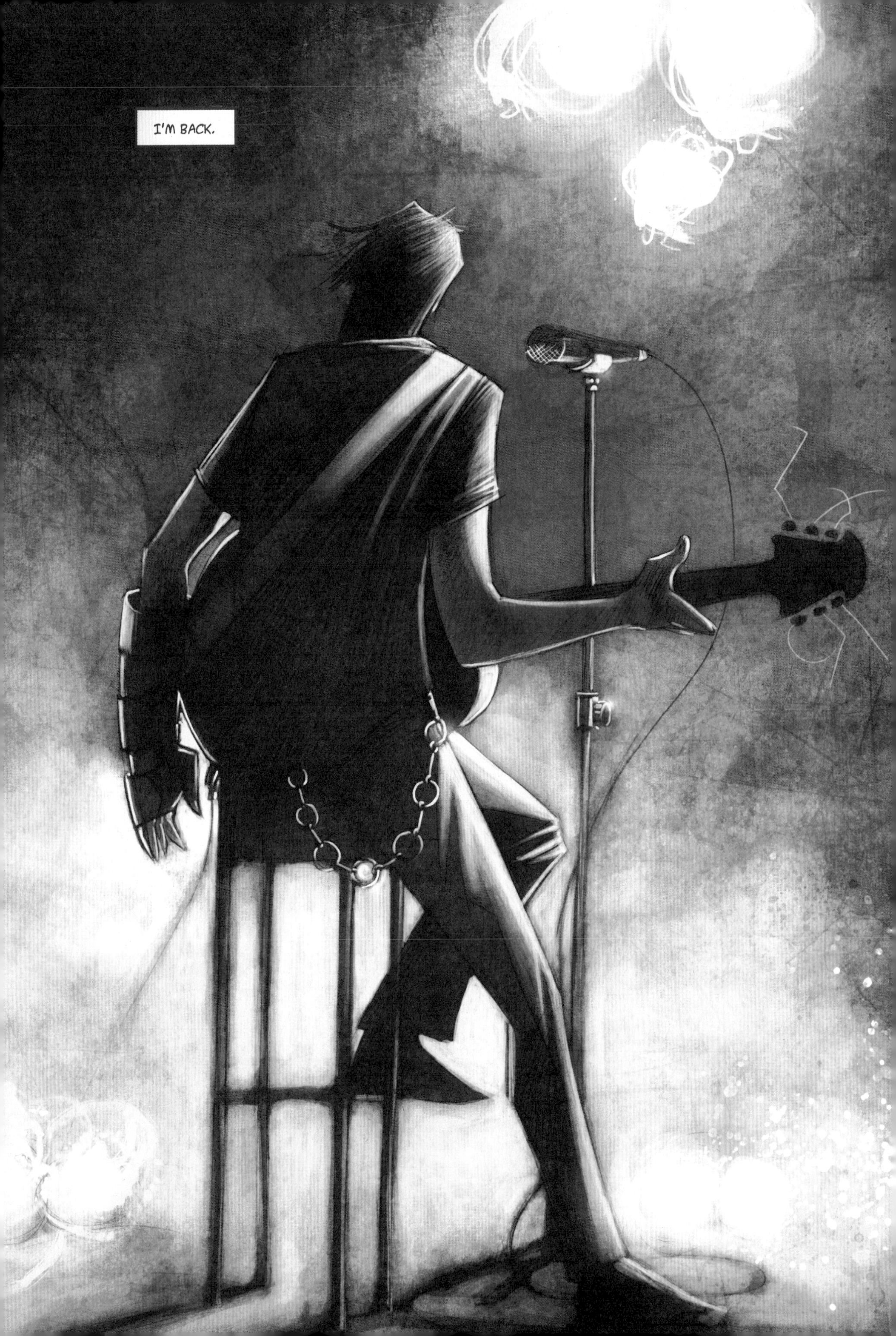
I'M BACK.

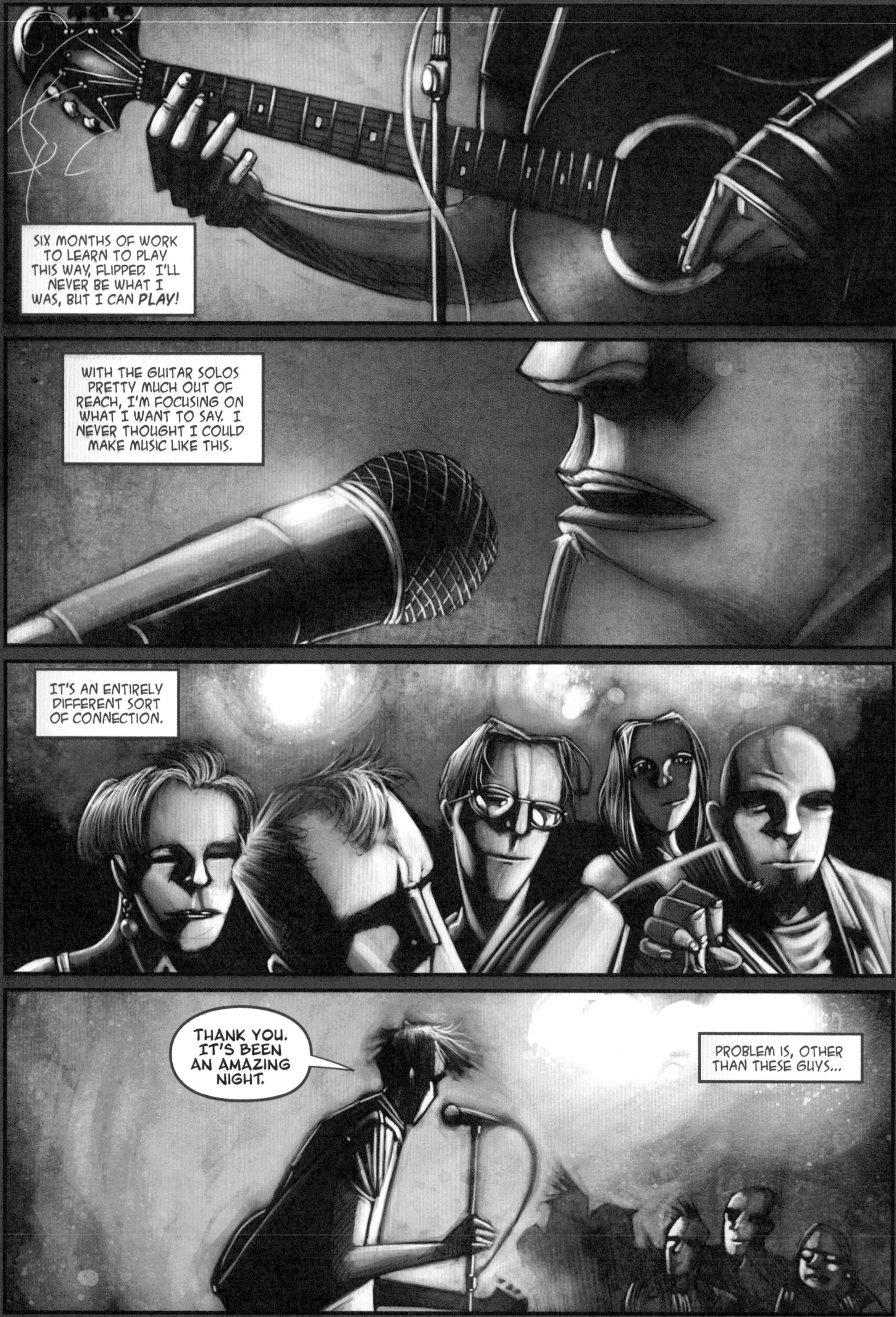
SIX MONTHS OF WORK TO LEARN TO PLAY THIS WAY, FLIPPED. I'LL NEVER BE WHAT I WAS, BUT I CAN PLAY!
WITH THE GUITAR SOLOS PRETTY MUCH OUT OF REACH, I'M FOCUSING ON WHAT I WANT TO SAY. I NEVER THOUGHT I COULD MAKE MUSIC LIKE THIS.
IT'S AN ENTIRELY DIFFERENT SORT OF CONNECTION.
THANK YOU. IT'S BEEN AN AMAZING NIGHT.
PROBLEM IS, OTHER THAN THESE GUYS...

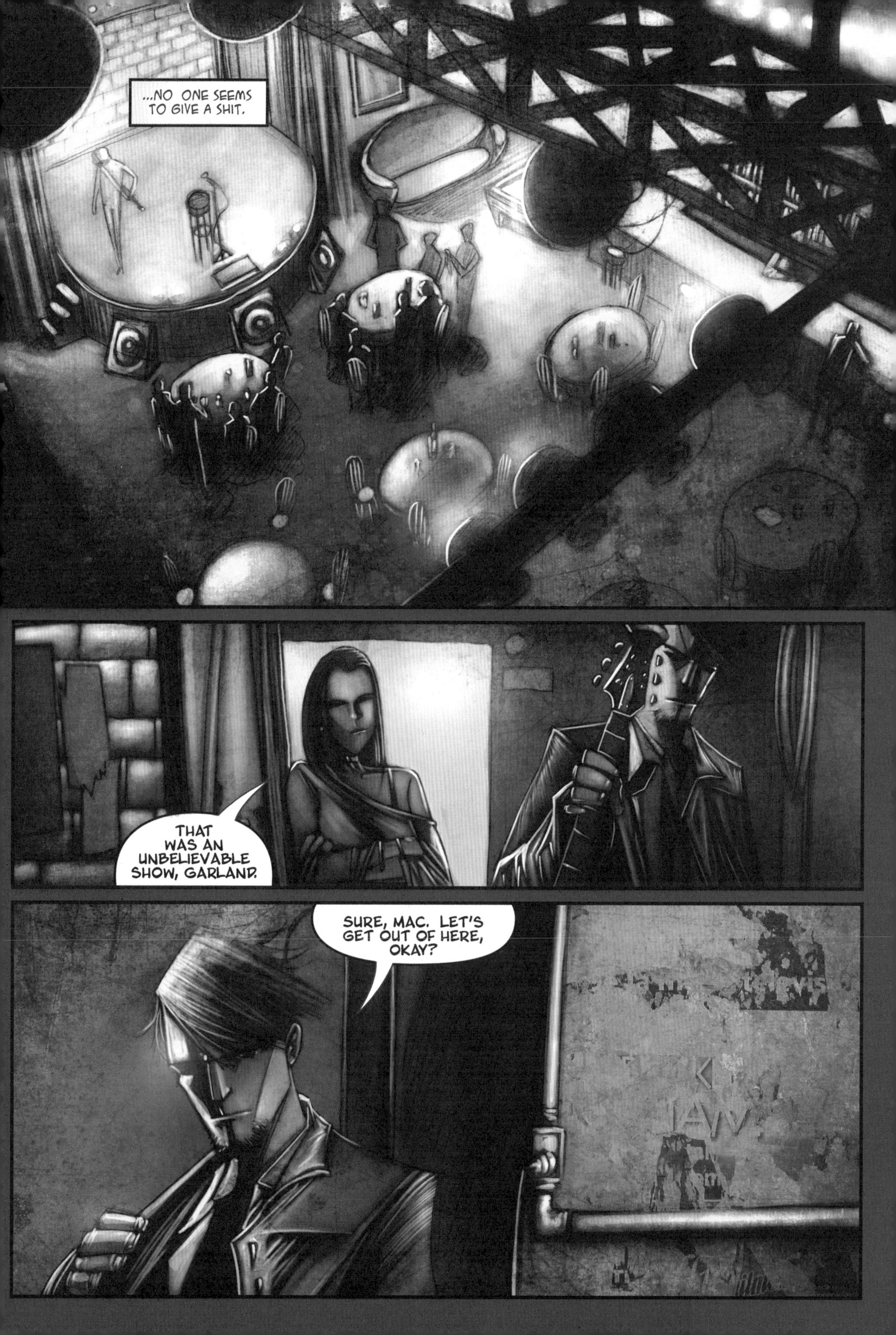
...NO ONE SEEMS TO GIVE A SHIT.
THAT WAS AN UNBELIEVABLE SHOW, GARLAND.
SURE, MAC. LET'S GET OUT OF HERE, OKAY?

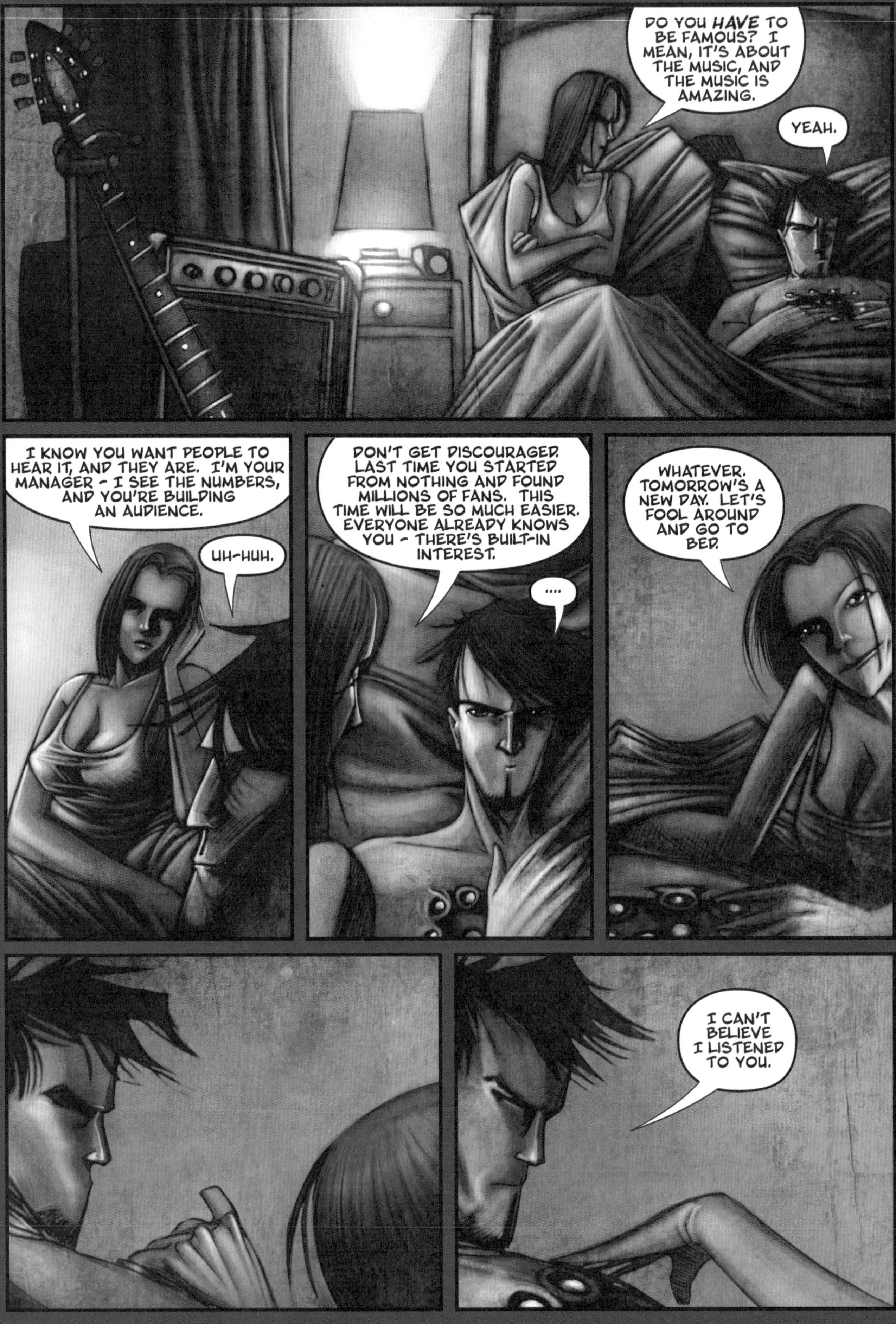
DO YOU HAVE TO BE FAMOUS? I MEAN, IT'S ABOUT THE MUSIC, AND THE MUSIC IS AMAZING.
YEAH.
I KNOW YOU WANT PEOPLE TO HEAR IT, AND THEY ARE. I'M YOUR MANAGER - I SEE THE NUMBERS, AND YOU'RE BUILDING AN AUDIENCE.
UH-HUH.
DON'T GET DISCOURAGED. LAST TIME YOU STARTED FROM NOTHING AND FOUND MILLIONS OF FANS. THIS TIME WILL BE SO MUCH EASIER. EVERYONE ALREADY KNOWS YOU - THERE'S BUILT-IN INTEREST.
....
WHATEVER. TOMORROW'S A NEW DAY. LET'S FOOL AROUND AND GO TO BED.
I CAN'T BELIEVE I LISTENED TO YOU.

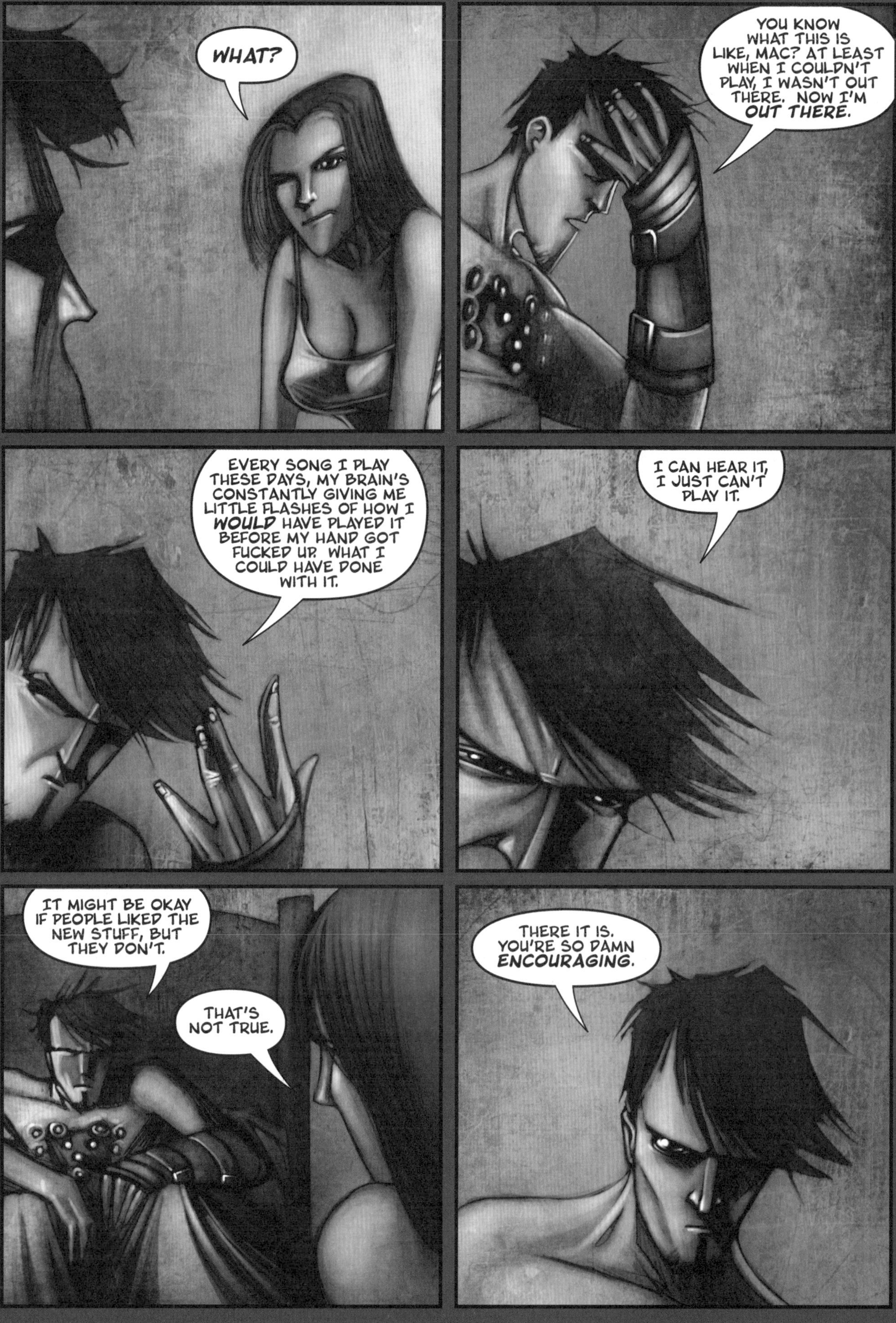
WHAT?
YOU KNOW WHAT THIS IS LIKE, MAC? AT LEAST WHEN I COULDN'T PLAY, I WASN'T OUT THERE. NOW I'M OUT THERE.
EVERY SONG I PLAY THESE DAYS, MY BRAIN'S CONSTANTLY GIVING ME LITTLE FLASHES OF HOW I WOULD HAVE PLAYED IT BEFORE MY HAND GOT FUCKED UP. WHAT I COULD HAVE DONE WITH IT.
I CAN HEAR IT, I JUST CAN'T PLAY IT.
IT MIGHT BE OKAY IF PEOPLE LIKED THE NEW STUFF, BUT THEY DON'T.
THAT'S NOT TRUE.
THERE IT IS. YOU'RE SO DAMN ENCOURAGING.

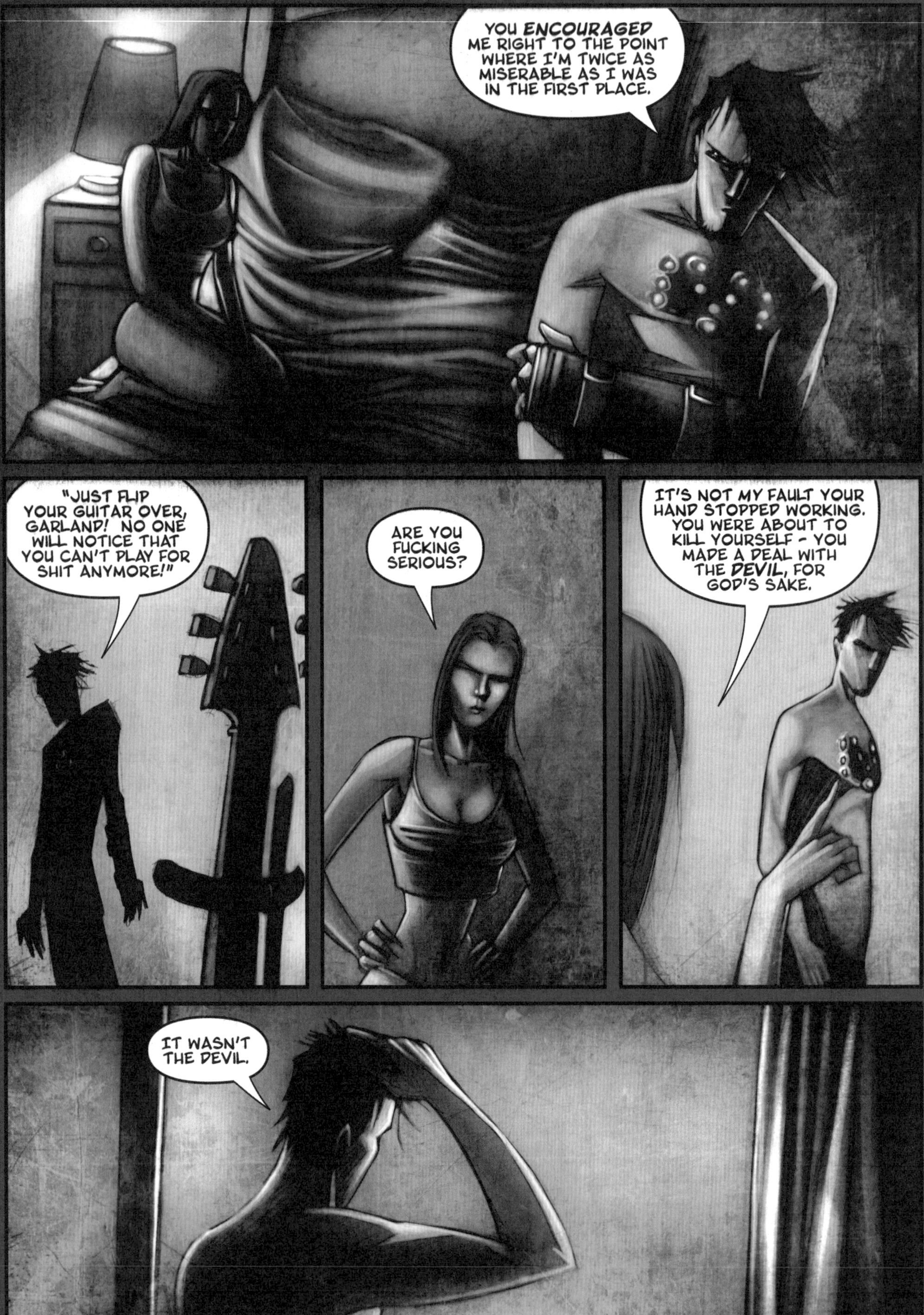
YOU ENCOURAGED ME RIGHT TO THE POINT WHERE I'M TWICE AS MISERABLE AS I WAS IN THE FIRST PLACE.
"JUST FLIP YOUR GUITAR OVER, GARLAND! NO ONE WILL NOTICE THAT YOU CAN'T PLAY FOR SHIT ANYMORE!"
ARE YOU FUCKING SERIOUS?
IT'S NOT MY FAULT YOUR HAND STOPPED WORKING. YOU WERE ABOUT TO KILL YOURSELF - YOU MADE A DEAL WITH THE DEVIL, FOR GOD'S SAKE.
IT WASN'T THE DEVIL.

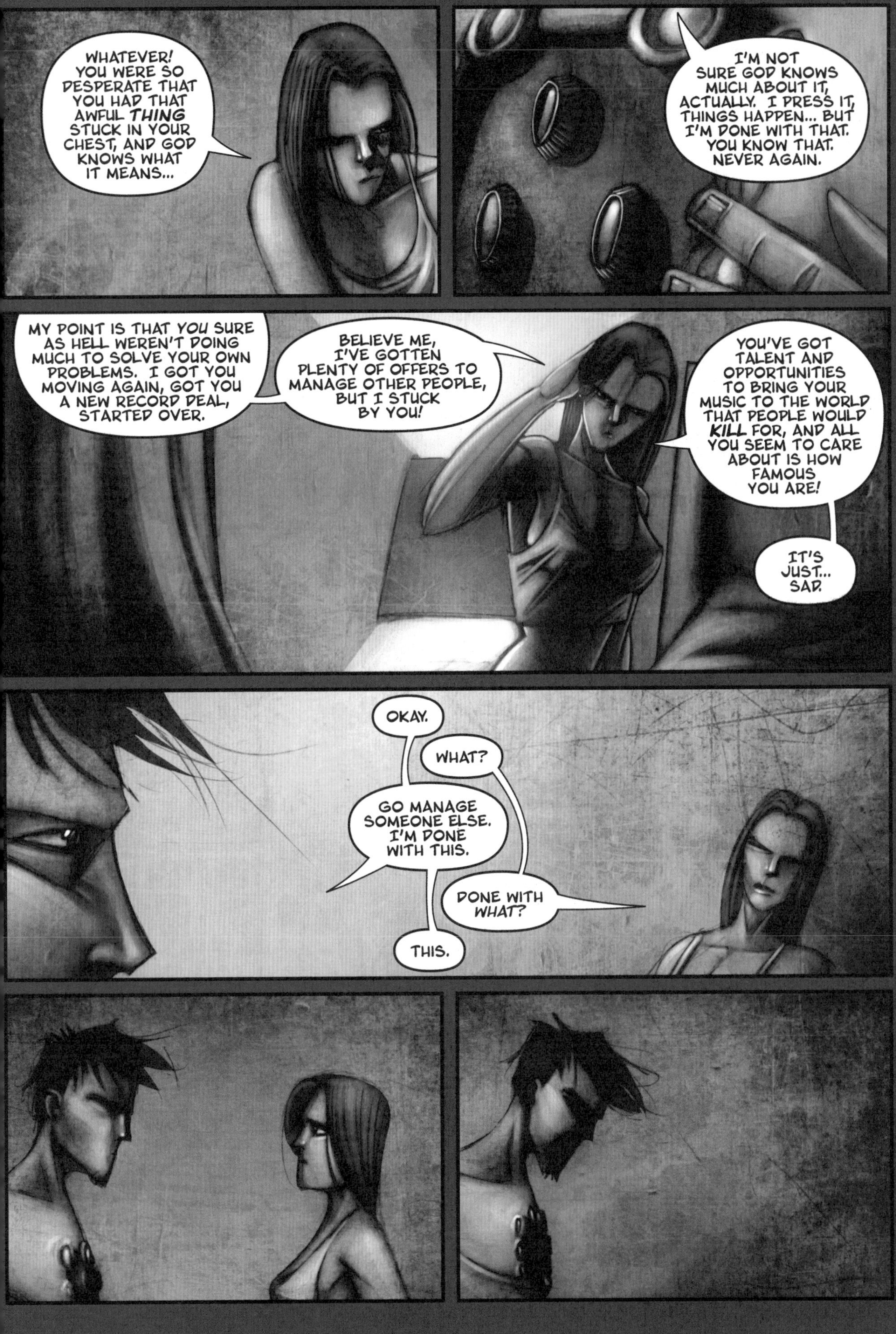
WHATEVER! YOU WERE SO DESPERATE THAT YOU HAD THAT AWFUL THING STUCK IN YOUR CHEST, AND GOD KNOWS WHAT IT MEANS...
I'M NOT SURE GOD KNOWS MUCH ABOUT IT, ACTUALLY. I PRESS IT, THINGS HAPPEN... BUT I'M DONE WITH THAT. YOU KNOW THAT. NEVER AGAIN.
MY POINT IS THAT YOU SURE AS HELL WEREN'T DOING MUCH TO SOLVE YOUR OWN PROBLEMS. I GOT YOU MOVING AGAIN, GOT YOU A NEW RECORD DEAL, STARTED OVER.
BELIEVE ME, I'VE GOTTEN PLENTY OF OFFERS TO MANAGE OTHER PEOPLE, BUT I STUCK BY YOU!
YOU'VE GOT TALENT AND OPPORTUNITIES TO BRING YOUR MUSIC TO THE WORLD THAT PEOPLE WOULD KILL FOR, AND ALL YOU SEEM TO CARE ABOUT IS HOW FAMOUS YOU ARE!
IT'S JUST... SAD.
OKAY.
WHAT?
GO MANAGE SOMEONE ELSE. I'M DONE WITH THIS.
DONE WITH WHAT?
THIS.

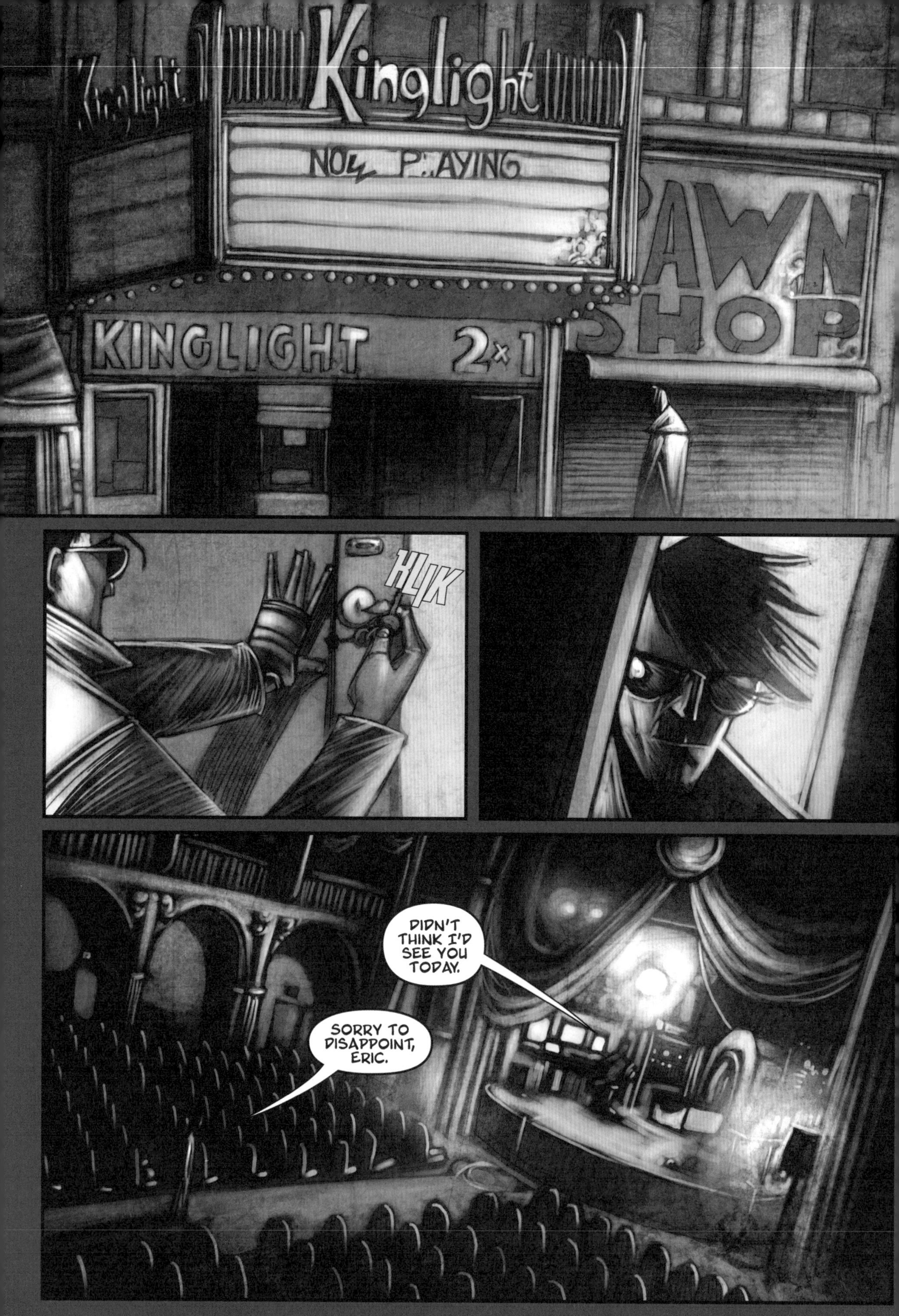
Kinglight
Kinglight
NOW P.AYING
KINGLIGHT 2x1
KLIK
DIDN'T THINK I'D SEE YOU TODAY.
SORRY TO DISAPPOINT, ERIC.

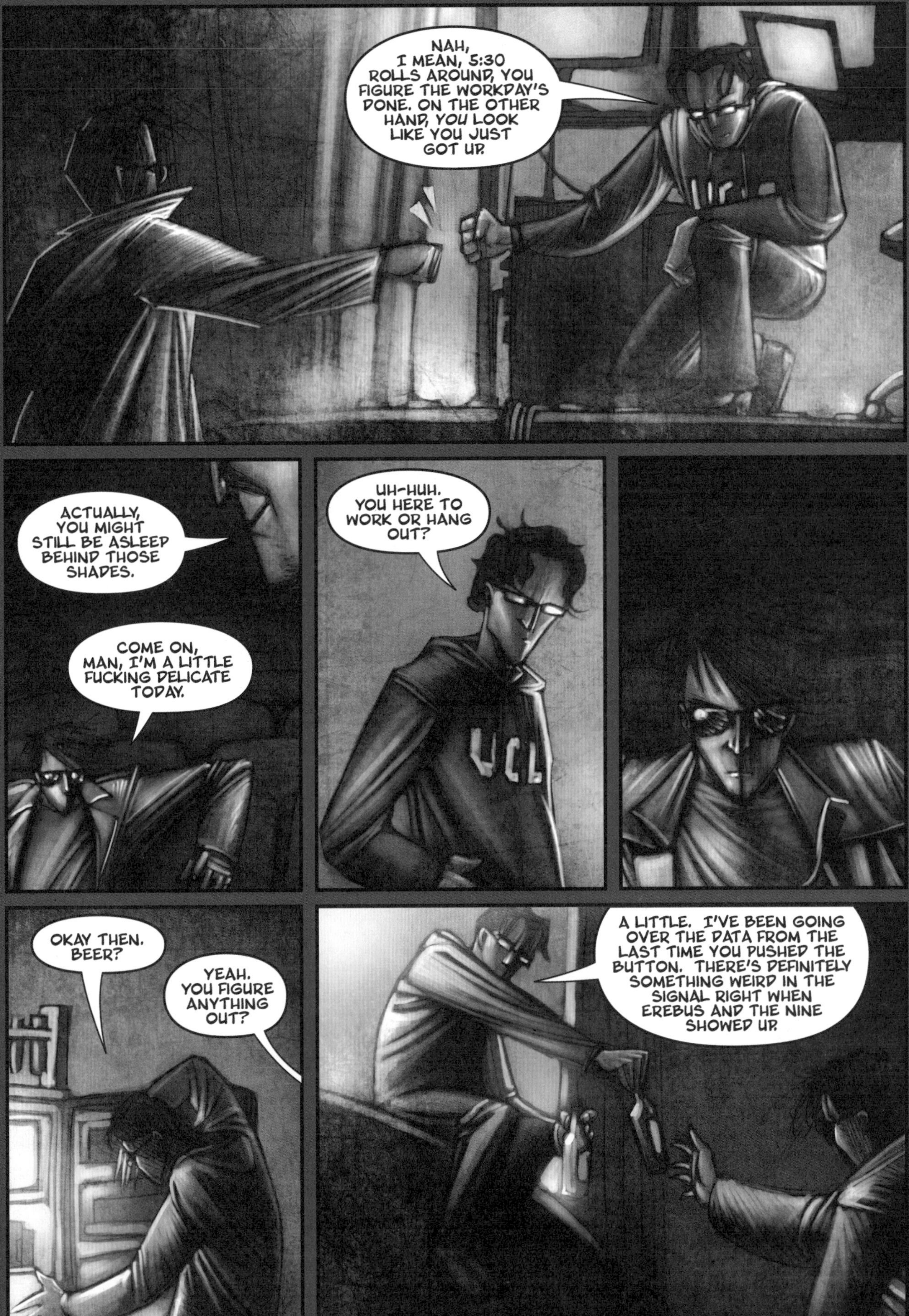
NAH, I MEAN, 5:30 ROLLS AROUND, YOU FIGURE THE WORKDAY'S DONE. ON THE OTHER HAND, *YOU* LOOK LIKE YOU JUST GOT UP.
ACTUALLY, YOU MIGHT STILL BE ASLEEP BEHIND THOSE SHADES.
COME ON, MAN, I'M A LITTLE FUCKING DELICATE TODAY.
UH-HUH. YOU HERE TO WORK OR HANG OUT?
OKAY THEN. BEER?
YEAH. YOU FIGURE ANYTHING OUT?
A LITTLE. I'VE BEEN GOING OVER THE DATA FROM THE LAST TIME YOU PUSHED THE BUTTON. THERE'S DEFINITELY SOMETHING WEIRD IN THE SIGNAL RIGHT WHEN EREBUS AND THE NINE SHOWED UP.

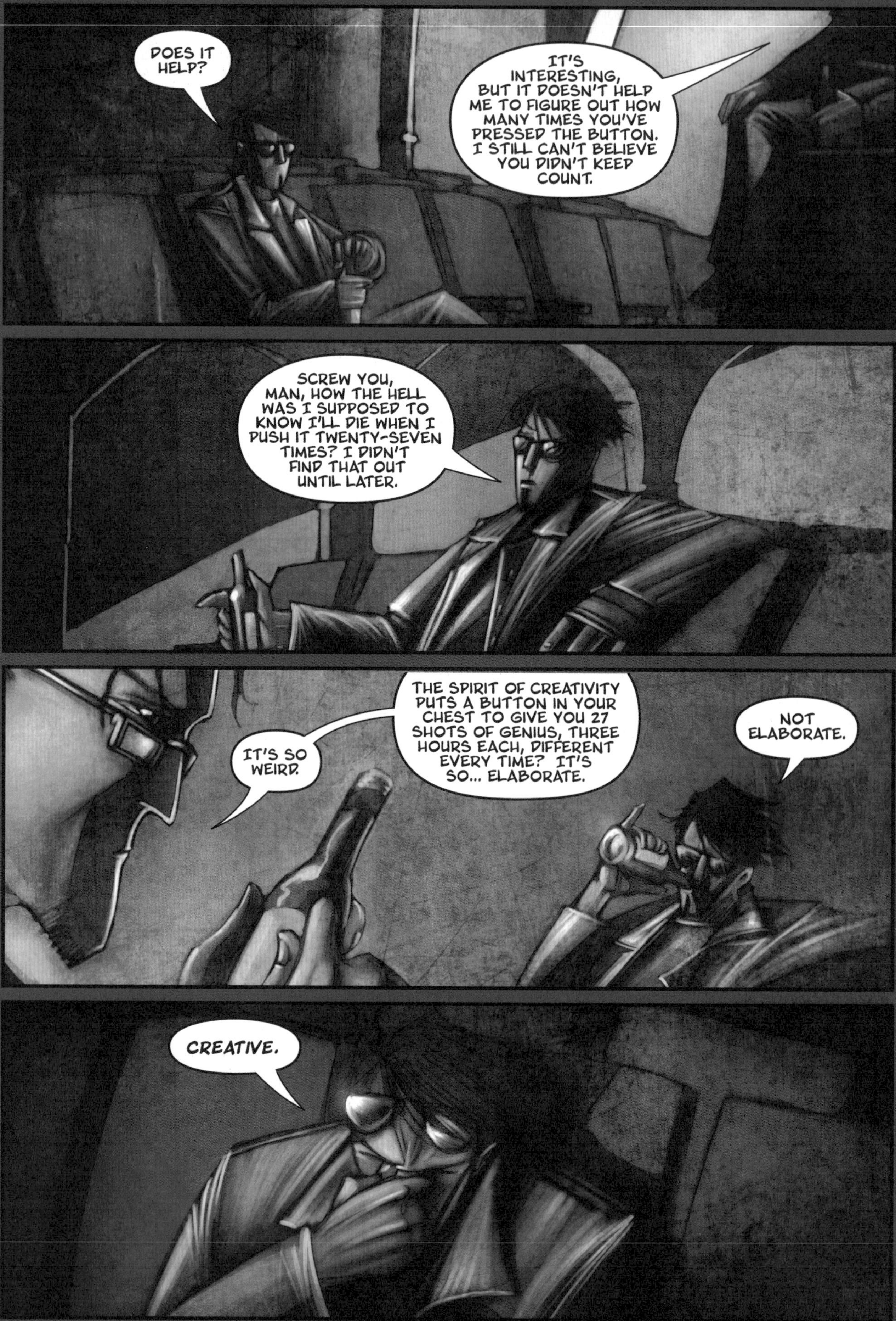
DOES IT HELP?
IT'S INTERESTING, BUT IT DOESN'T HELP ME TO FIGURE OUT HOW MANY TIMES YOU'VE PRESSED THE BUTTON. I STILL CAN'T BELIEVE YOU DIDN'T KEEP COUNT.
SCREW YOU, MAN, HOW THE HELL WAS I SUPPOSED TO KNOW I'LL DIE WHEN I PUSH IT TWENTY-SEVEN TIMES? I DIDN'T FIND THAT OUT UNTIL LATER.
IT'S SO WEIRD.
THE SPIRIT OF CREATIVITY PUTS A BUTTON IN YOUR CHEST TO GIVE YOU 27 SHOTS OF GENIUS, THREE HOURS EACH, DIFFERENT EVERY TIME? IT'S SO... ELABORATE.
NOT ELABORATE.
CREATIVE.

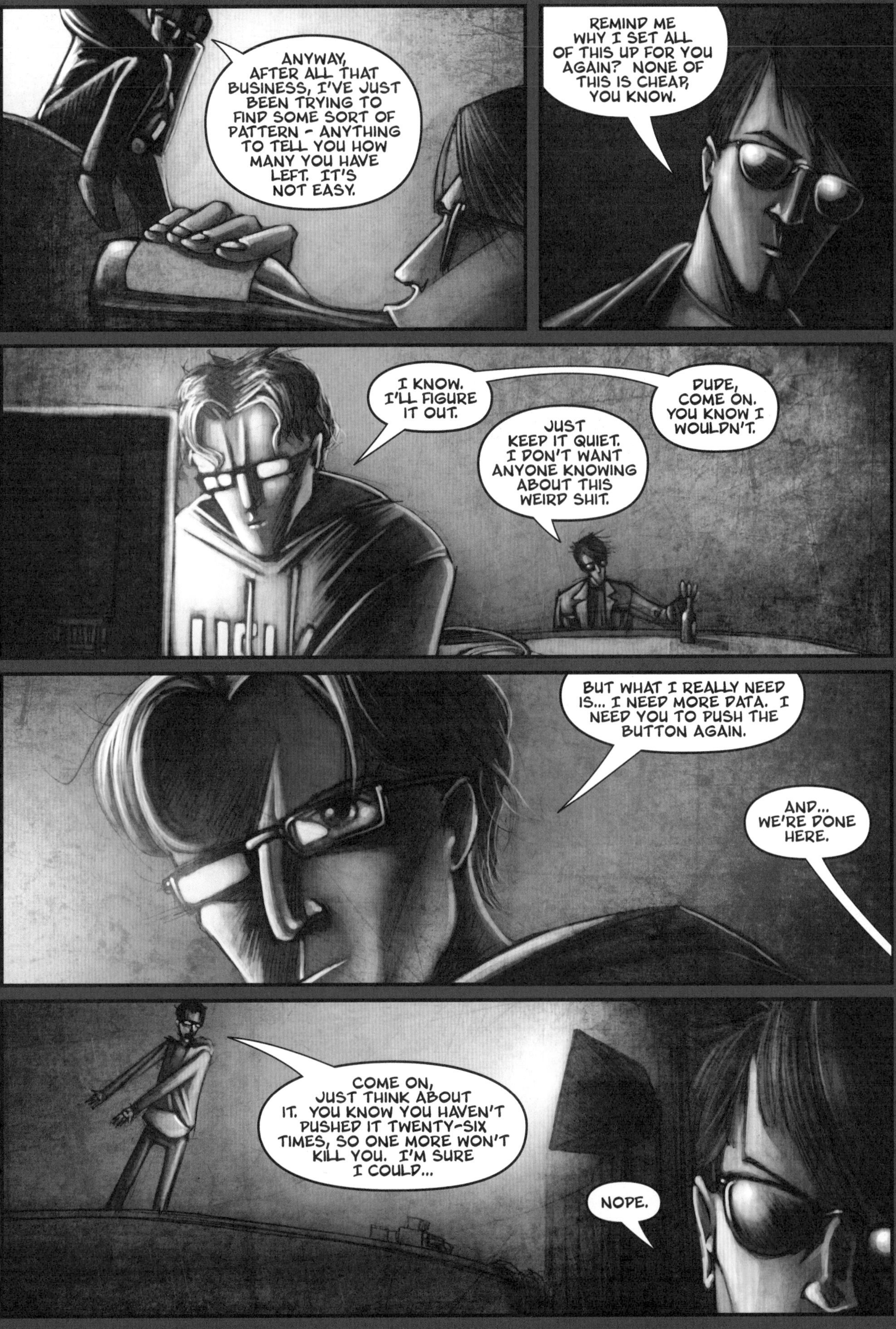
ANYWAY, AFTER ALL THAT BUSINESS, I'VE JUST BEEN TRYING TO FIND SOME SORT OF PATTERN - ANYTHING TO TELL YOU HOW MANY YOU HAVE LEFT. IT'S NOT EASY.
REMIND ME WHY I SET ALL OF THIS UP FOR YOU AGAIN? NONE OF THIS IS CHEAP, YOU KNOW.
I KNOW. I'LL FIGURE IT OUT.
DUDE, COME ON. YOU KNOW I WOULDN'T.
JUST KEEP IT QUIET. I DON'T WANT ANYONE KNOWING ABOUT THIS WEIRD SHIT.
BUT WHAT I REALLY NEED IS... I NEED MORE DATA. I NEED YOU TO PUSH THE BUTTON AGAIN.
AND... WE'RE DONE HERE.
COME ON, JUST THINK ABOUT IT. YOU KNOW YOU HAVEN'T PUSHED IT TWENTY-SIX TIMES, SO ONE MORE WON'T KILL YOU. I'M SURE I COULD...
NOPE.

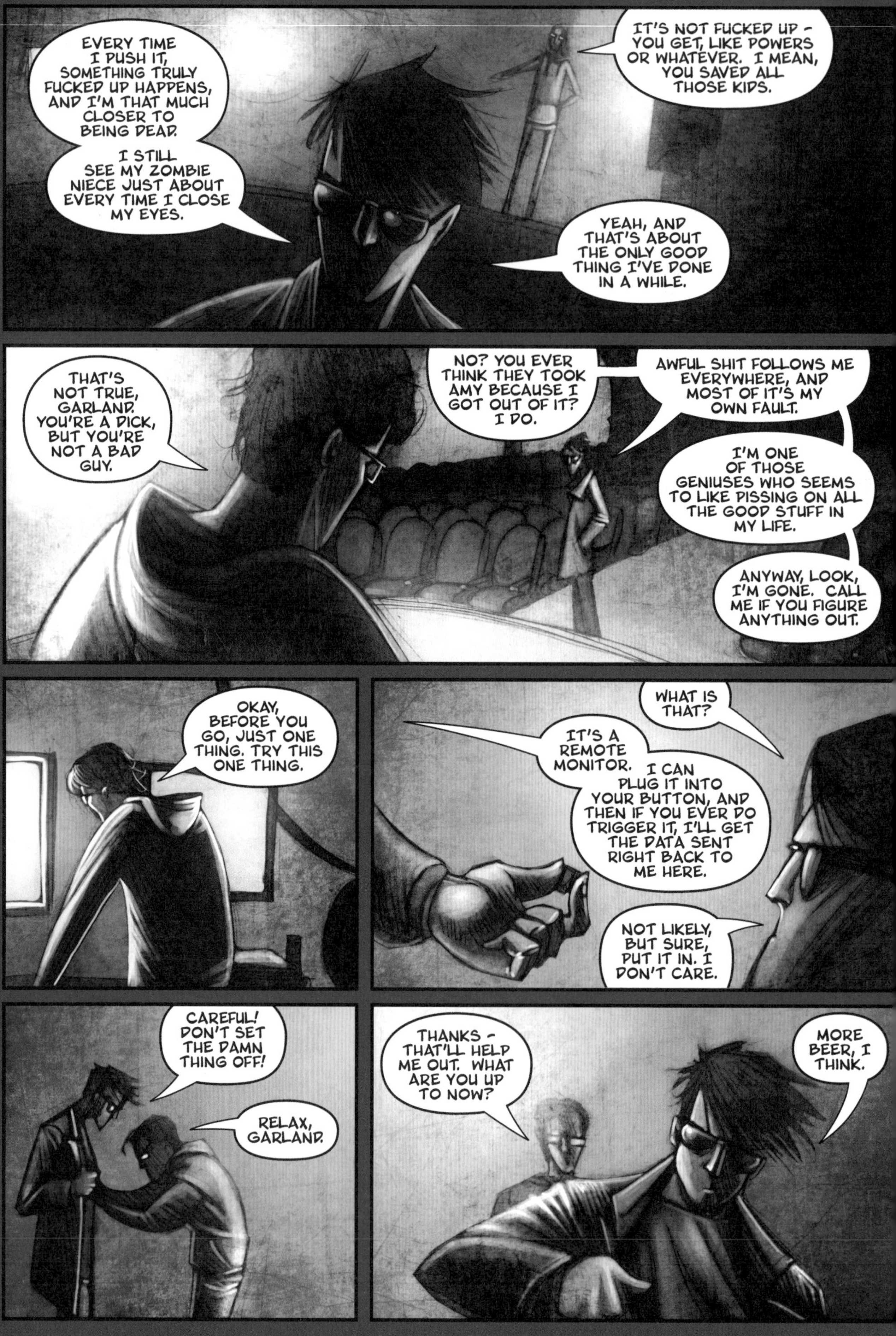
EVERY TIME I PUSH IT, SOMETHING TRULY FUCKED UP HAPPENS, AND I'M THAT MUCH CLOSER TO BEING DEAD.
I STILL SEE MY ZOMBIE NIECE JUST ABOUT EVERY TIME I CLOSE MY EYES.
IT'S NOT FUCKED UP - YOU GET, LIKE POWERS OR WHATEVER. I MEAN, YOU SAVED ALL THOSE KIDS.
YEAH, AND THAT'S ABOUT THE ONLY GOOD THING I'VE DONE IN A WHILE.
THAT'S NOT TRUE, GARLAND. YOU'RE A DICK, BUT YOU'RE NOT A BAD GUY.
NO? YOU EVER THINK THEY TOOK AMY BECAUSE I GOT OUT OF IT? I DO.
AWFUL SHIT FOLLOWS ME EVERYWHERE, AND MOST OF IT'S MY OWN FAULT.
I'M ONE OF THOSE GENIUSES WHO SEEMS TO LIKE PISSING ON ALL THE GOOD STUFF IN MY LIFE.
ANYWAY, LOOK, I'M GONE. CALL ME IF YOU FIGURE ANYTHING OUT.
OKAY, BEFORE YOU GO, JUST ONE THING. TRY THIS ONE THING.
WHAT IS THAT?
IT'S A REMOTE MONITOR.
I CAN PLUG IT INTO YOUR BUTTON, AND THEN IF YOU EVER DO TRIGGER IT, I'LL GET THE DATA SENT RIGHT BACK TO ME HERE.
NOT LIKELY, BUT SURE, PUT IT IN. I DON'T CARE.
CAREFUL! DON'T SET THE DAMN THING OFF!
RELAX, GARLAND.
THANKS - THAT'LL HELP ME OUT. WHAT ARE YOU UP TO NOW?
MORE BEER, I THINK.

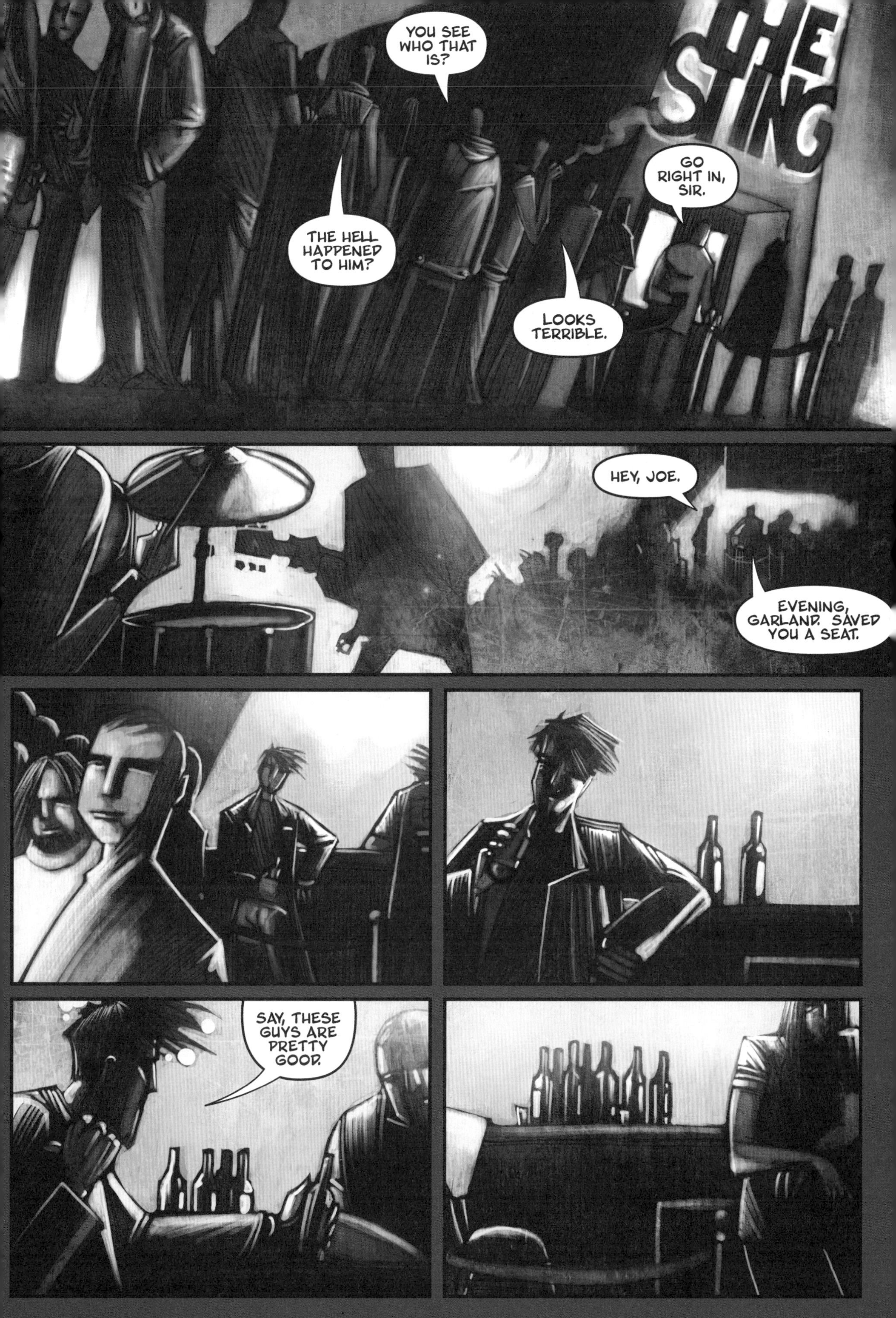
THE SWING
YOU SEE WHO THAT IS?
THE HELL HAPPENED TO HIM?
GO RIGHT IN, SIR.
LOOKS TERRIBLE.
HEY, JOE.
EVENING, GARLAND. SAVED YOU A SEAT.
SAY, THESE GUYS ARE PRETTY GOOD.

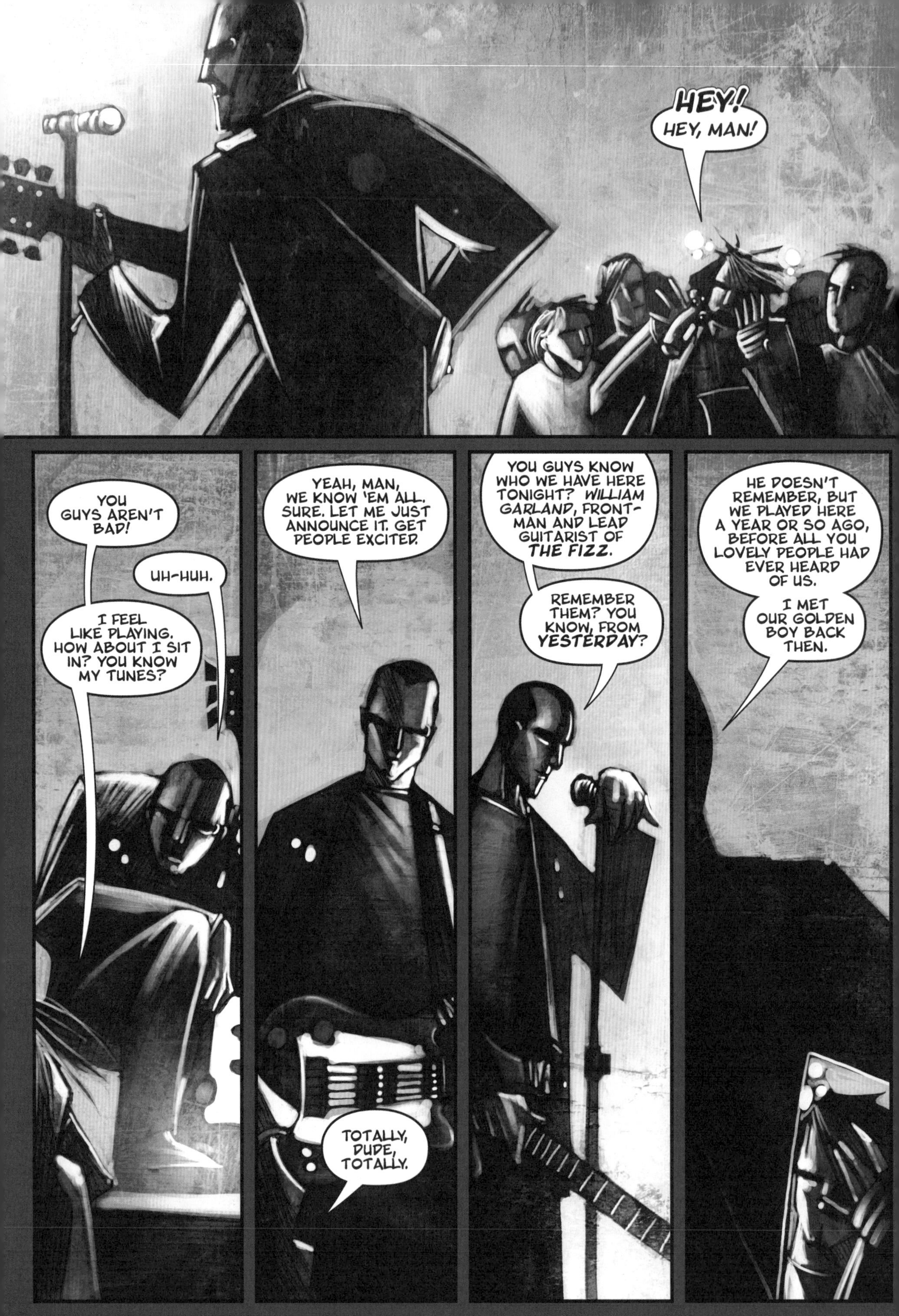
HEY! HEY, MAN!
YOU GUYS AREN'T BAD!
UH-HUH.
I FEEL LIKE PLAYING. HOW ABOUT I SIT IN? YOU KNOW MY TUNES?
YEAH, MAN, WE KNOW 'EM ALL. SURE. LET ME JUST ANNOUNCE IT. GET PEOPLE EXCITED.
TOTALLY, DUDE, TOTALLY.
YOU GUYS KNOW WHO WE HAVE HERE TONIGHT? WILLIAM GARLAND, FRONT-MAN AND LEAD GUITARIST OF THE FIZZ.
REMEMBER THEM? YOU KNOW, FROM YESTERDAY?
HE DOESN'T REMEMBER, BUT WE PLAYED HERE A YEAR OR SO AGO, BEFORE ALL YOU LOVELY PEOPLE HAD EVER HEARD OF US.
I MET OUR GOLDEN BOY BACK THEN.

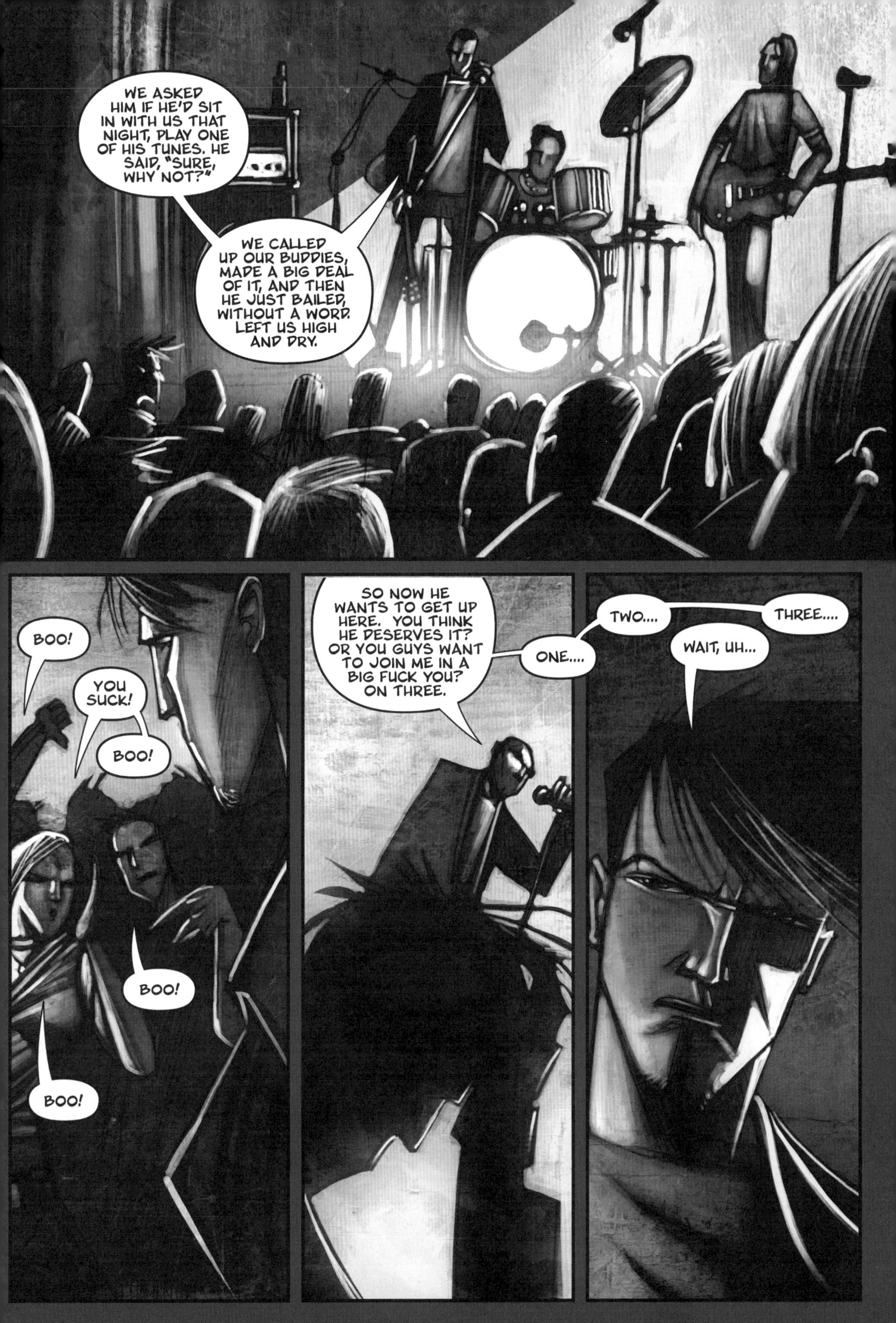
WE ASKED HIM IF HE'D SIT IN WITH US THAT NIGHT, PLAY ONE OF HIS TUNES. HE SAID, "SURE, WHY NOT?"
WE CALLED UP OUR BUDDIES, MADE A BIG DEAL OF IT, AND THEN HE JUST BAILED, WITHOUT A WORD. LEFT US HIGH AND DRY.
BOO!
YOU SUCK!
BOO!
BOO!
BOO!
SO NOW HE WANTS TO GET UP HERE. YOU THINK HE DESERVES IT? OR YOU GUYS WANT TO JOIN ME IN A BIG FUCK YOU? ON THREE.
ONE....
TWO....
THREE....
WAIT, UH...

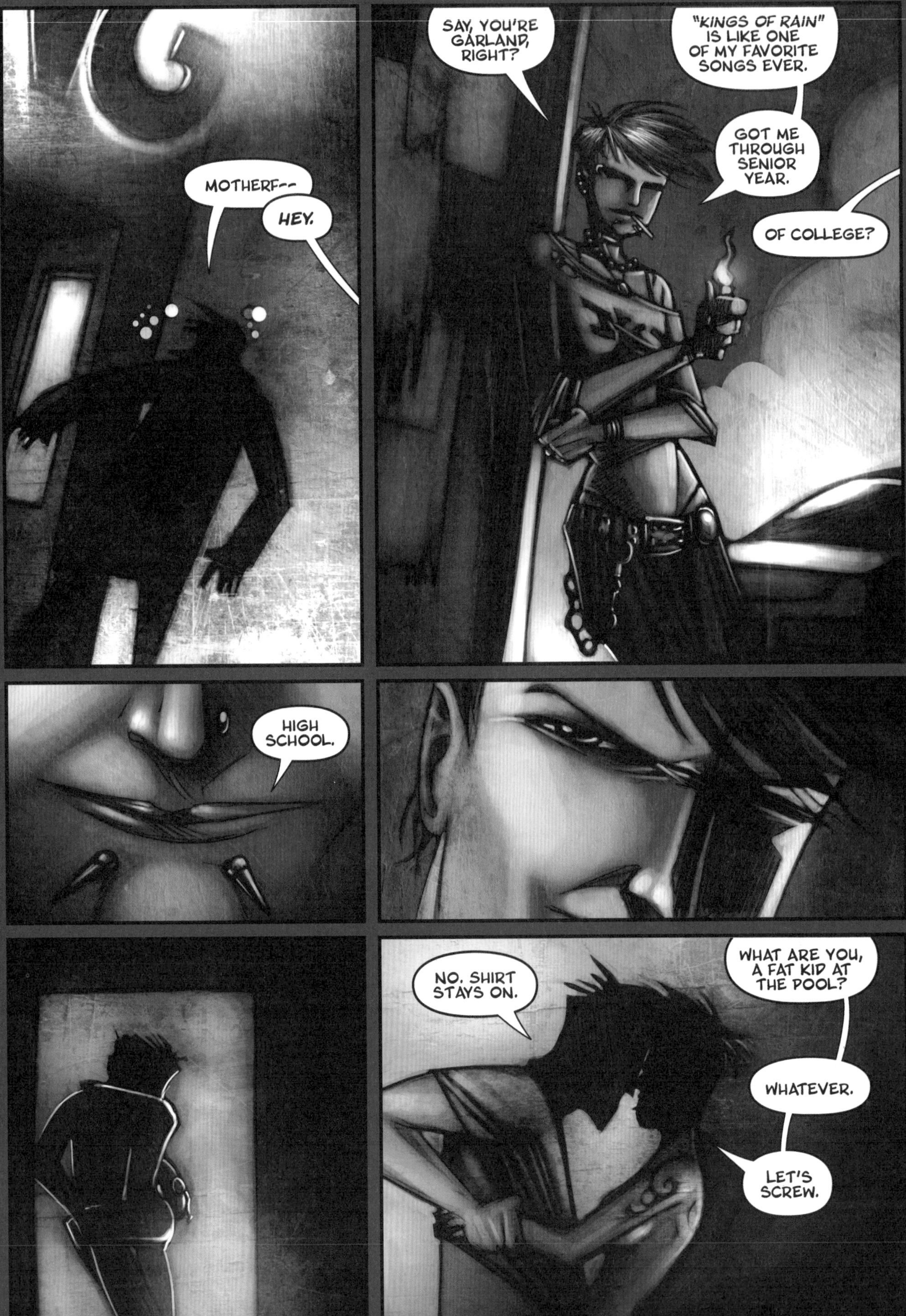
MOTHERF--
HEY.
SAY, YOU'RE GARLAND, RIGHT?
"KINGS OF RAIN" IS LIKE ONE OF MY FAVORITE SONGS EVER.
GOT ME THROUGH SENIOR YEAR.
OF COLLEGE?
HIGH SCHOOL.
NO. SHIRT STAYS ON.
WHAT ARE YOU, A FAT KID AT THE POOL?
WHATEVER.
LET'S SCREW.

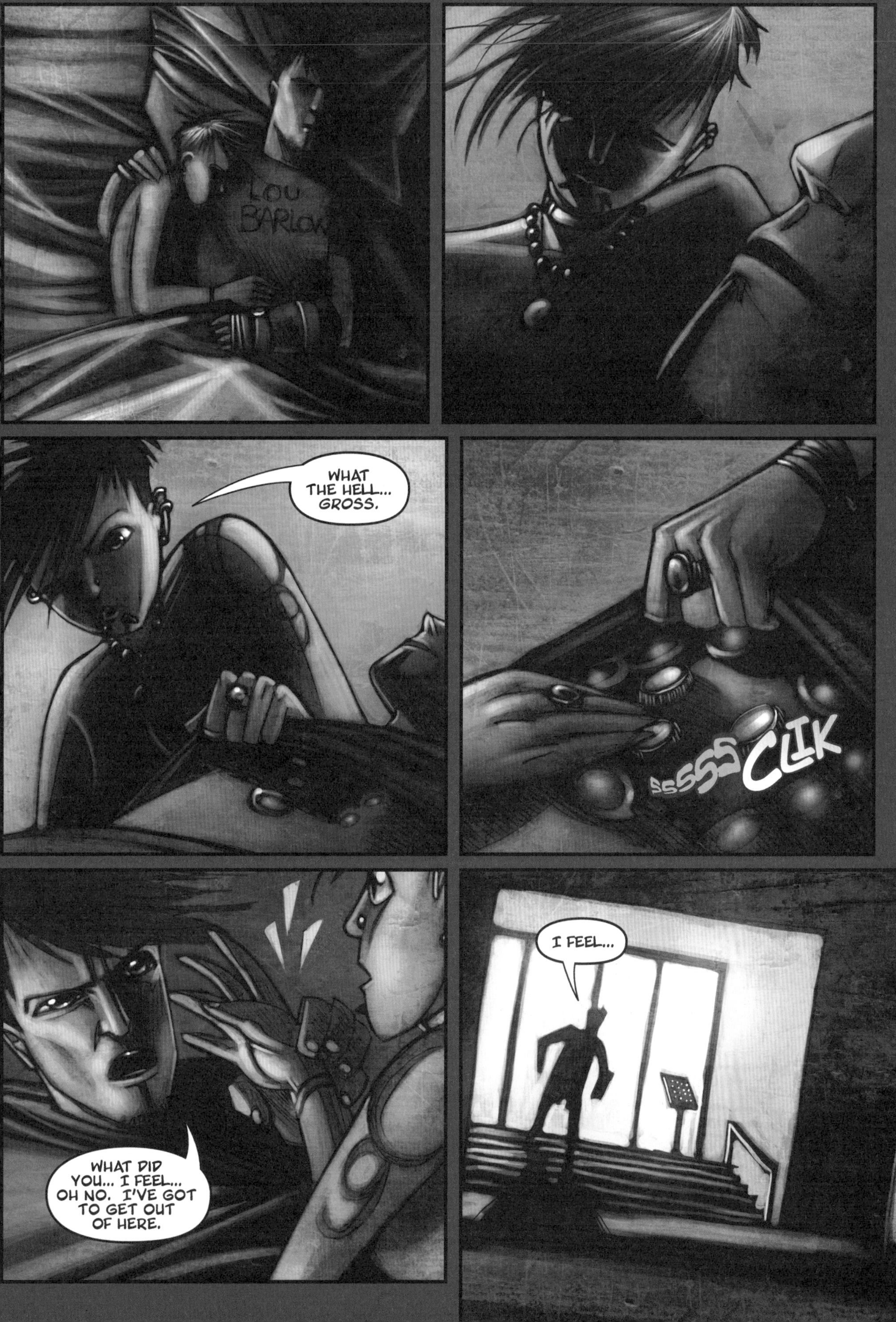
LOU BARLOW
WHAT THE HELL... GROSS.
SSSSS CLIK
WHAT DID YOU... I FEEL... OH NO. I'VE GOT TO GET OUT OF HERE.
I FEEL...

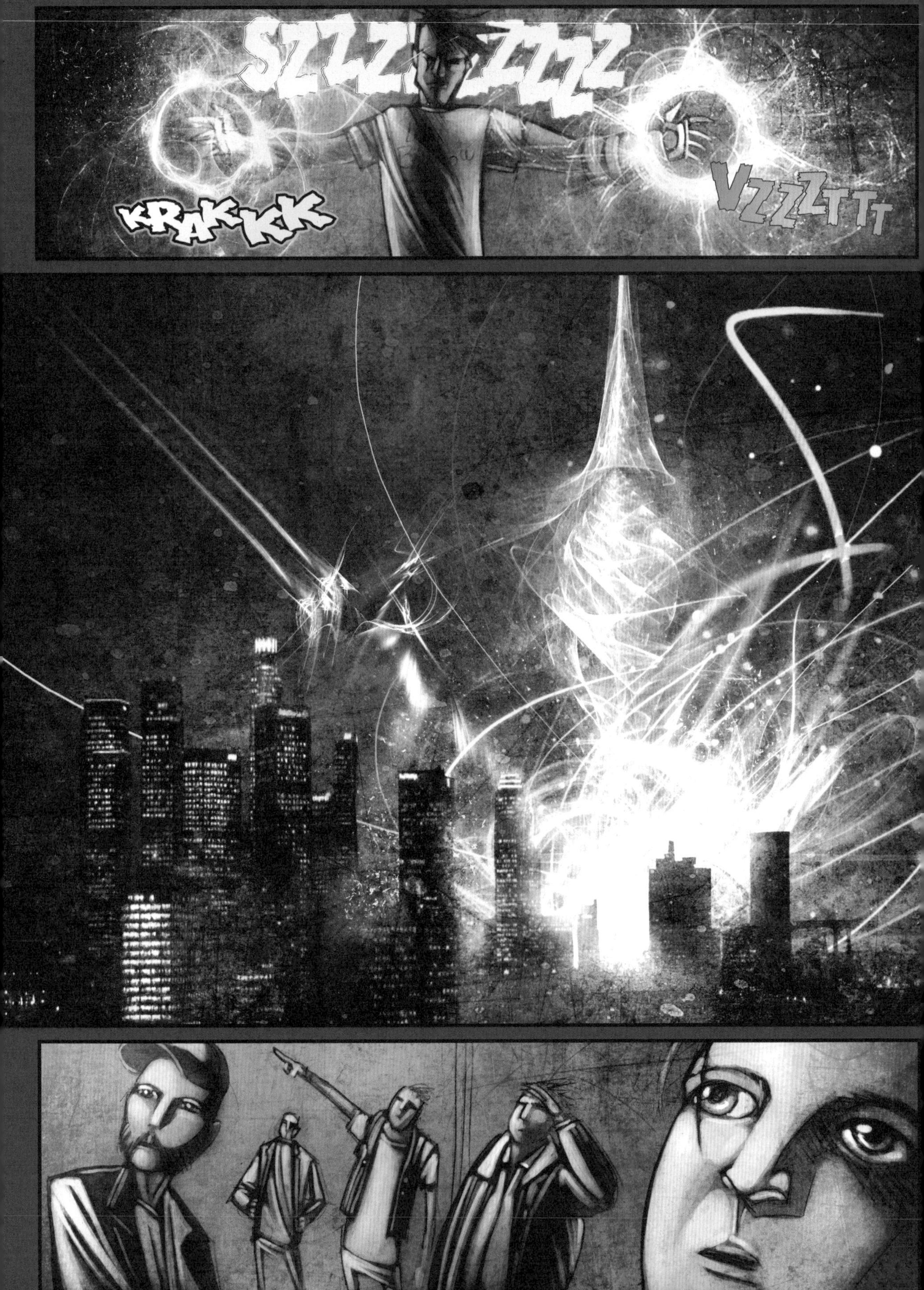
SZZZZZZZ
KRAKKK
VZZZTTT

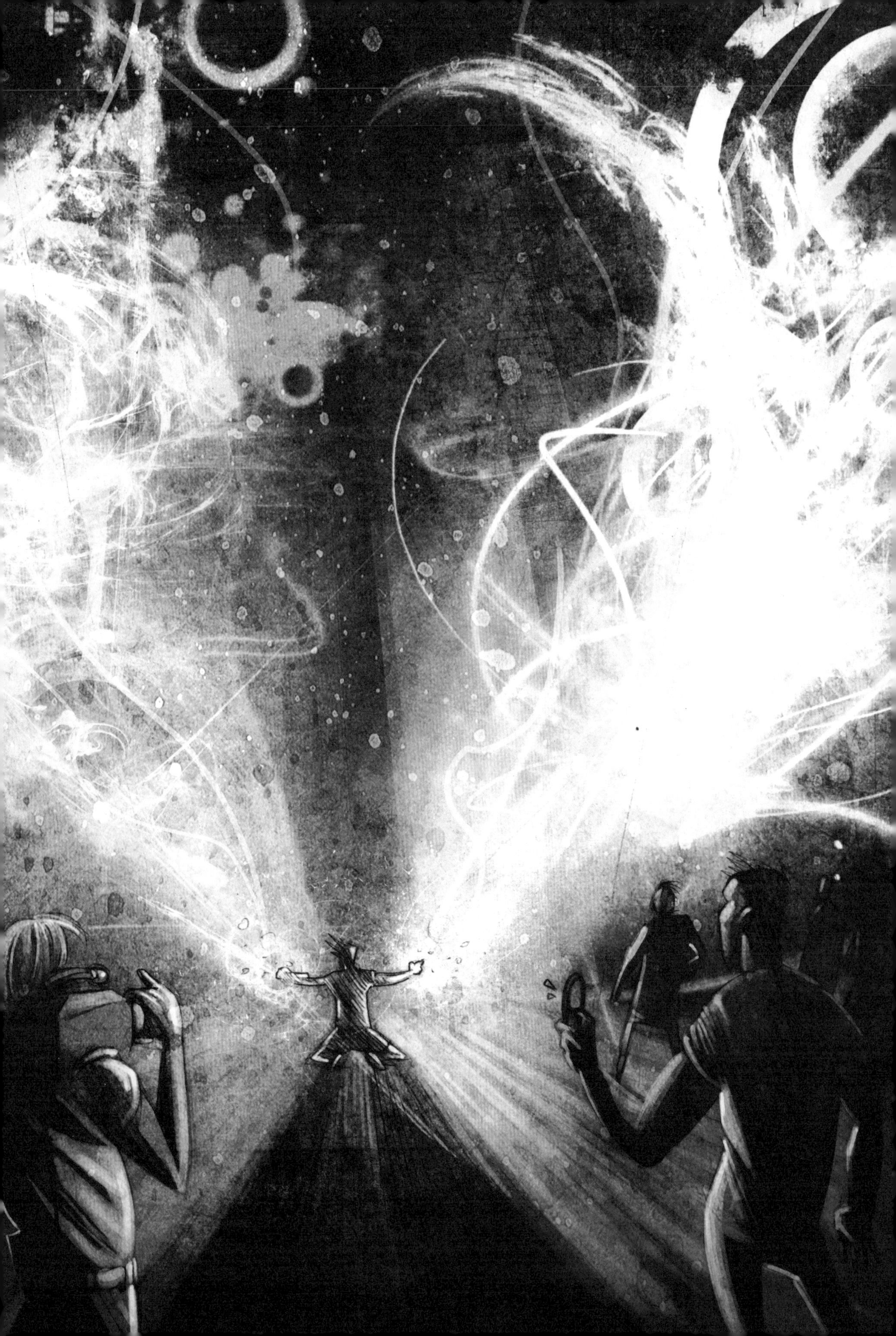

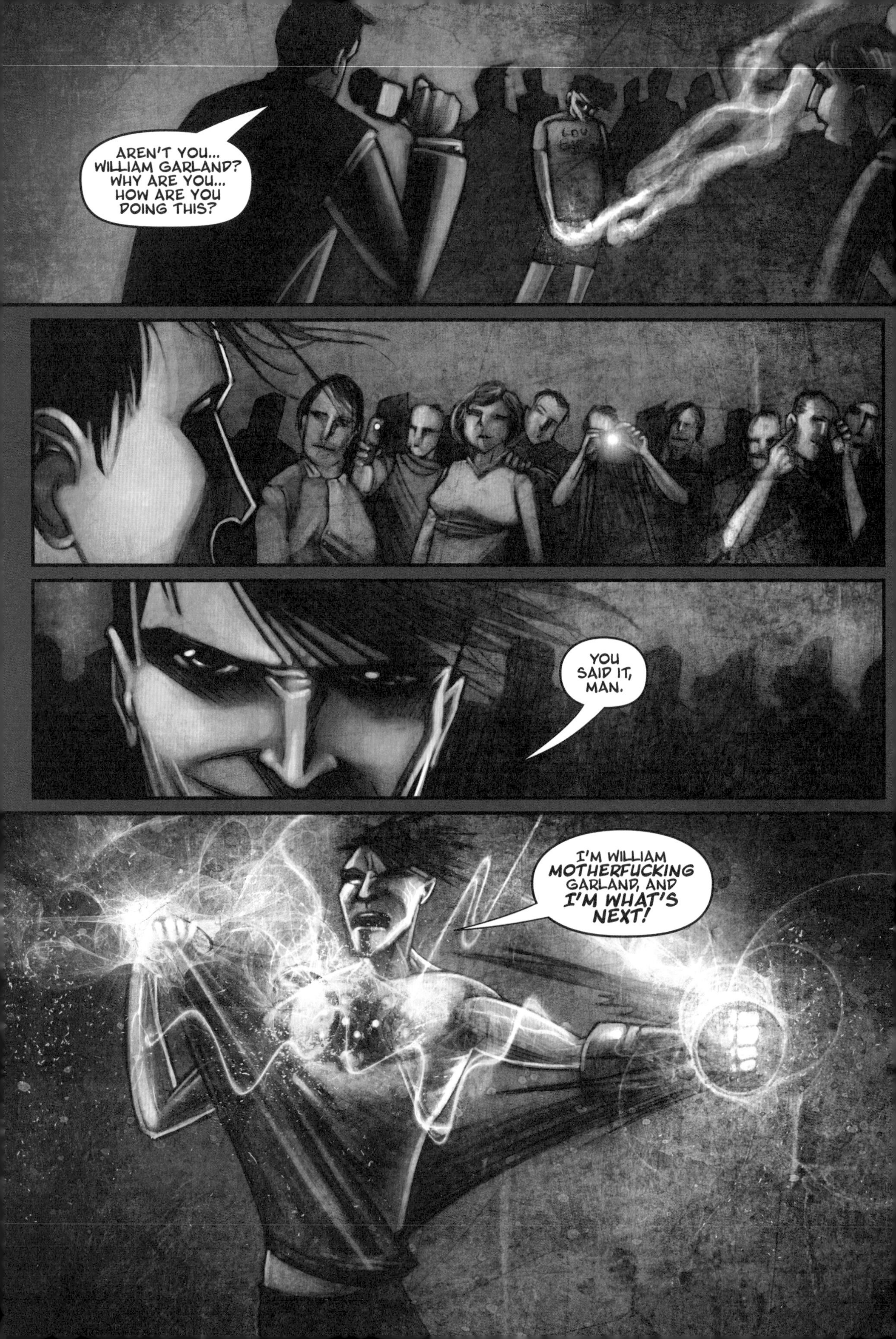
AREN'T YOU... WILLIAM GARLAND? WHY ARE YOU... HOW ARE YOU DOING THIS?
YOU SAID IT, MAN.
I'M WILLIAM MOTHERFUCKING GARLAND, AND I'M WHAT'S NEXT!

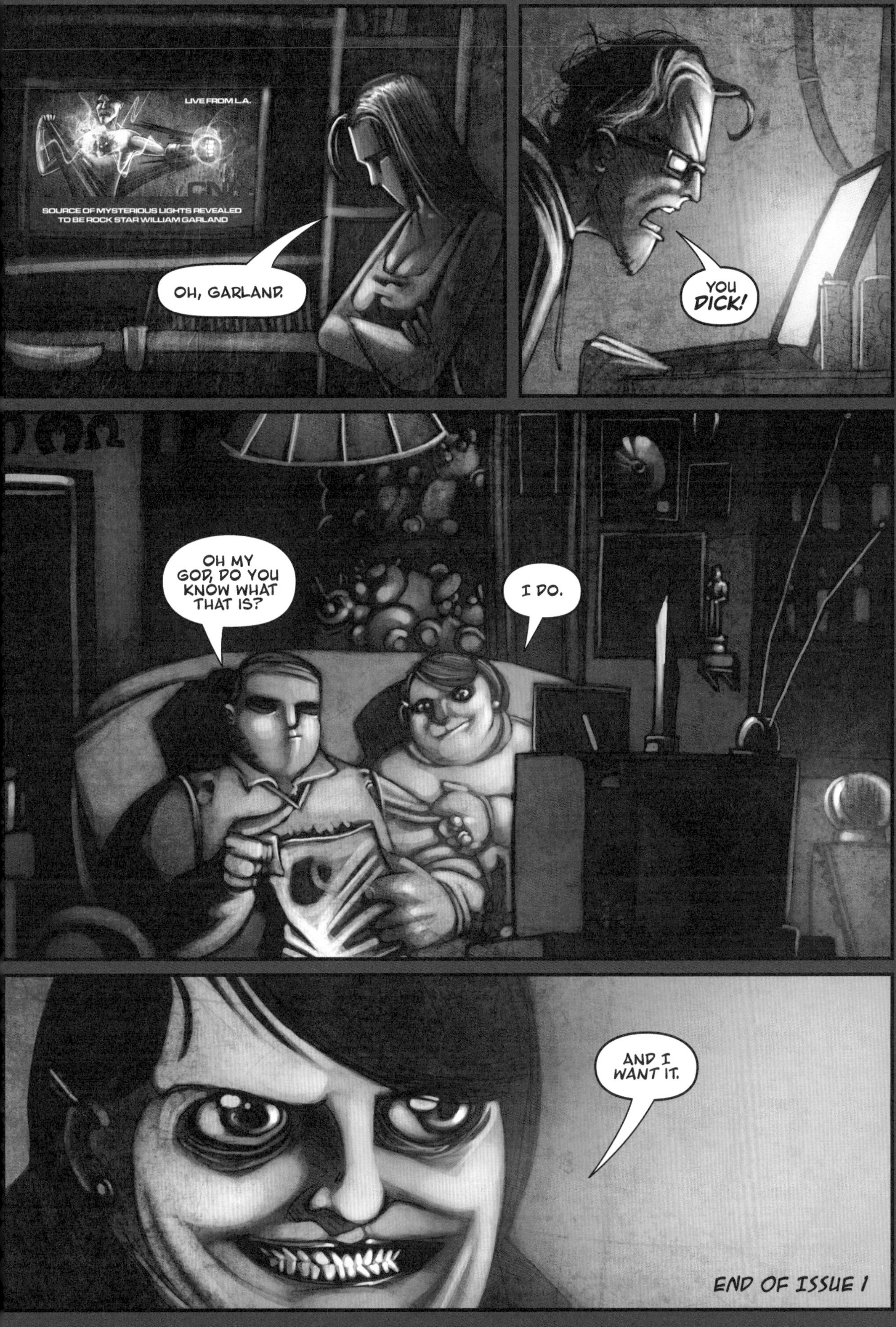
LIVE FROM L.A.
SOURCE OF MYSTERIOUS LIGHTS REVEALED TO BE ROCK STAR WILLIAM GARLAND
OH, GARLAND.
YOU DICK!
OH MY GOD, DO YOU KNOW WHAT THAT IS?
I DO.
AND I WANT IT.
END OF ISSUE 1

27 SECOND SET #2 cover by W. SCOTT FORBES
Based on "Video Killed the Radio Star" by The Buggles

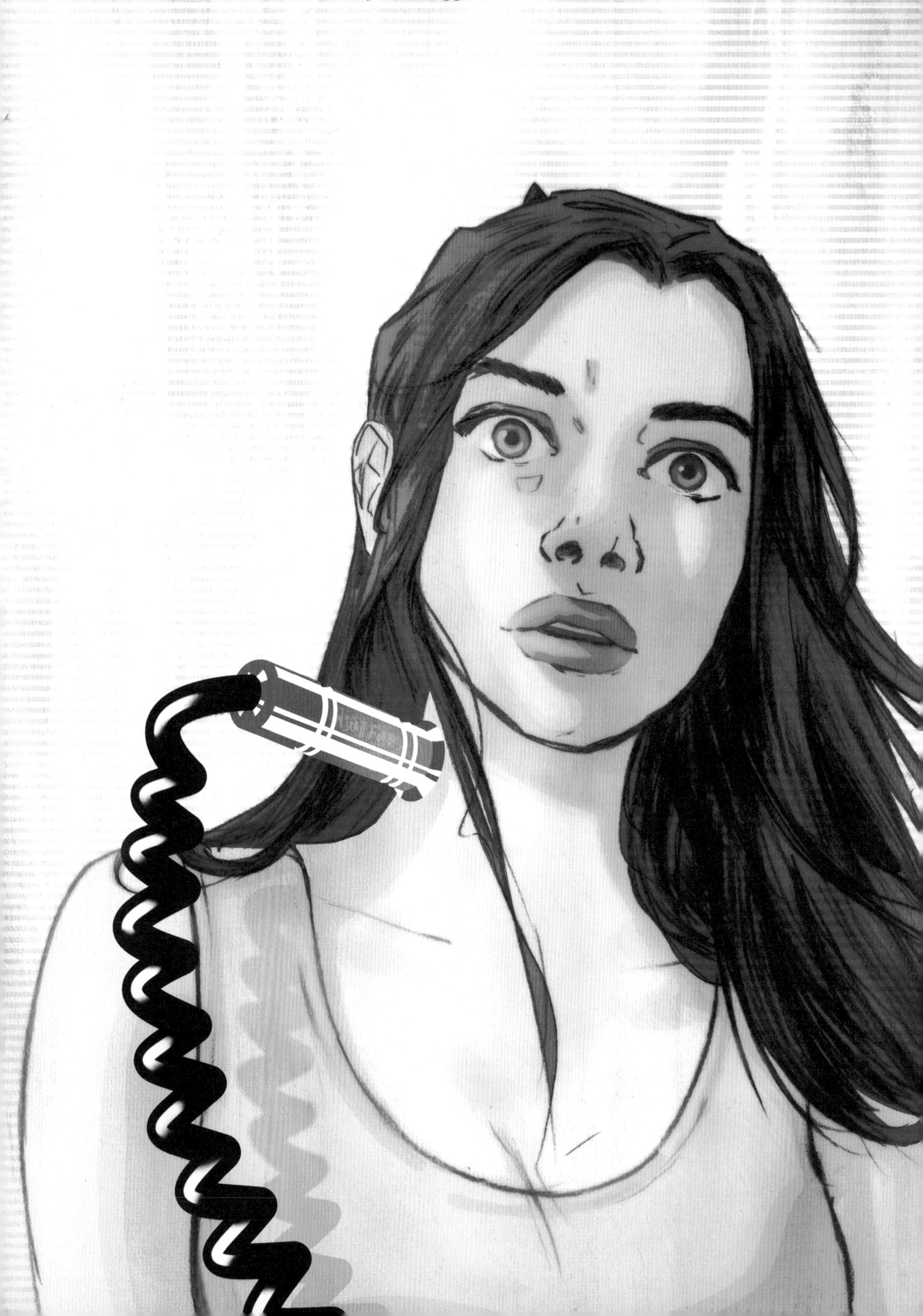

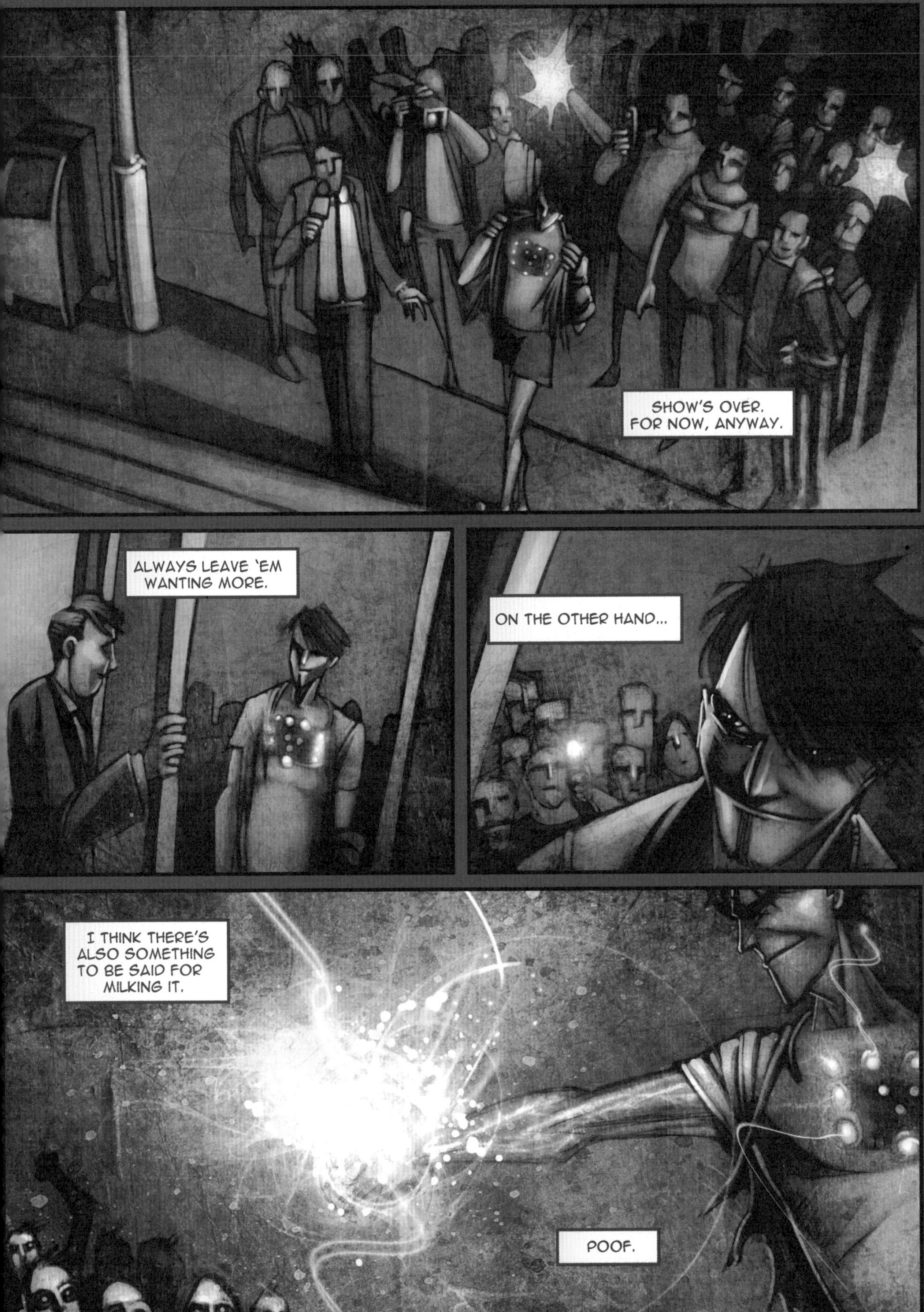
SHOW'S OVER. FOR NOW, ANYWAY.
ALWAYS LEAVE 'EM WANTING MORE.
ON THE OTHER HAND...
I THINK THERE'S ALSO SOMETHING TO BE SAID FOR MILKING IT.
POOF.

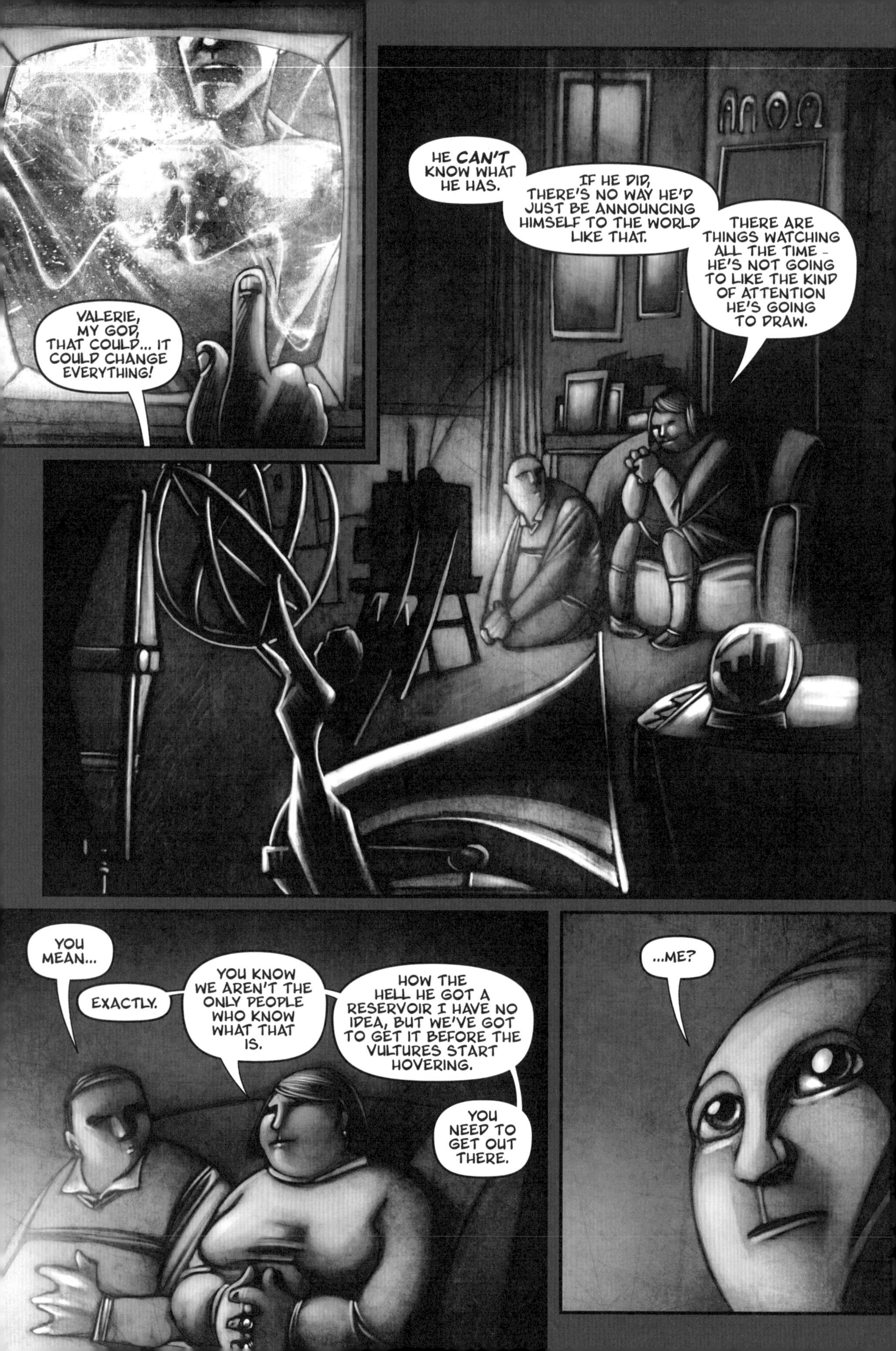
VALERIE, MY GOD, THAT COULD... IT COULD CHANGE EVERYTHING!
HE CAN'T KNOW WHAT HE HAS.
IF HE DID, THERE'S NO WAY HE'D JUST BE ANNOUNCING HIMSELF TO THE WORLD LIKE THAT.
THERE ARE THINGS WATCHING ALL THE TIME - HE'S NOT GOING TO LIKE THE KIND OF ATTENTION HE'S GOING TO DRAW.
YOU MEAN...
EXACTLY.
YOU KNOW WE AREN'T THE ONLY PEOPLE WHO KNOW WHAT THAT IS.
HOW THE HELL HE GOT A RESERVOIR I HAVE NO IDEA, BUT WE'VE GOT TO GET IT BEFORE THE VULTURES START HOVERING.
YOU NEED TO GET OUT THERE.
...ME?

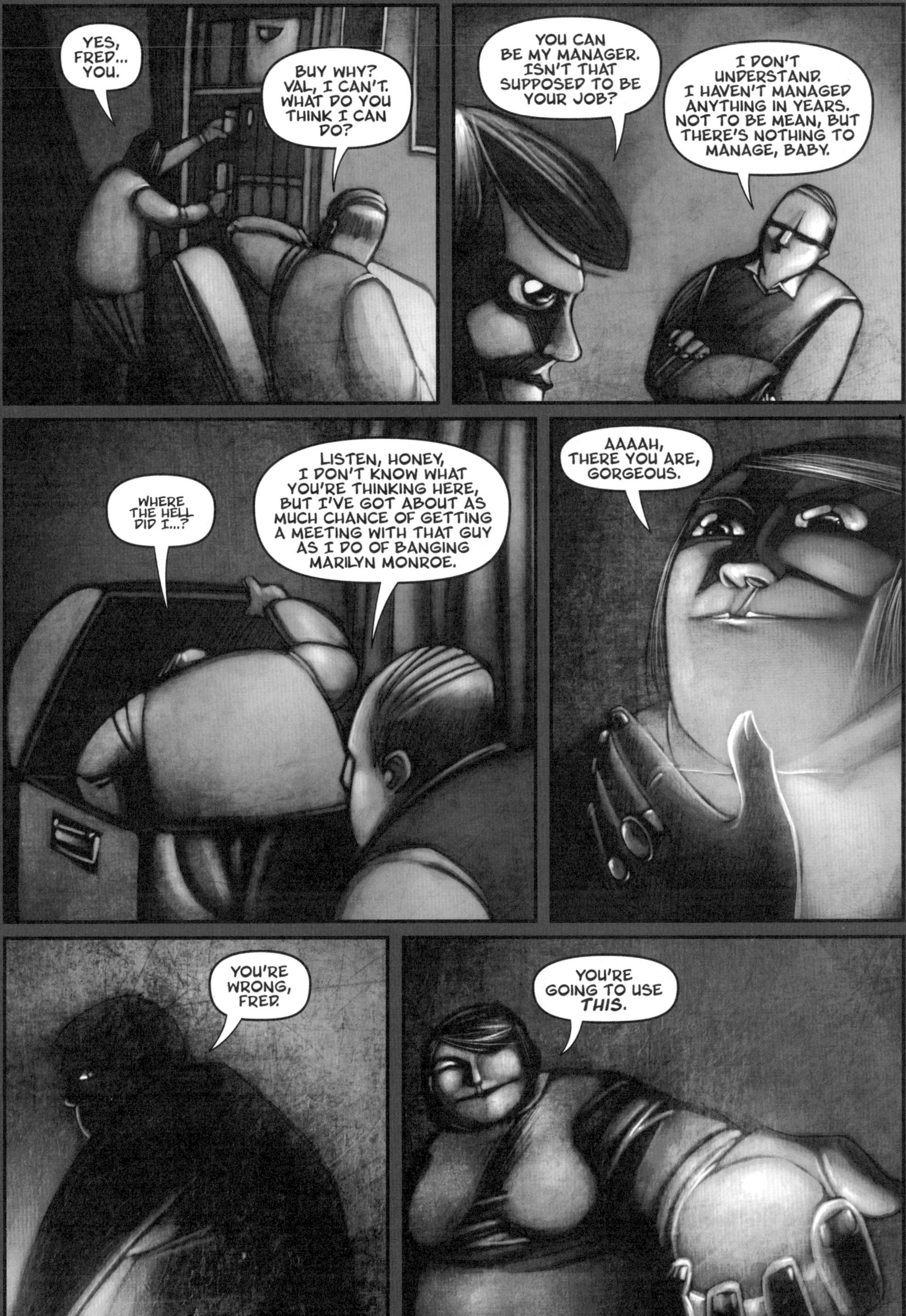
YES, FRED... YOU.
BUY WHY? VAL, I CAN'T. WHAT DO YOU THINK I CAN DO?
YOU CAN BE MY MANAGER. ISN'T THAT SUPPOSED TO BE YOUR JOB?
I DON'T UNDERSTAND. I HAVEN'T MANAGED ANYTHING IN YEARS. NOT TO BE MEAN, BUT THERE'S NOTHING TO MANAGE, BABY.
WHERE THE HELL DID I...?
LISTEN, HONEY, I DON'T KNOW WHAT YOU'RE THINKING HERE, BUT I'VE GOT ABOUT AS MUCH CHANCE OF GETTING A MEETING WITH THAT GUY AS I DO OF BANGING MARILYN MONROE.
AAAAH, THERE YOU ARE, GORGEOUS.
YOU'RE WRONG, FRED.
YOU'RE GOING TO USE THIS.

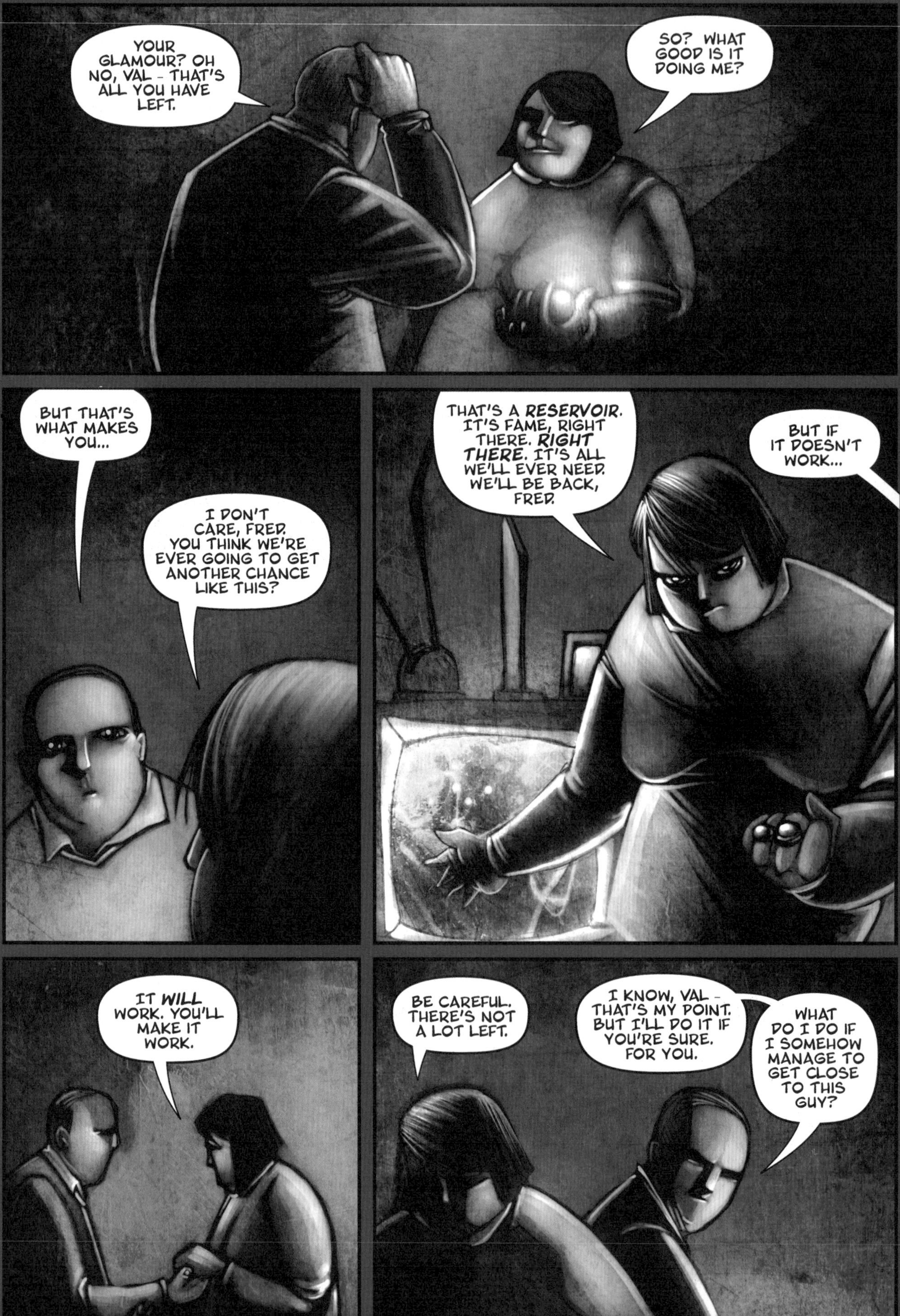
YOUR GLAMOUR? OH NO, VAL - THAT'S ALL YOU HAVE LEFT.
SO? WHAT GOOD IS IT DOING ME?
BUT THAT'S WHAT MAKES YOU...
I DON'T CARE, FRED. YOU THINK WE'RE EVER GOING TO GET ANOTHER CHANCE LIKE THIS?
THAT'S A RESERVOIR. IT'S FAME, RIGHT THERE. RIGHT THERE. IT'S ALL WE'LL EVER NEED. WE'LL BE BACK, FRED.
BUT IF IT DOESN'T WORK...
IT WILL WORK. YOU'LL MAKE IT WORK.
BE CAREFUL. THERE'S NOT A LOT LEFT.
I KNOW, VAL - THAT'S MY POINT. BUT I'LL DO IT IF YOU'RE SURE. FOR YOU.
WHAT DO I DO IF I SOMEHOW MANAGE TO GET CLOSE TO THIS GUY?

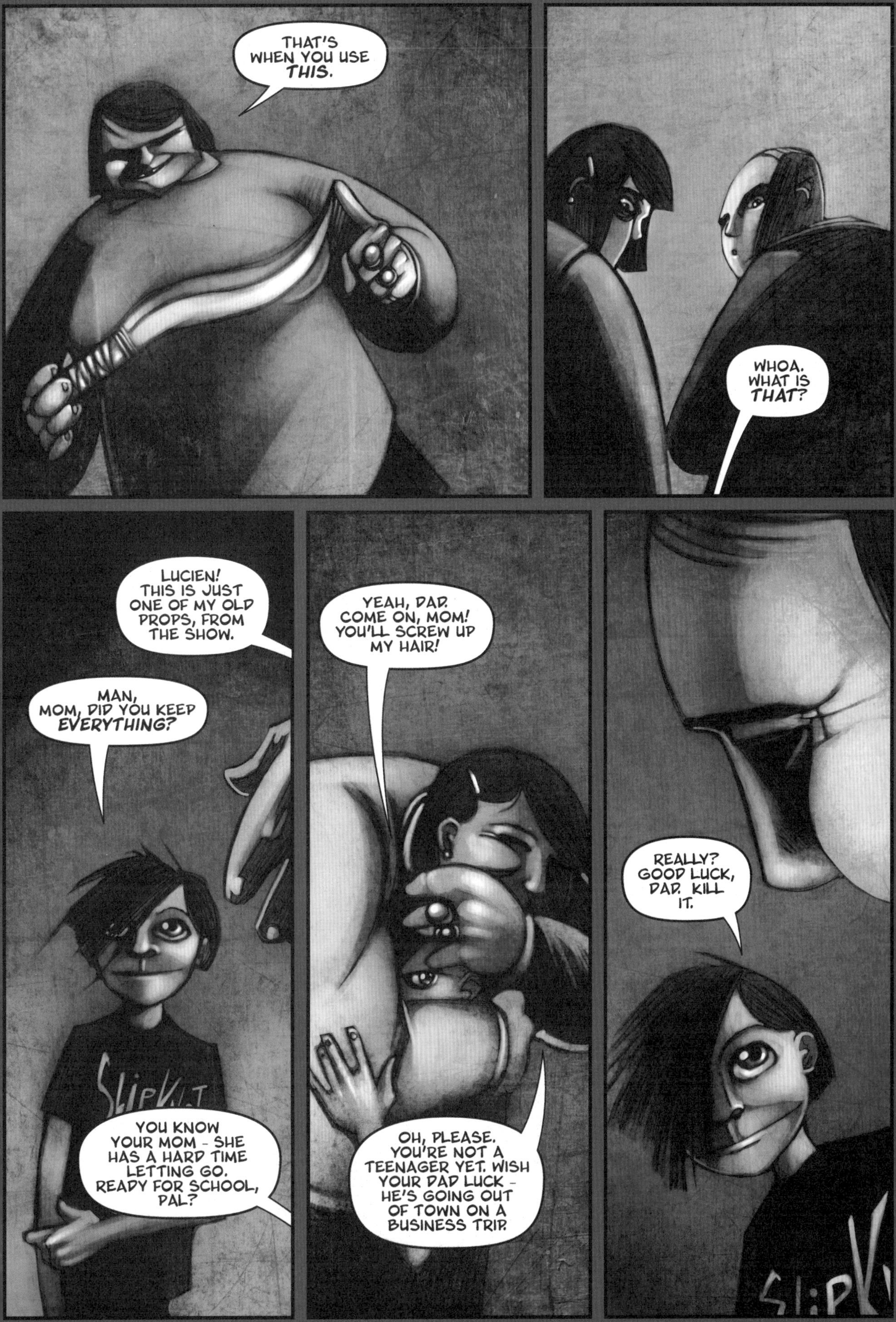
THAT'S WHEN YOU USE THIS.
WHOA. WHAT IS THAT?
LUCIEN! THIS IS JUST ONE OF MY OLD PROPS, FROM THE SHOW.
MAN, MOM, DID YOU KEEP EVERYTHING?
YOU KNOW YOUR MOM - SHE HAS A HARD TIME LETTING GO. READY FOR SCHOOL, PAL?
YEAH, DAD. COME ON, MOM! YOU'LL SCREW UP MY HAIR!
OH, PLEASE. YOU'RE NOT A TEENAGER YET. WISH YOUR DAD LUCK - HE'S GOING OUT OF TOWN ON A BUSINESS TRIP.
REALLY? GOOD LUCK, DAD. KILL IT.

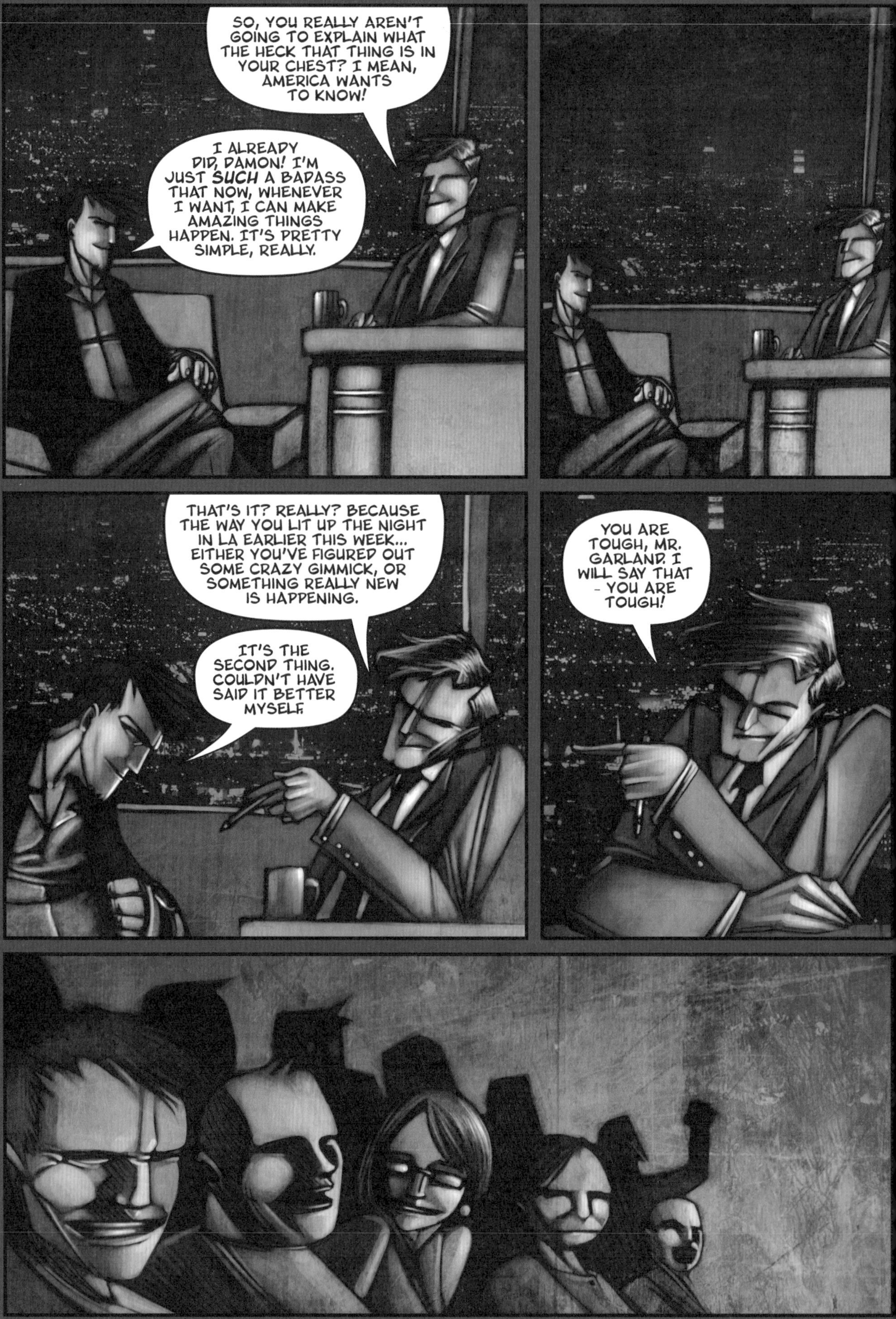
SO, YOU REALLY AREN'T GOING TO EXPLAIN WHAT THE HECK THAT THING IS IN YOUR CHEST? I MEAN, AMERICA WANTS TO KNOW!
I ALREADY DID, DAMON! I'M JUST SUCH A BADASS THAT NOW, WHENEVER I WANT, I CAN MAKE AMAZING THINGS HAPPEN. IT'S PRETTY SIMPLE, REALLY.
THAT'S IT? REALLY? BECAUSE THE WAY YOU LIT UP THE NIGHT IN LA EARLIER THIS WEEK... EITHER YOU'VE FIGURED OUT SOME CRAZY GIMMICK, OR SOMETHING REALLY NEW IS HAPPENING.
IT'S THE SECOND THING. COULDN'T HAVE SAID IT BETTER MYSELF.
YOU ARE TOUGH, MR. GARLAND. I WILL SAY THAT - YOU ARE TOUGH!

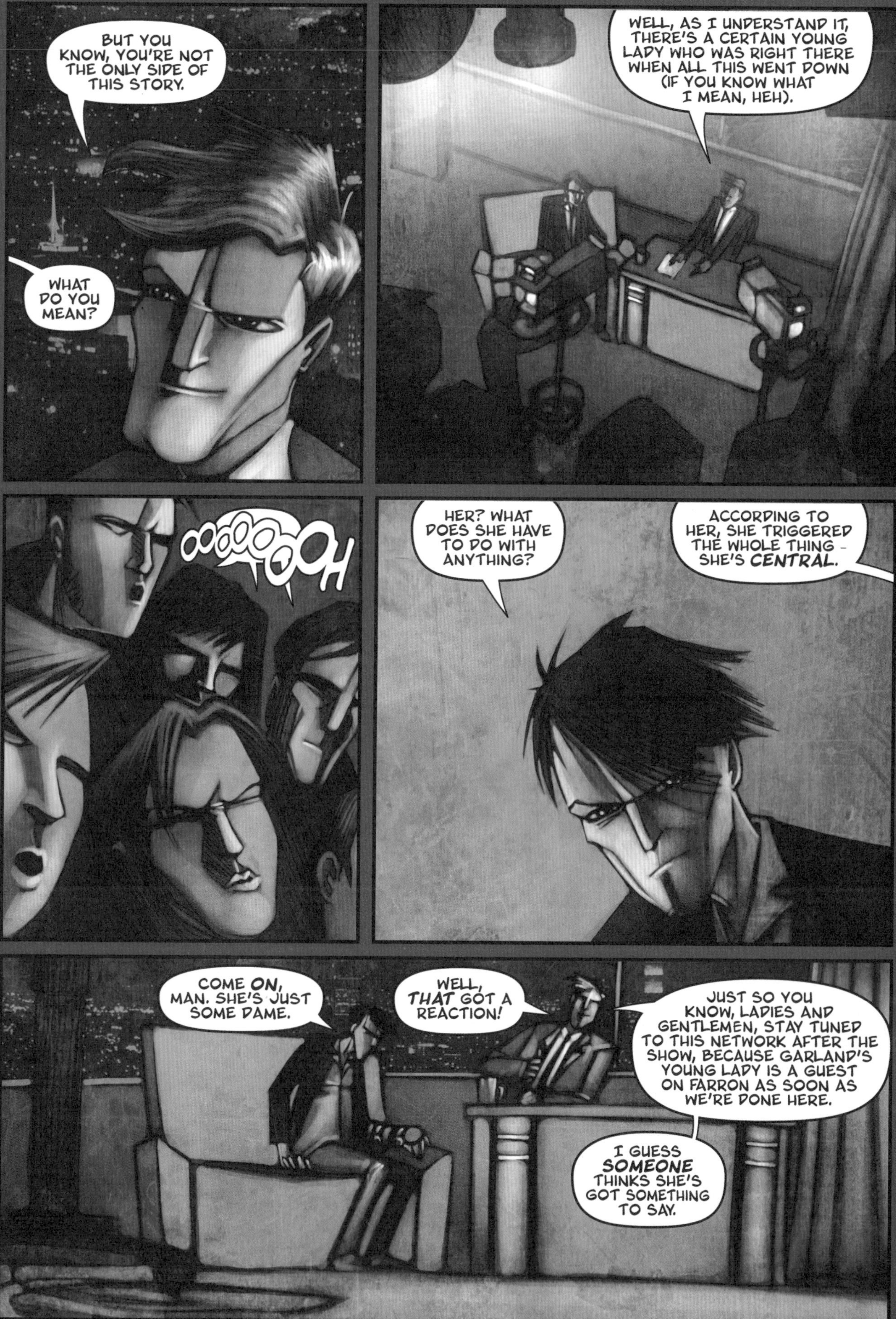
BUT YOU KNOW, YOU'RE NOT THE ONLY SIDE OF THIS STORY.
WHAT DO YOU MEAN?
WELL, AS I UNDERSTAND IT, THERE'S A CERTAIN YOUNG LADY WHO WAS RIGHT THERE WHEN ALL THIS WENT DOWN (IF YOU KNOW WHAT I MEAN, HEH).
OOOOOOOOH
HER? WHAT DOES SHE HAVE TO DO WITH ANYTHING?
ACCORDING TO HER, SHE TRIGGERED THE WHOLE THING - SHE'S CENTRAL.
COME ON, MAN. SHE'S JUST SOME DAME.
WELL, THAT GOT A REACTION!
JUST SO YOU KNOW, LADIES AND GENTLEMEN, STAY TUNED TO THIS NETWORK AFTER THE SHOW, BECAUSE GARLAND'S YOUNG LADY IS A GUEST ON FARRON AS SOON AS WE'RE DONE HERE.
I GUESS SOMEONE THINKS SHE'S GOT SOMETHING TO SAY.

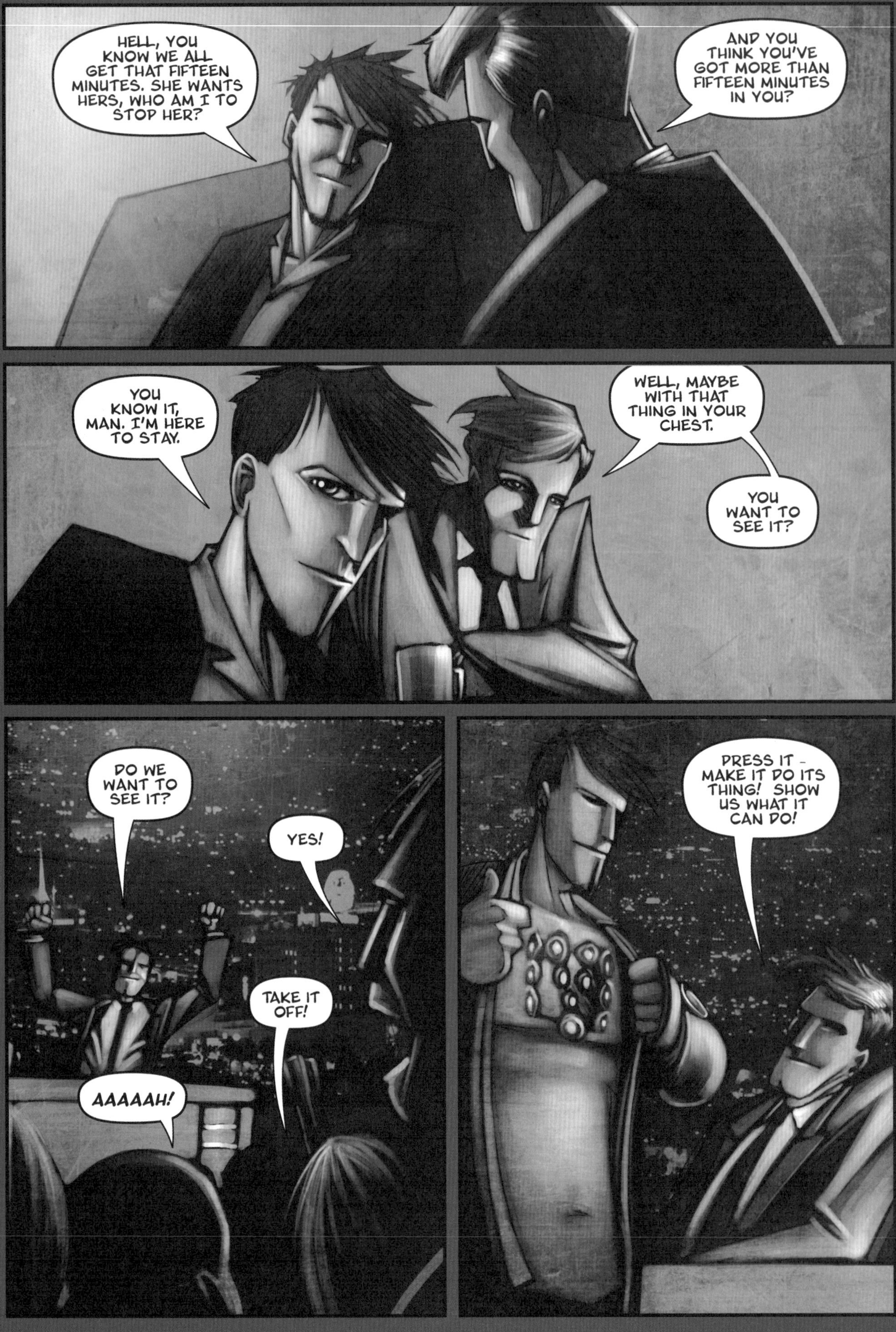
HELL, YOU KNOW WE ALL GET THAT FIFTEEN MINUTES. SHE WANTS HERS, WHO AM I TO STOP HER?
AND YOU THINK YOU'VE GOT MORE THAN FIFTEEN MINUTES IN YOU?
YOU KNOW IT, MAN. I'M HERE TO STAY.
WELL, MAYBE WITH THAT THING IN YOUR CHEST.
YOU WANT TO SEE IT?
DO WE WANT TO SEE IT?
YES!
TAKE IT OFF!
AAAAAH!
PRESS IT - MAKE IT DO ITS THING! SHOW US WHAT IT CAN DO!

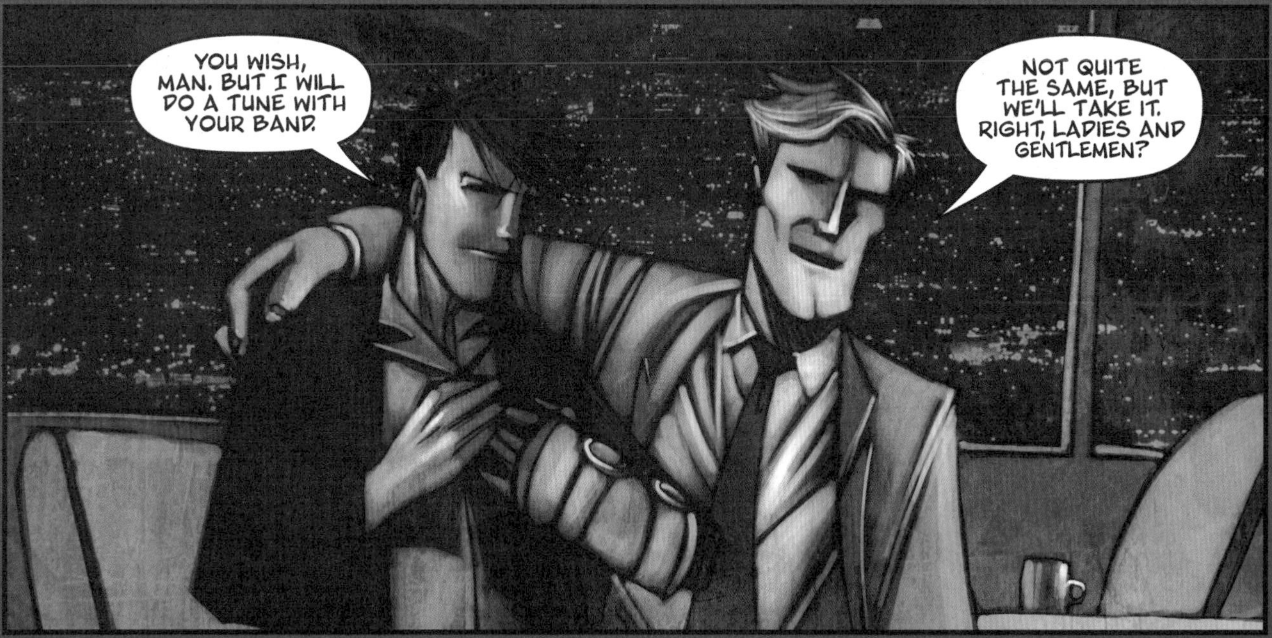
YOU WISH, MAN. BUT I WILL DO A TUNE WITH YOUR BAND.
NOT QUITE THE SAME, BUT WE'LL TAKE IT. RIGHT, LADIES AND GENTLEMEN?
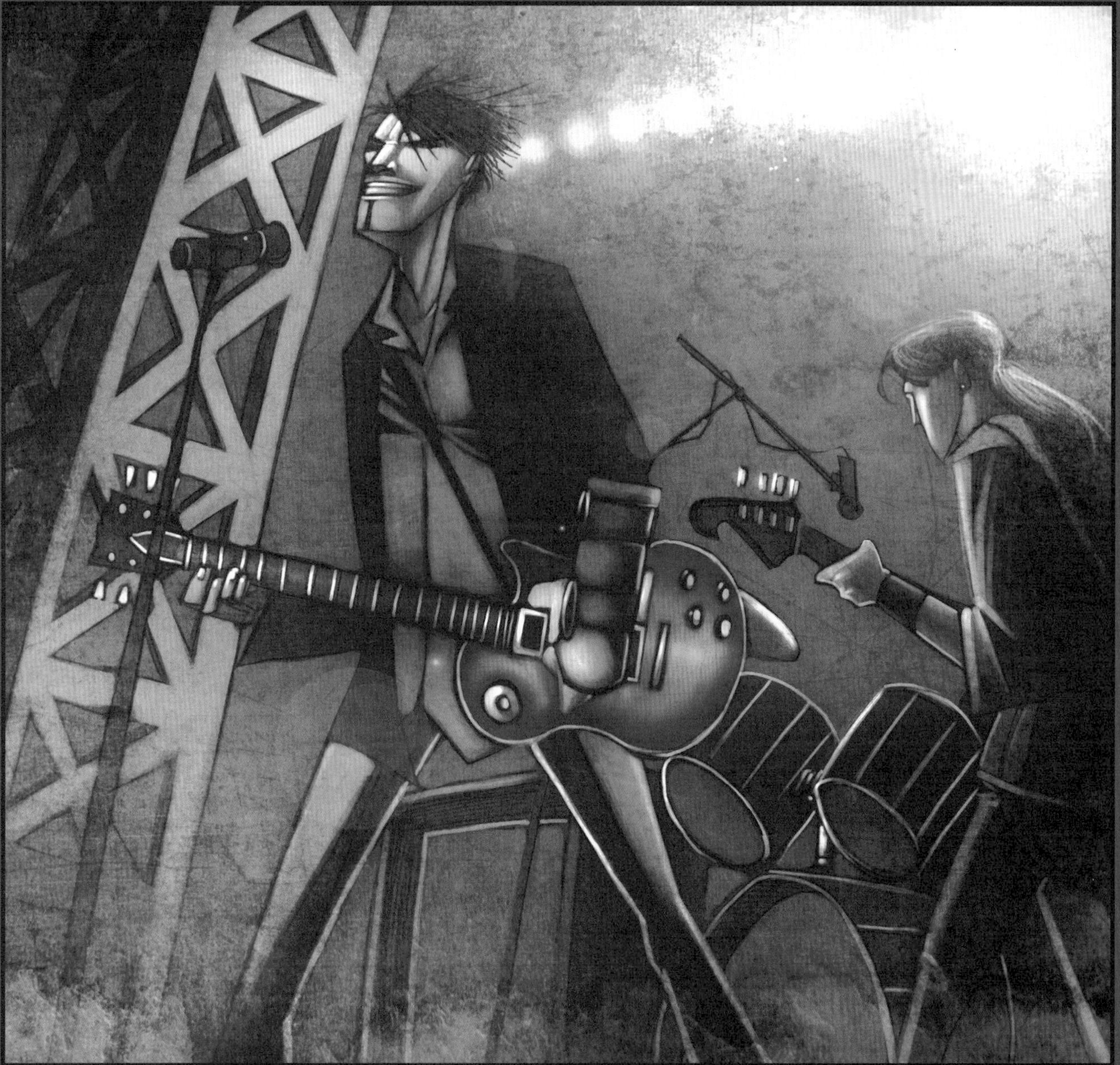

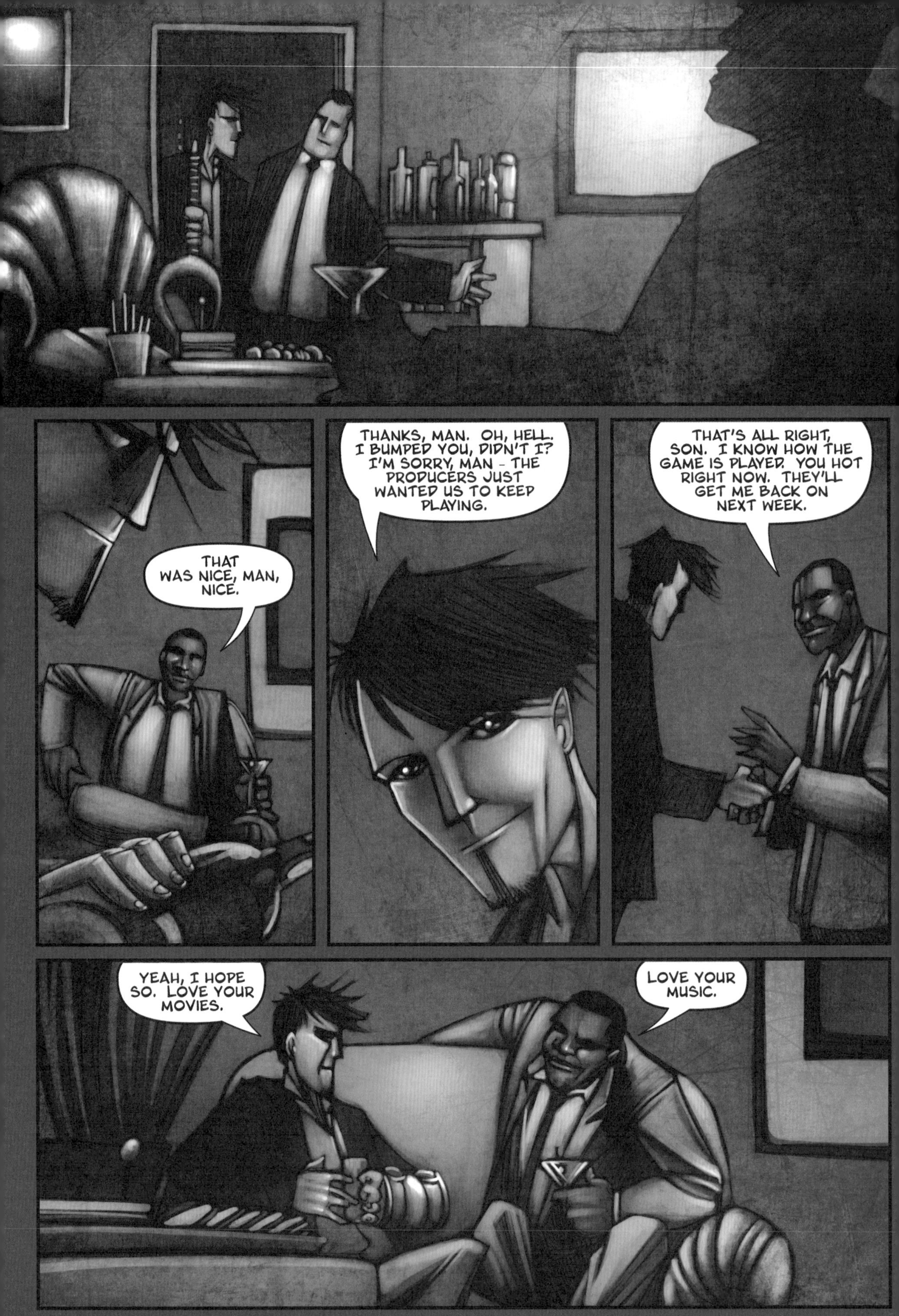
THAT WAS NICE, MAN, NICE.
THANKS, MAN. OH, HELL. I BUMPED YOU, DIDN'T I? I'M SORRY, MAN - THE PRODUCERS JUST WANTED US TO KEEP PLAYING.
THAT'S ALL RIGHT, SON. I KNOW HOW THE GAME IS PLAYED. YOU HOT RIGHT NOW. THEY'LL GET ME BACK ON NEXT WEEK.
YEAH, I HOPE SO. LOVE YOUR MOVIES.
LOVE YOUR MUSIC.

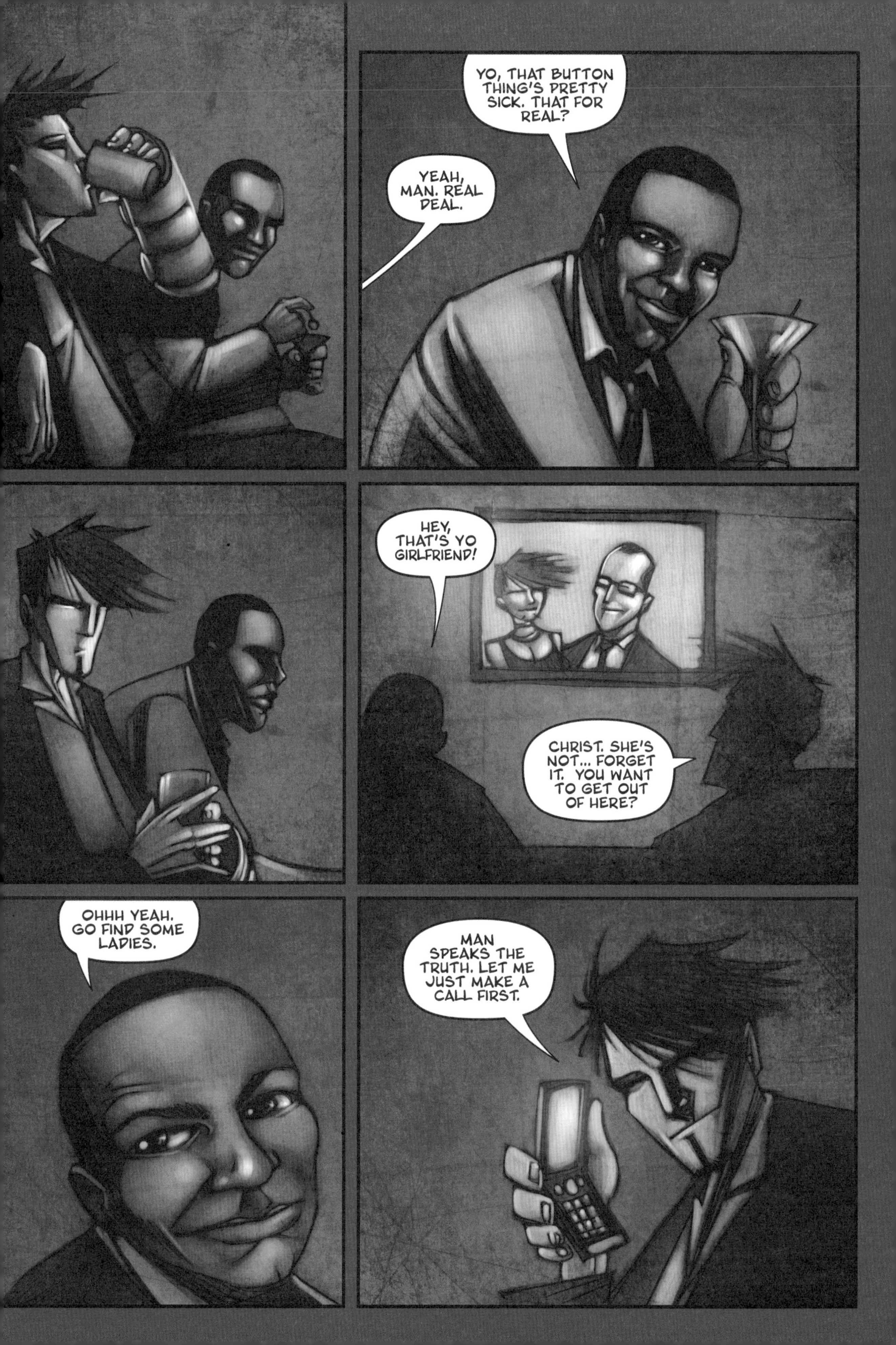
YO, THAT BUTTON THING'S PRETTY SICK. THAT FOR REAL?
YEAH, MAN. REAL DEAL.
HEY, THAT'S YO GIRLFRIEND!
CHRIST. SHE'S NOT... FORGET IT. YOU WANT TO GET OUT OF HERE?
OHHH YEAH. GO FIND SOME LADIES.
MAN SPEAKS THE TRUTH. LET ME JUST MAKE A CALL FIRST.

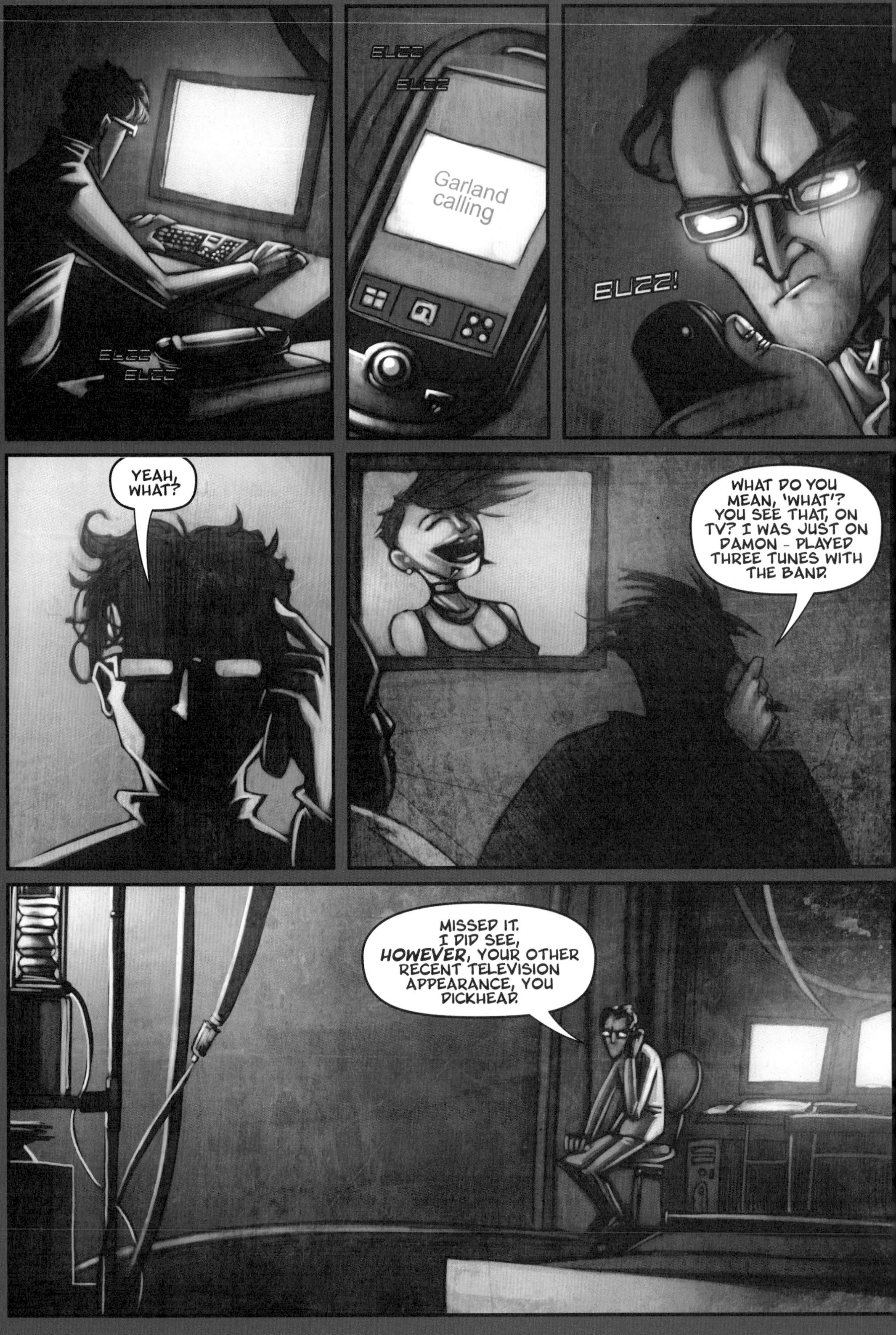
BUZZ
BUZZ
BUZZ
BUZZ
Garland calling
BUZZ!
YEAH, WHAT?
WHAT DO YOU MEAN, 'WHAT'? YOU SEE THAT, ON TV? I WAS JUST ON DAMON - PLAYED THREE TUNES WITH THE BAND.
MISSED IT. I DID SEE, **HOWEVER**, YOUR OTHER RECENT TELEVISION APPEARANCE, YOU DICKHEAD.

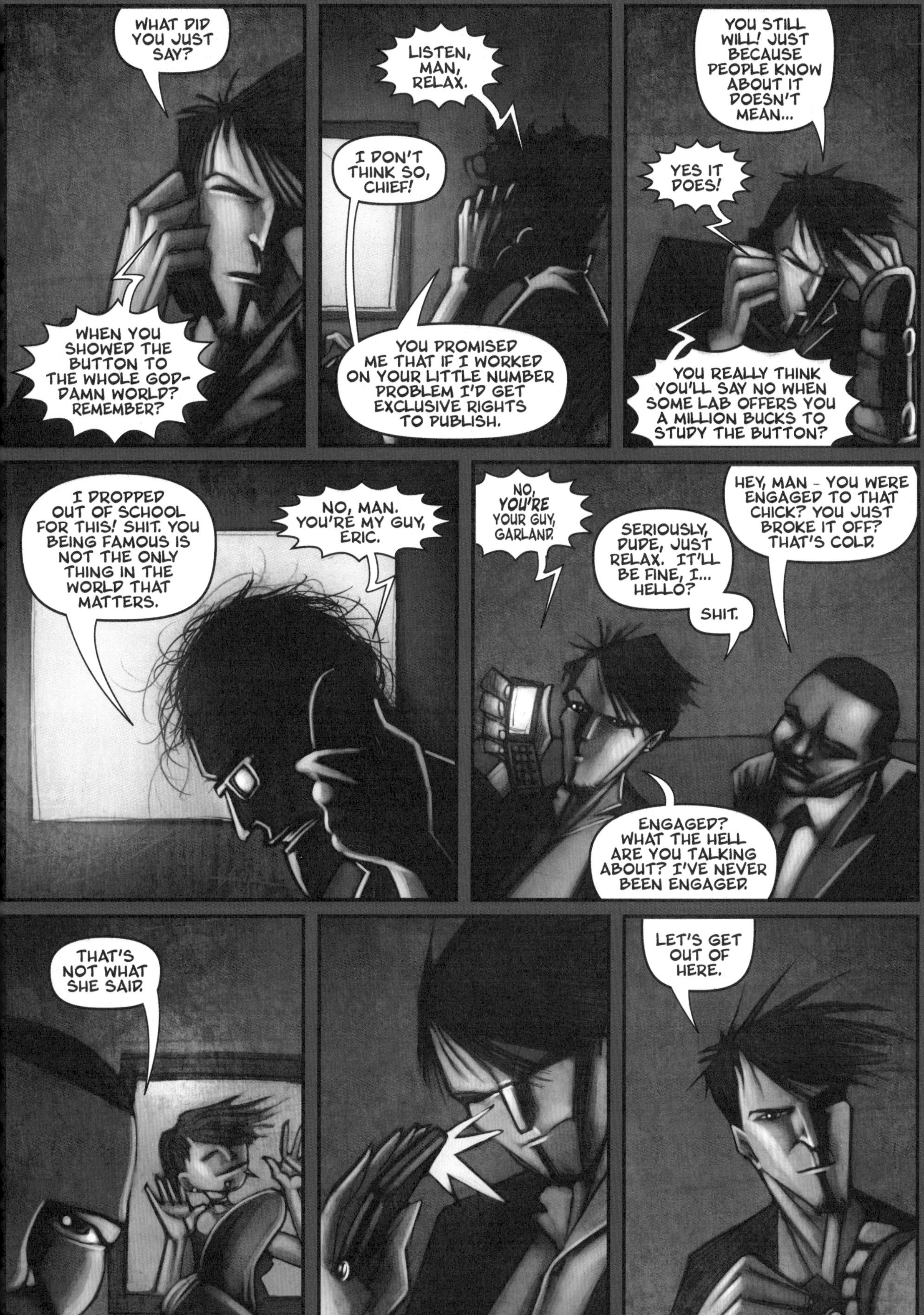

WHAT DID YOU JUST SAY?
WHEN YOU SHOWED THE BUTTON TO THE WHOLE GOD-DAMN WORLD? REMEMBER?
LISTEN, MAN, RELAX.
I DON'T THINK SO, CHIEF!
YOU PROMISED ME THAT IF I WORKED ON YOUR LITTLE NUMBER PROBLEM I'D GET EXCLUSIVE RIGHTS TO PUBLISH.
YOU STILL WILL! JUST BECAUSE PEOPLE KNOW ABOUT IT DOESN'T MEAN...
YES IT DOES!
YOU REALLY THINK YOU'LL SAY NO WHEN SOME LAB OFFERS YOU A MILLION BUCKS TO STUDY THE BUTTON?
I DROPPED OUT OF SCHOOL FOR THIS! SHIT. YOU BEING FAMOUS IS NOT THE ONLY THING IN THE WORLD THAT MATTERS.
NO, MAN. YOU'RE MY GUY, ERIC.
NO, YOU'RE YOUR GUY, GARLAND.
SERIOUSLY, DUDE, JUST RELAX. IT'LL BE FINE, I... HELLO?
SHIT.
HEY, MAN - YOU WERE ENGAGED TO THAT CHICK? YOU JUST BROKE IT OFF? THAT'S COLD.
ENGAGED? WHAT THE HELL ARE YOU TALKING ABOUT? I'VE NEVER BEEN ENGAGED.
THAT'S NOT WHAT SHE SAID.
LET'S GET OUT OF HERE.

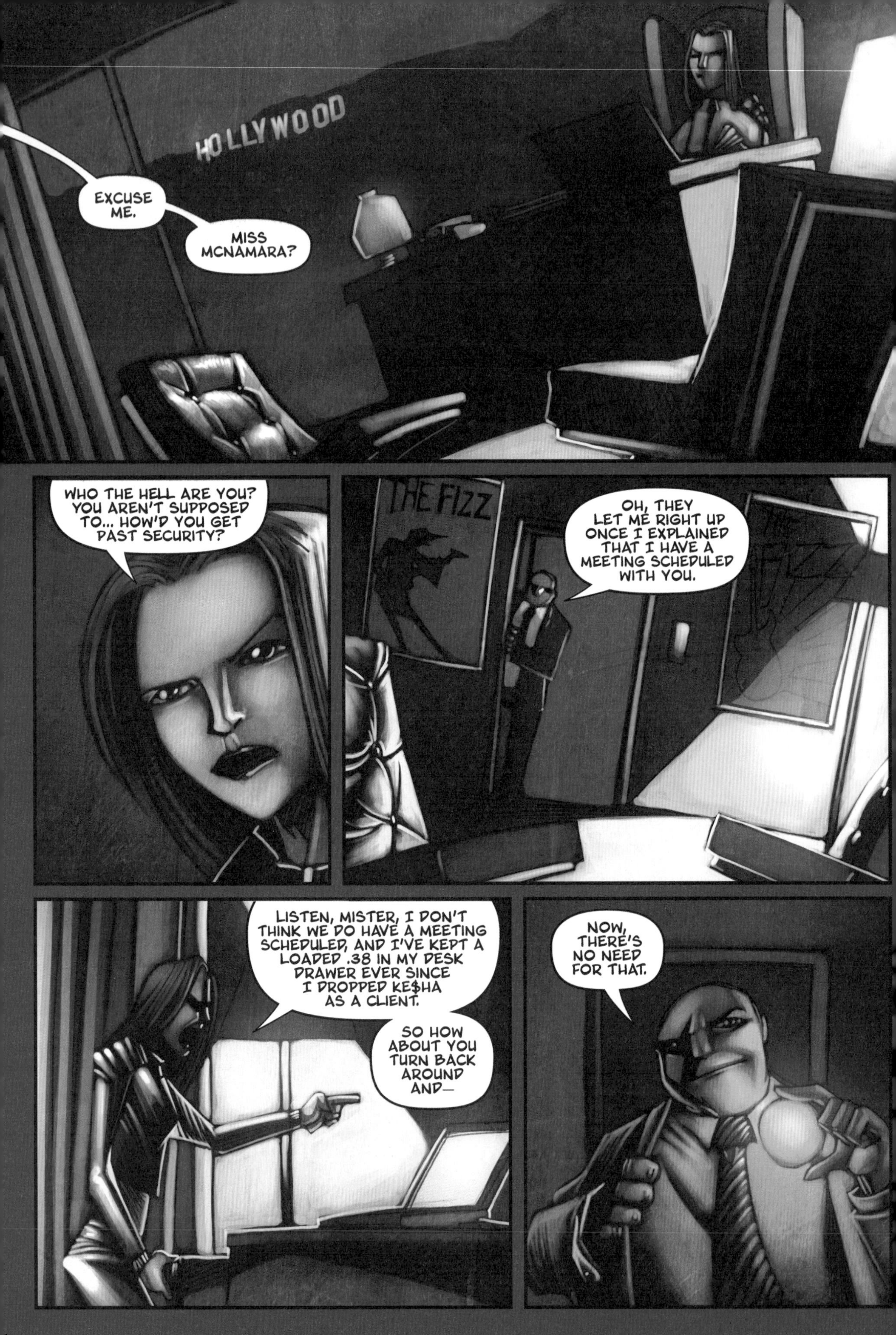

HOLLYWOOD
EXCUSE ME.
MISS MCNAMARA?
WHO THE HELL ARE YOU? YOU AREN'T SUPPOSED TO... HOW'D YOU GET PAST SECURITY?
THE FIZZ
OH, THEY LET ME RIGHT UP ONCE I EXPLAINED THAT I HAVE A MEETING SCHEDULED WITH YOU.
LISTEN, MISTER, I DON'T THINK WE DO HAVE A MEETING SCHEDULED, AND I'VE KEPT A LOADED .38 IN MY DESK DRAWER EVER SINCE I DROPPED KE$HA AS A CLIENT.
SO HOW ABOUT YOU TURN BACK AROUND AND—
NOW, THERE'S NO NEED FOR THAT.

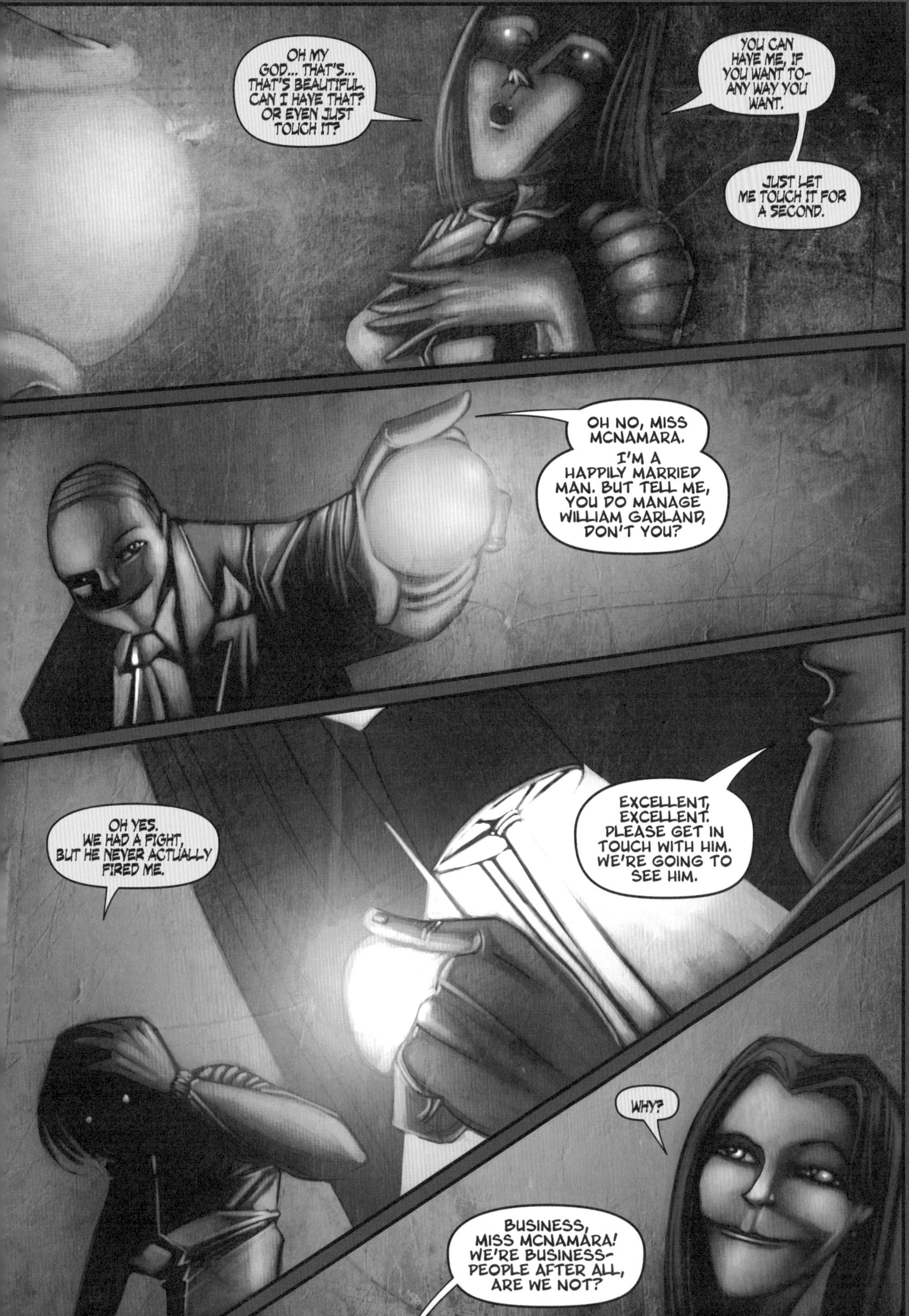

OH MY GOD... THAT'S... THAT'S BEAUTIFUL. CAN I HAVE THAT? OR EVEN JUST TOUCH IT?
YOU CAN HAVE ME, IF YOU WANT TO-ANY WAY YOU WANT.
JUST LET ME TOUCH IT FOR A SECOND.
OH NO, MISS MCNAMARA.
I'M A HAPPILY MARRIED MAN. BUT TELL ME, YOU DO MANAGE WILLIAM GARLAND, DON'T YOU?
OH YES. WE HAD A FIGHT, BUT HE NEVER ACTUALLY FIRED ME.
EXCELLENT, EXCELLENT. PLEASE GET IN TOUCH WITH HIM. WE'RE GOING TO SEE HIM.
WHY?
BUSINESS, MISS MCNAMARA! WE'RE BUSINESS-PEOPLE AFTER ALL, ARE WE NOT?

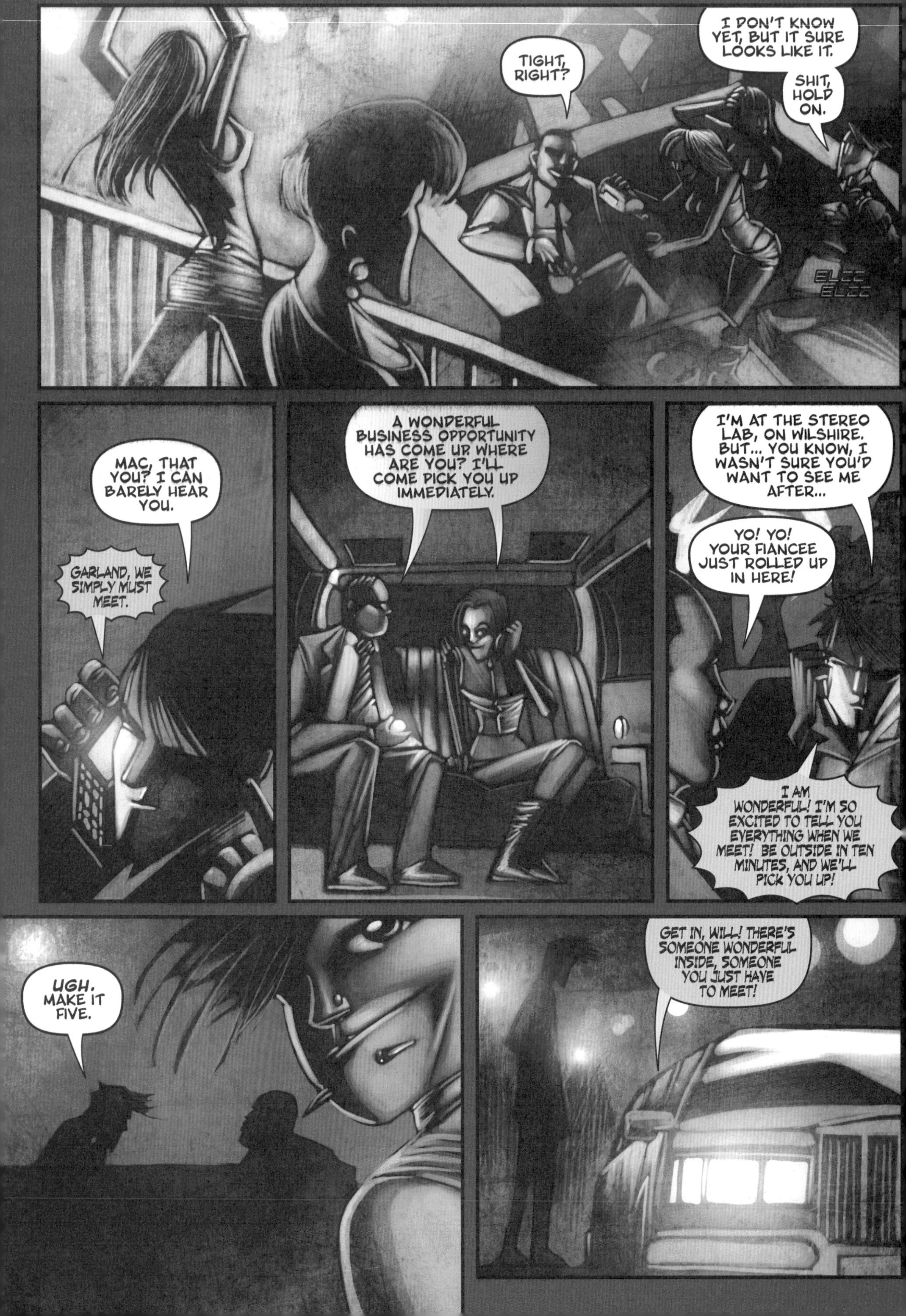
TIGHT, RIGHT?
I DON'T KNOW YET, BUT IT SURE LOOKS LIKE IT.
SHIT, HOLD ON.
MAC, THAT YOU? I CAN BARELY HEAR YOU.
GARLAND, WE SIMPLY MUST MEET.
A WONDERFUL BUSINESS OPPORTUNITY HAS COME UP. WHERE ARE YOU? I'LL COME PICK YOU UP IMMEDIATELY.
I'M AT THE STEREO LAB, ON WILSHIRE. BUT... YOU KNOW, I WASN'T SURE YOU'D WANT TO SEE ME AFTER...
YO! YO! YOUR FIANCEE JUST ROLLED UP IN HERE!
I AM WONDERFUL! I'M SO EXCITED TO TELL YOU EVERYTHING WHEN WE MEET! BE OUTSIDE IN TEN MINUTES, AND WE'LL PICK YOU UP!
UGH. MAKE IT FIVE.
GET IN, WILL! THERE'S SOMEONE WONDERFUL INSIDE, SOMEONE YOU JUST HAVE TO MEET!

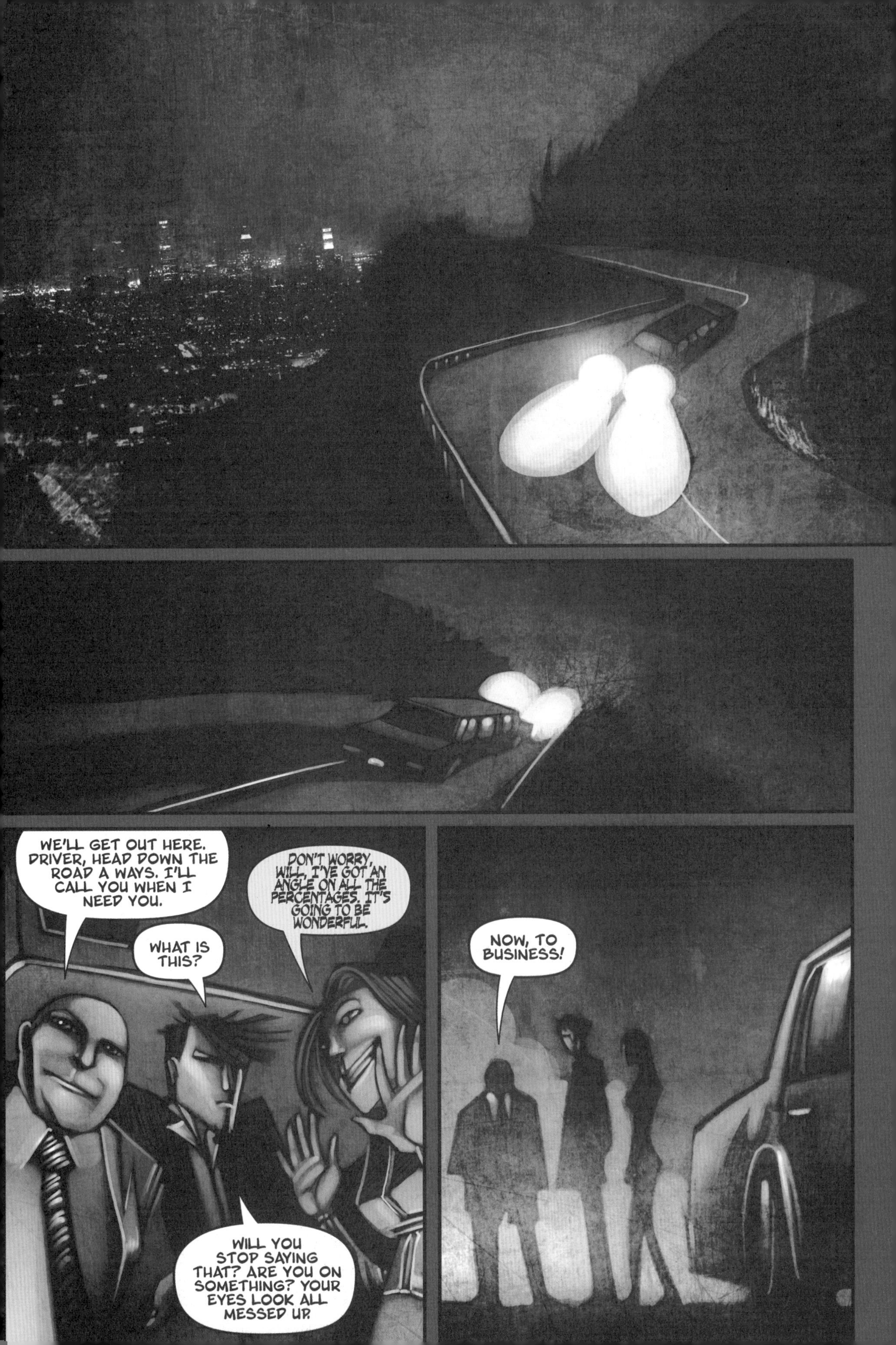
WE'LL GET OUT HERE. DRIVER, HEAD DOWN THE ROAD A WAYS. I'LL CALL YOU WHEN I NEED YOU.
WHAT IS THIS?
DON'T WORRY, WILL, I'VE GOT AN ANGLE ON ALL THE PERCENTAGES. IT'S GOING TO BE WONDERFUL.
WILL YOU STOP SAYING THAT? ARE YOU ON SOMETHING? YOUR EYES LOOK ALL MESSED UP.
NOW, TO BUSINESS!

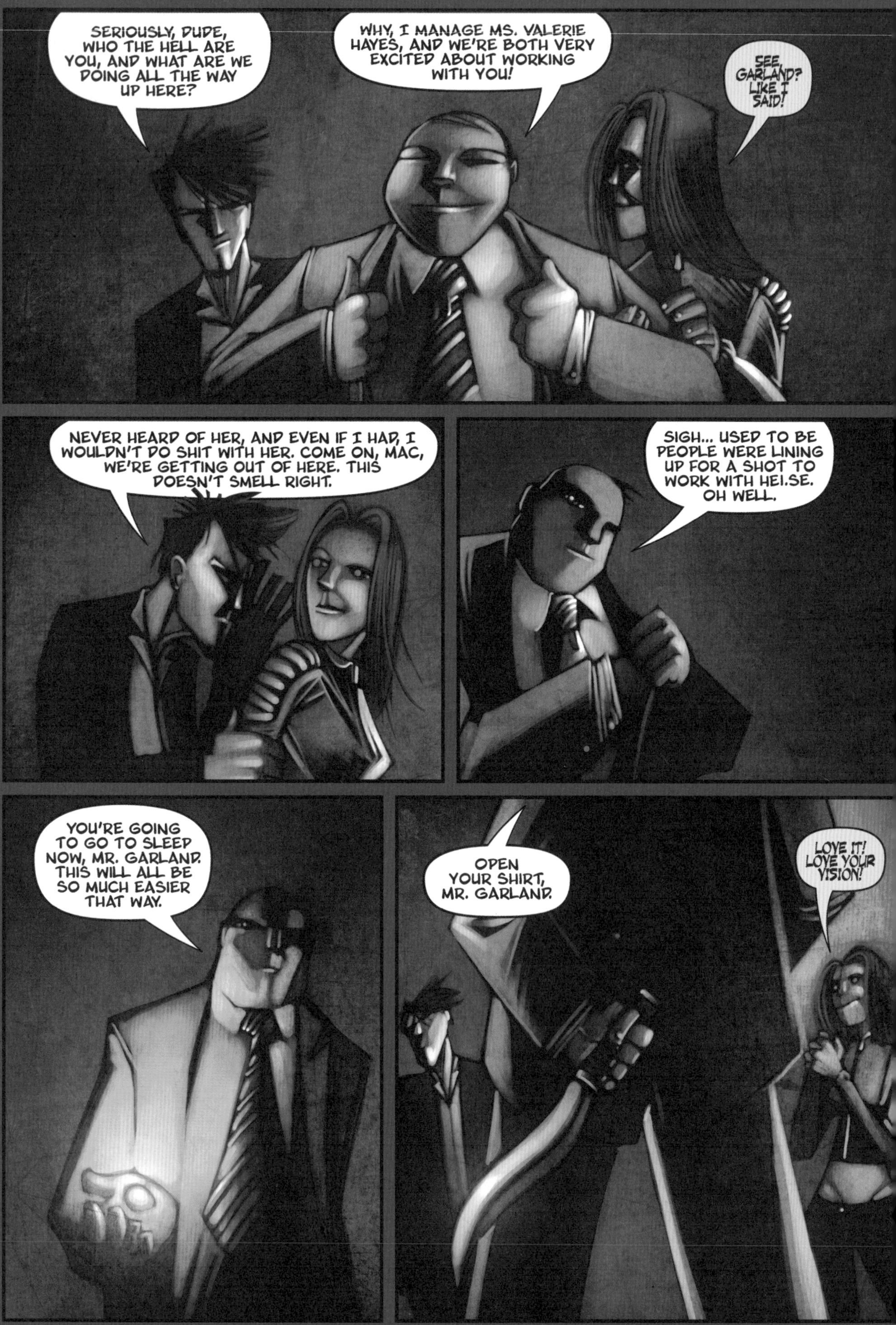
SERIOUSLY, DUDE, WHO THE HELL ARE YOU, AND WHAT ARE WE DOING ALL THE WAY UP HERE?
WHY, I MANAGE MS. VALERIE HAYES, AND WE'RE BOTH VERY EXCITED ABOUT WORKING WITH YOU!
SEE, GARLAND? LIKE I SAID!
NEVER HEARD OF HER, AND EVEN IF I HAD, I WOULDN'T DO SHIT WITH HER. COME ON, MAC, WE'RE GETTING OUT OF HERE. THIS DOESN'T SMELL RIGHT.
SIGH... USED TO BE PEOPLE WERE LINING UP FOR A SHOT TO WORK WITH HEI.SE. OH WELL.
YOU'RE GOING TO GO TO SLEEP NOW, MR. GARLAND. THIS WILL ALL BE SO MUCH EASIER THAT WAY.
OPEN YOUR SHIRT, MR. GARLAND.
LOVE IT! LOVE YOUR VISION!

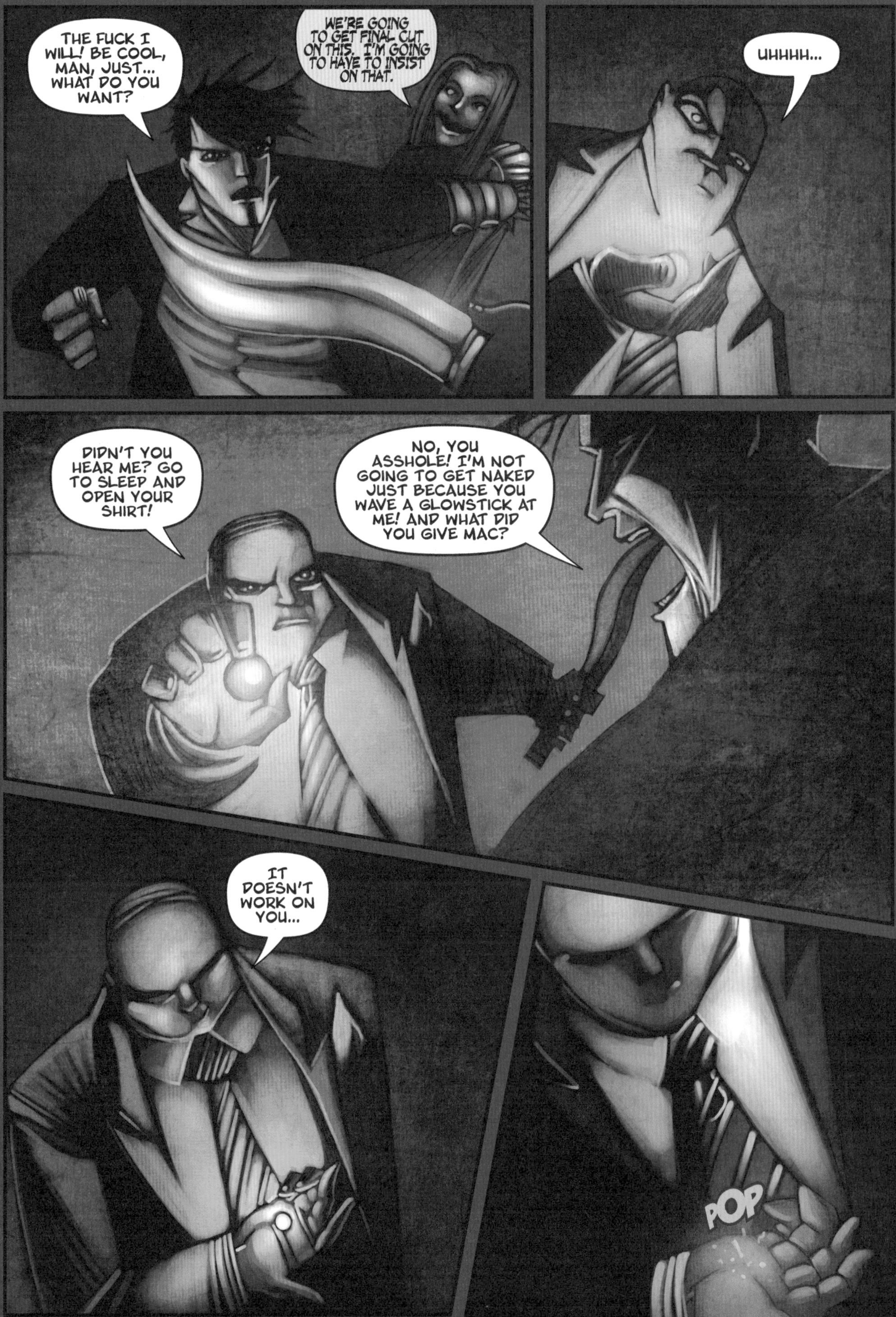
THE FUCK I WILL! BE COOL, MAN, JUST... WHAT DO YOU WANT?
WE'RE GOING TO GET FINAL CUT ON THIS. I'M GOING TO HAVE TO INSIST ON THAT.
UHHHH...
DIDN'T YOU HEAR ME? GO TO SLEEP AND OPEN YOUR SHIRT!
NO, YOU ASSHOLE! I'M NOT GOING TO GET NAKED JUST BECAUSE YOU WAVE A GLOWSTICK AT ME! AND WHAT DID YOU GIVE MAC?
IT DOESN'T WORK ON YOU...
POP

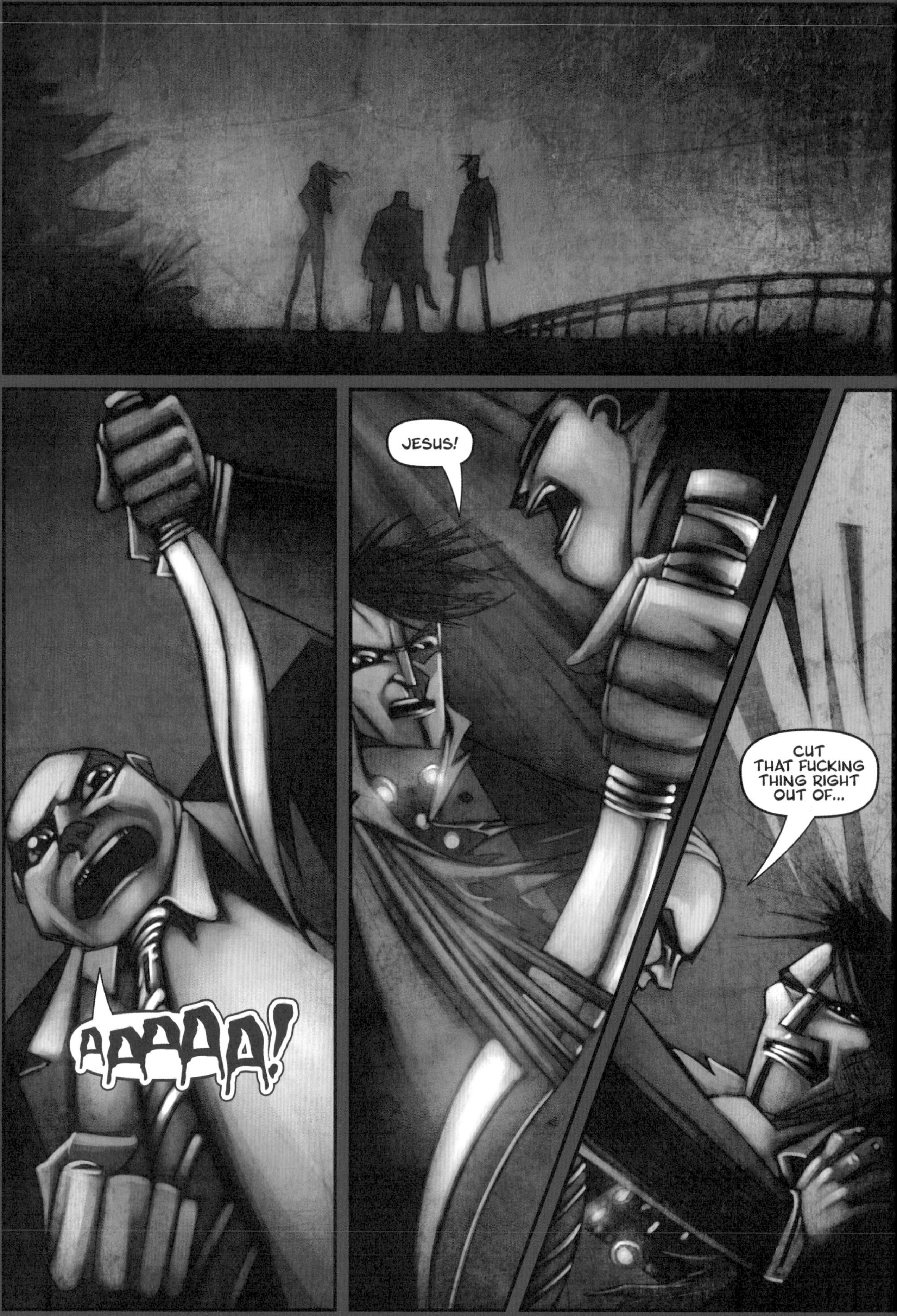
AAAAA!
JESUS!
CUT THAT FUCKING THING RIGHT OUT OF...

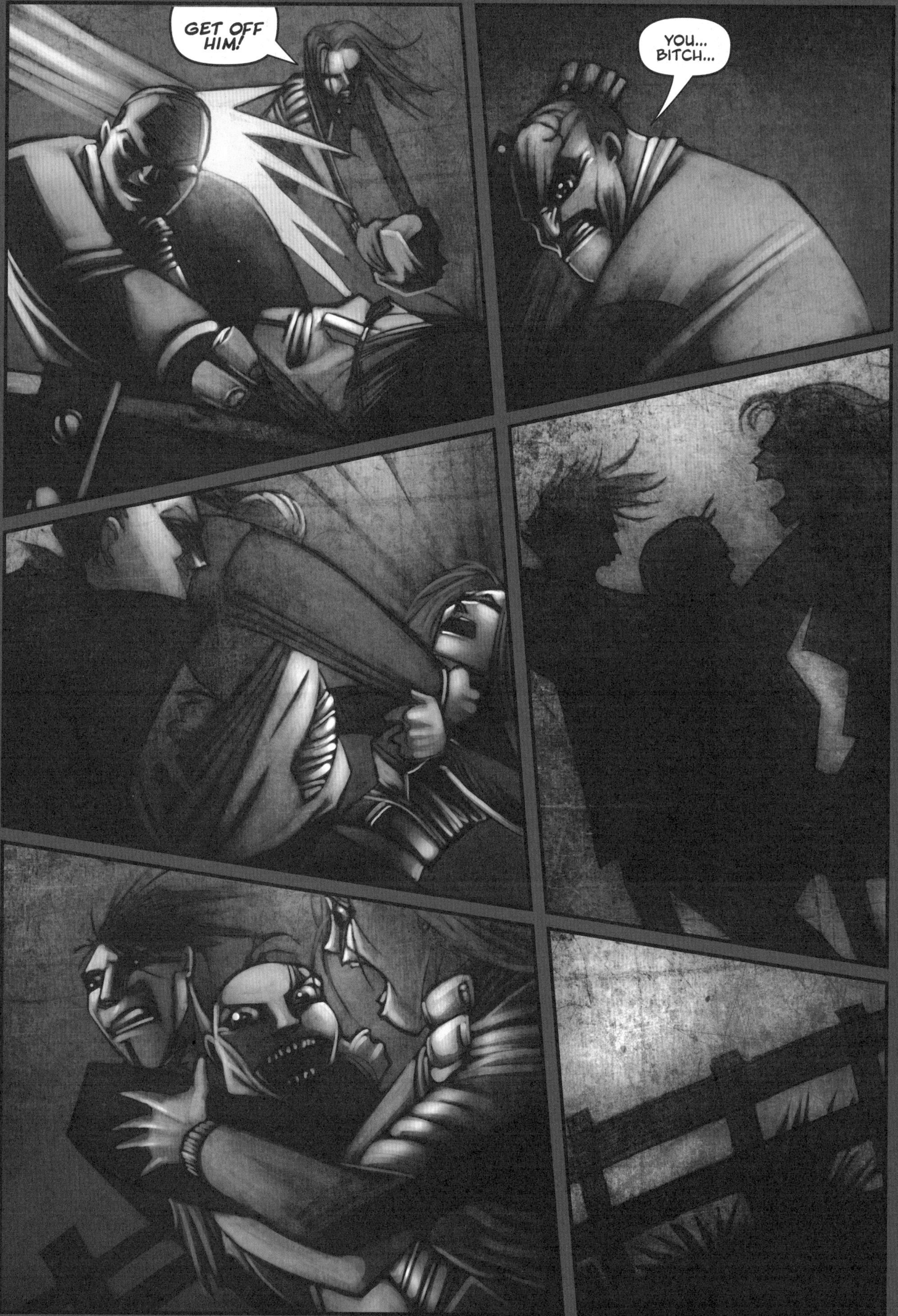
GET OFF HIM!
YOU... BITCH...

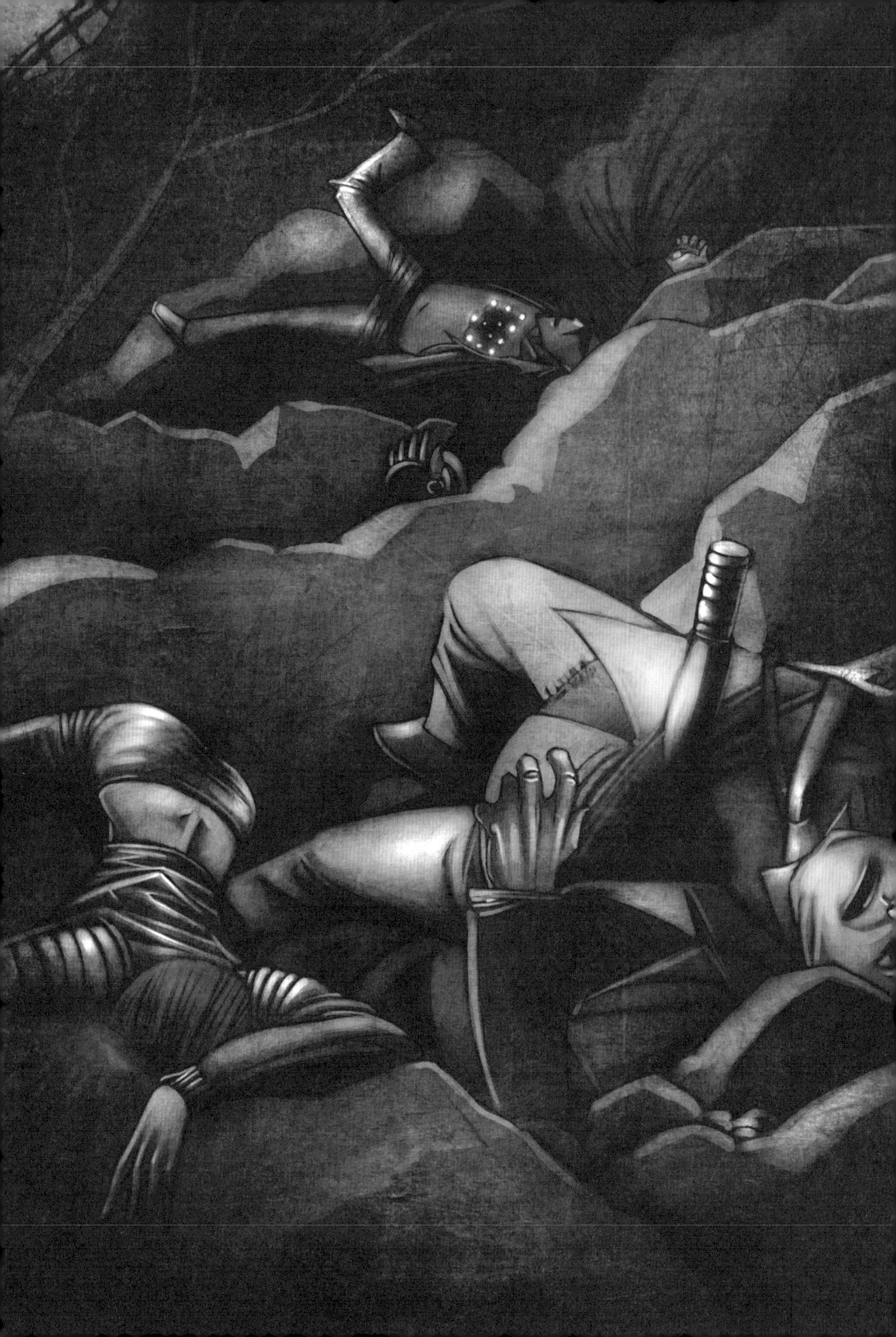

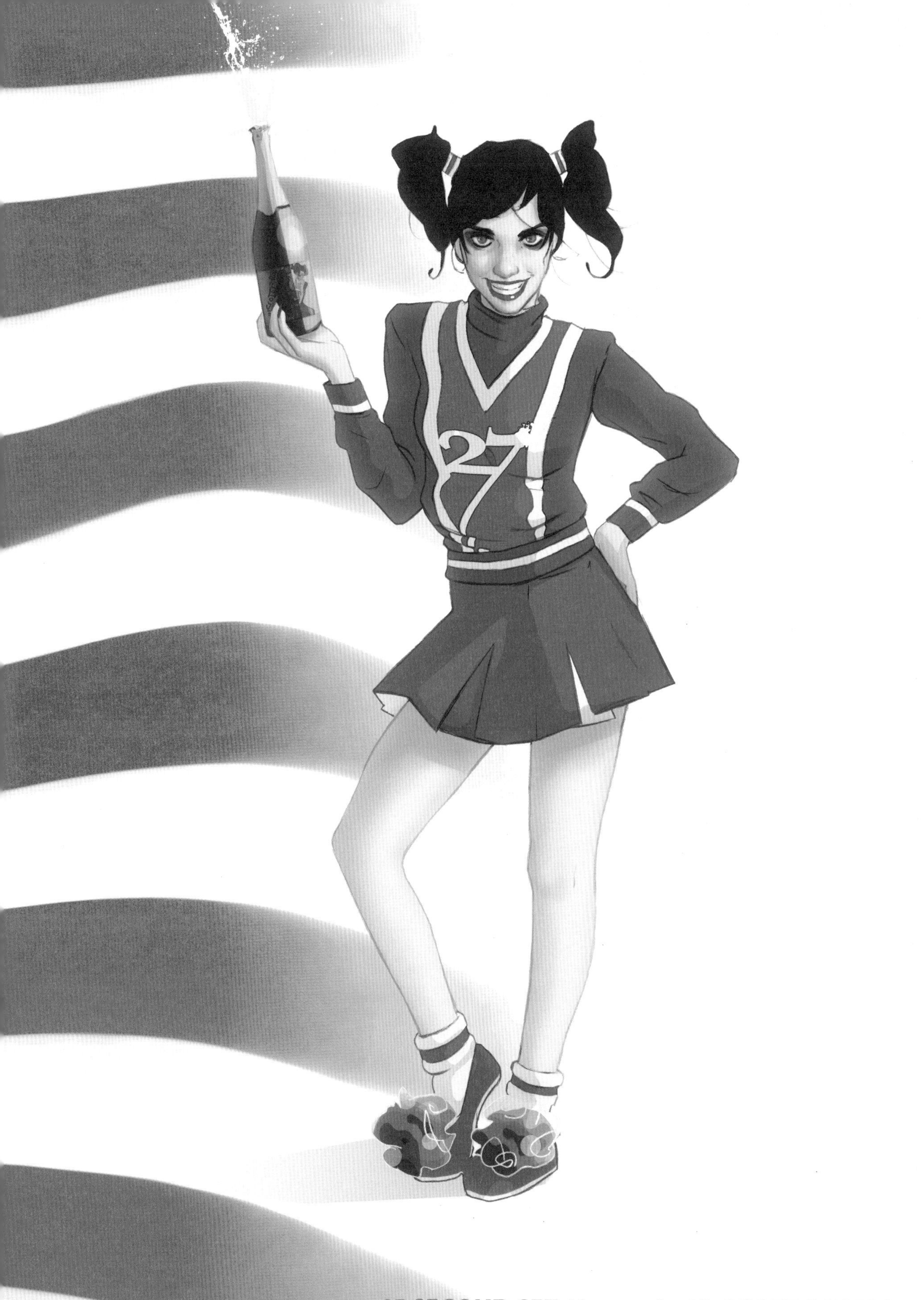

27 SECOND SET #3 cover by W. SCOTT FORBES
Based on "Mickey" by Toni Basil

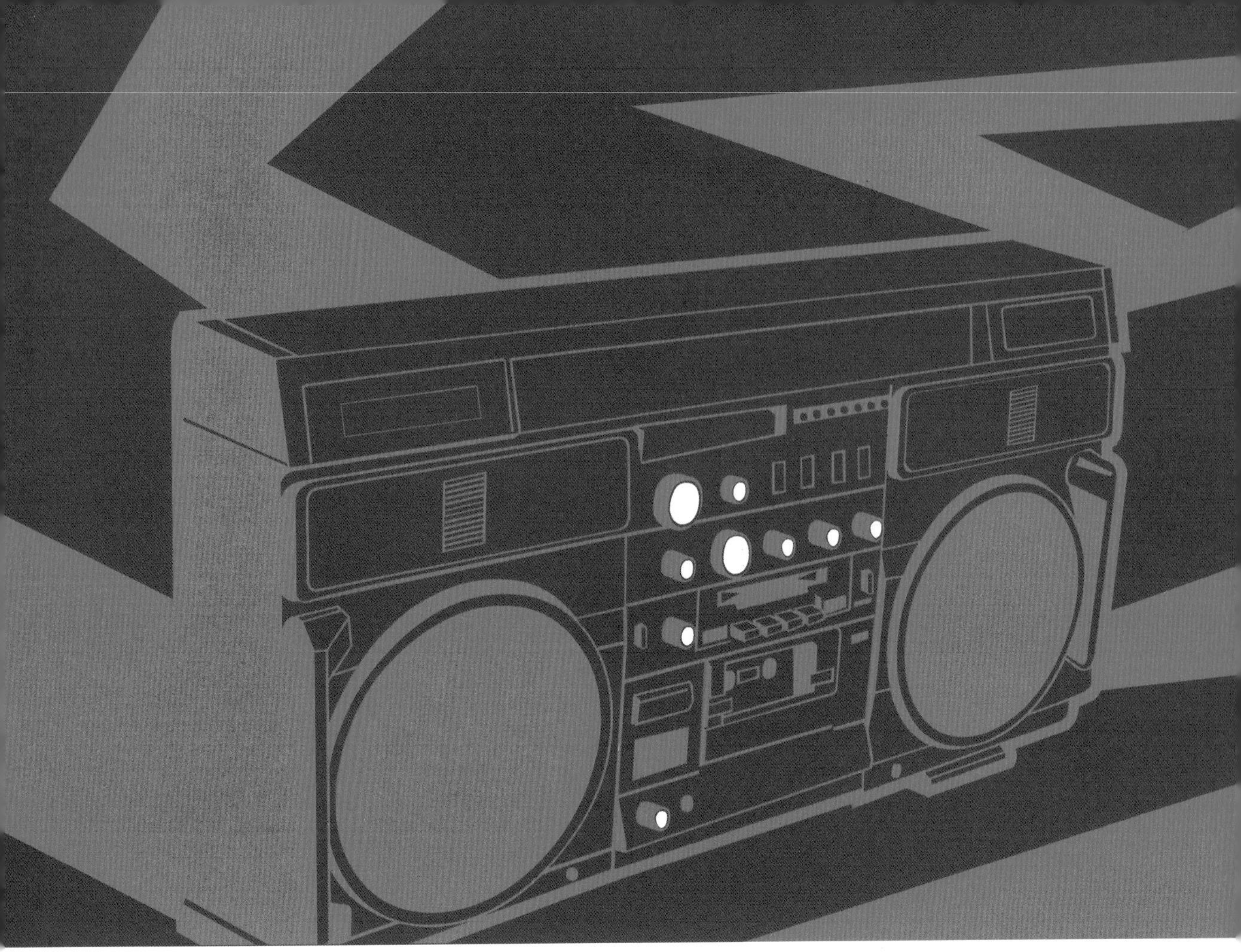

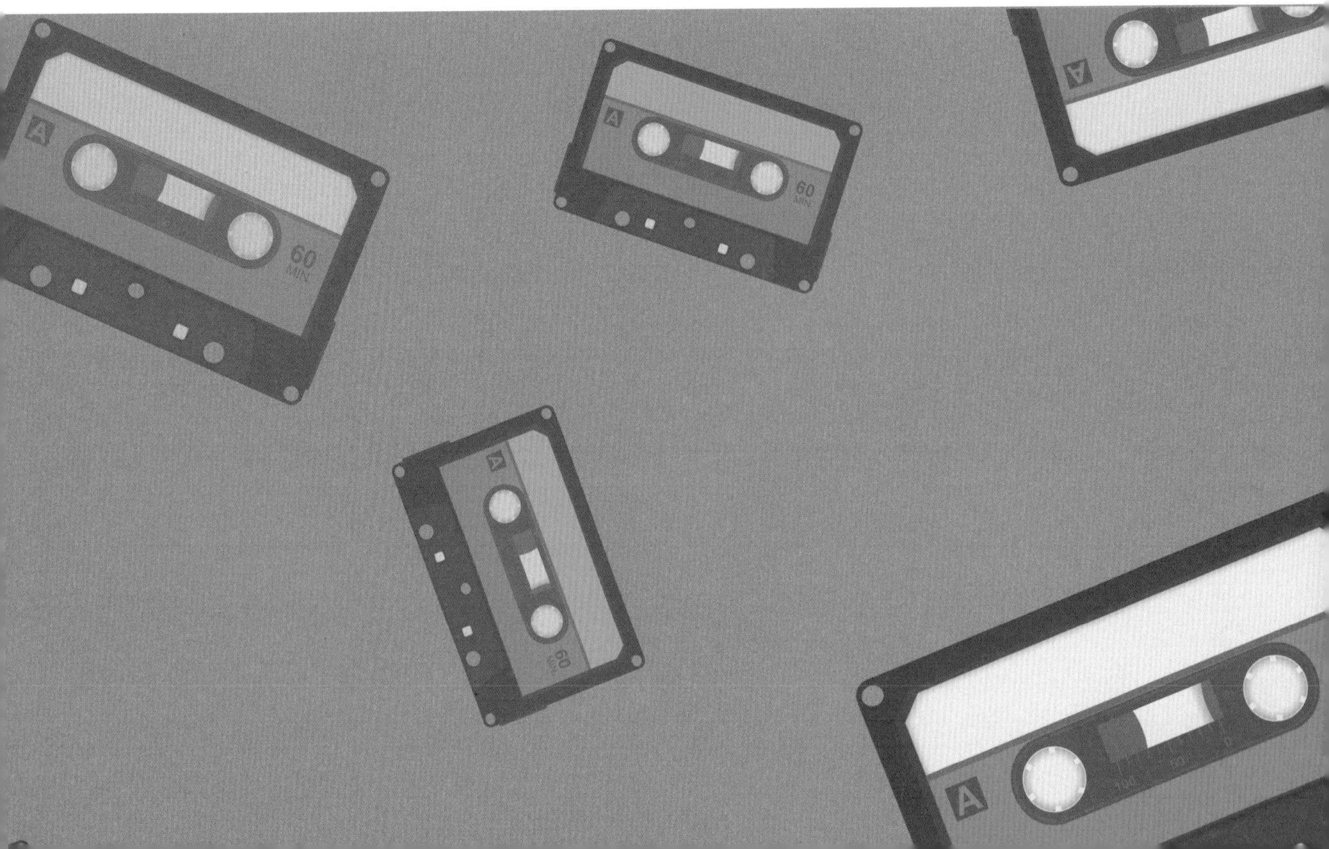
A
60
MIN

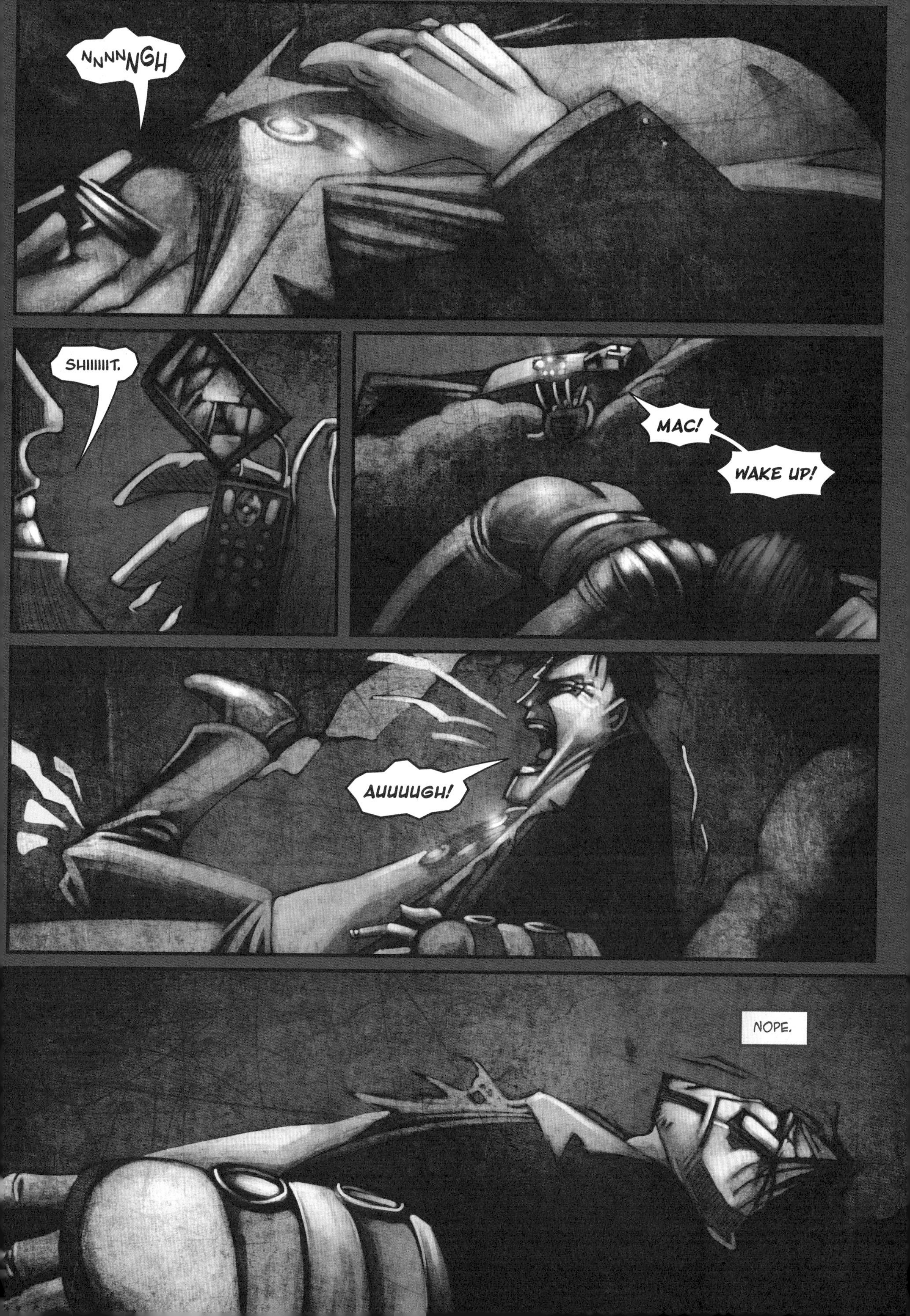
NNNNNGH
SHIIIIIIT.
MAC!
WAKE UP!
AUUUUGH!
NOPE.

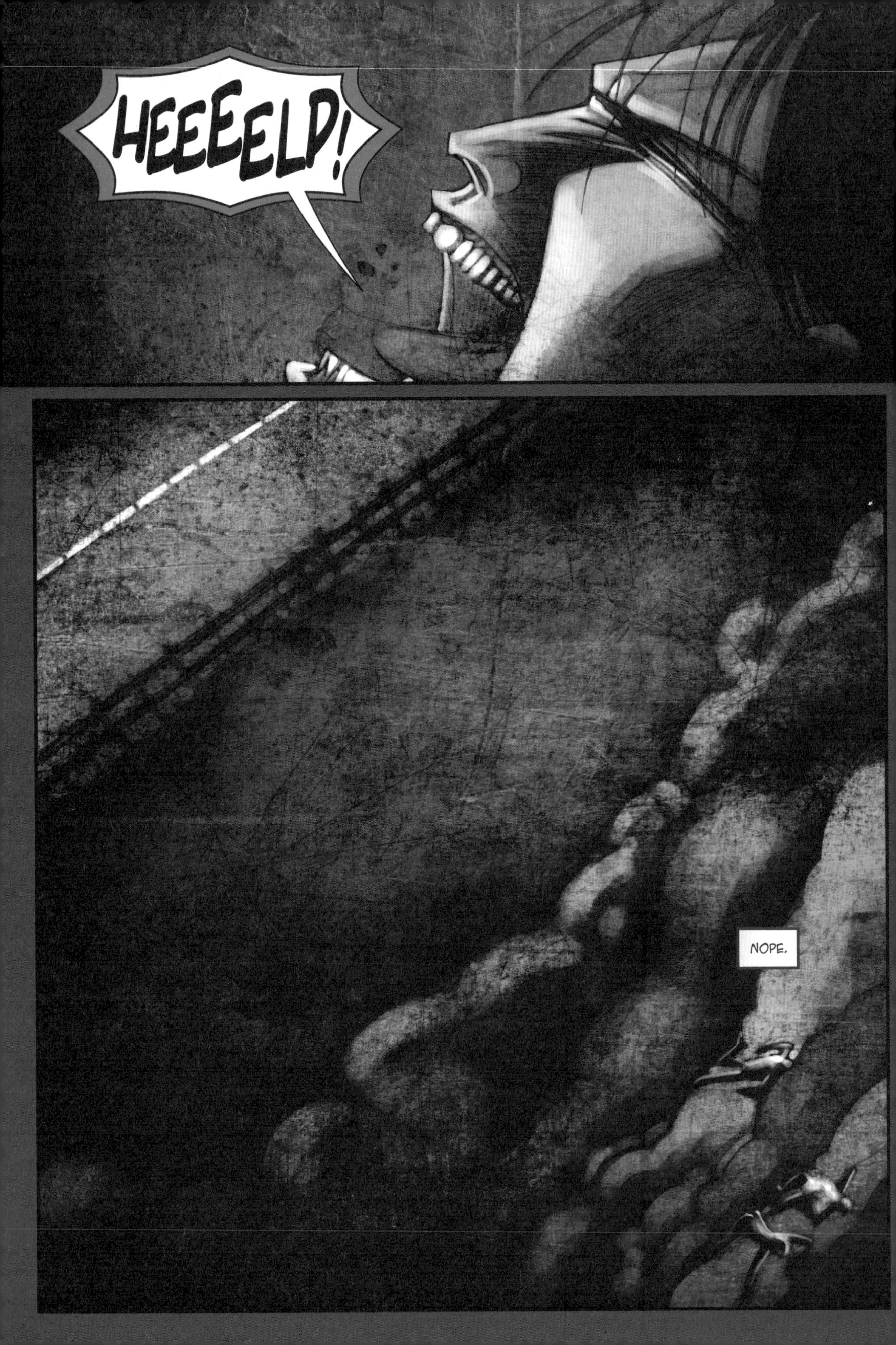
HEEEELP!
NOPE.

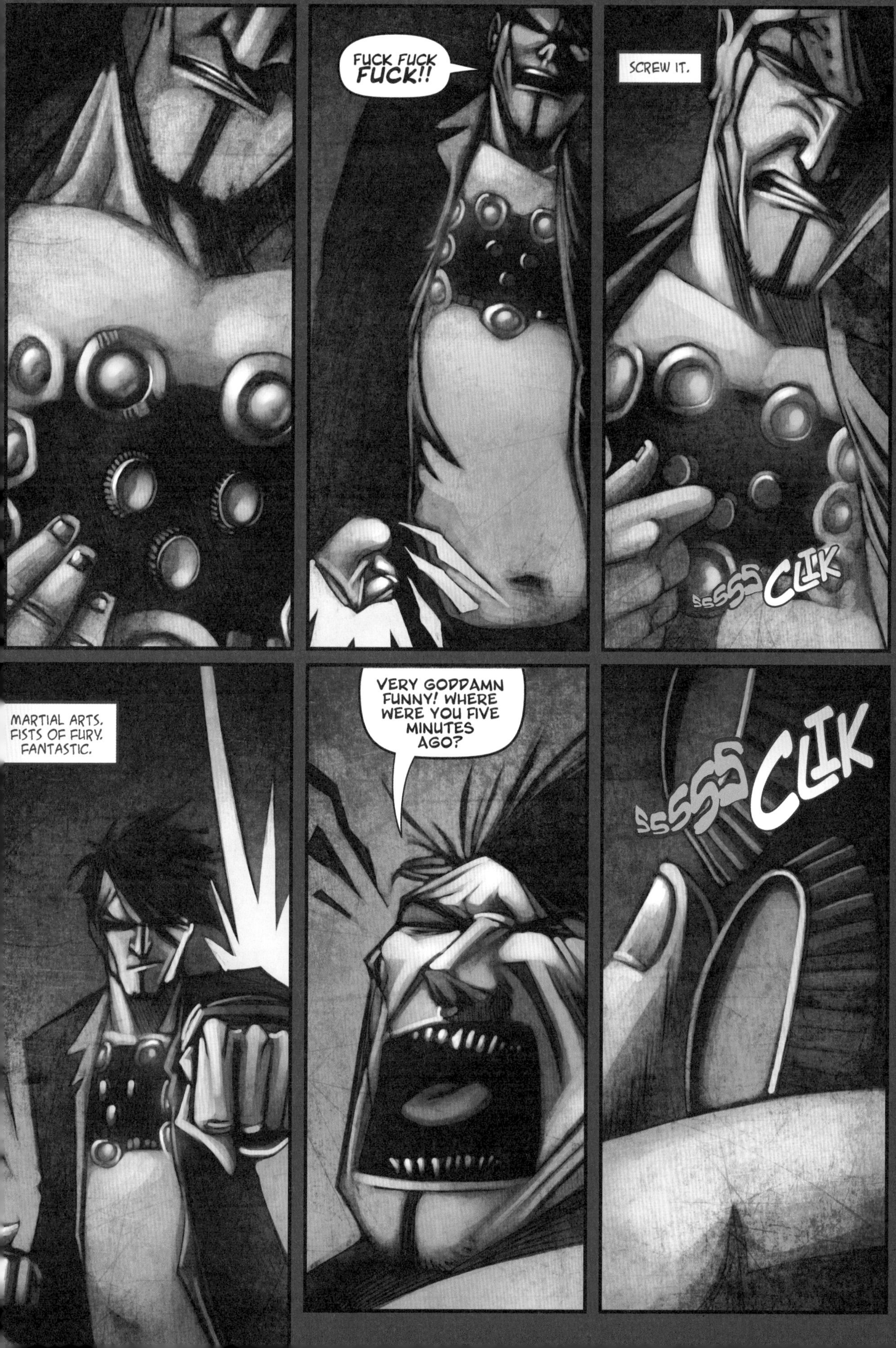
FUCK FUCK FUCK!!
SCREW IT.
SSSSS CLIK
MARTIAL ARTS. FISTS OF FURY. FANTASTIC.
VERY GODDAMN FUNNY! WHERE WERE YOU FIVE MINUTES AGO?
SSSSS CLIK

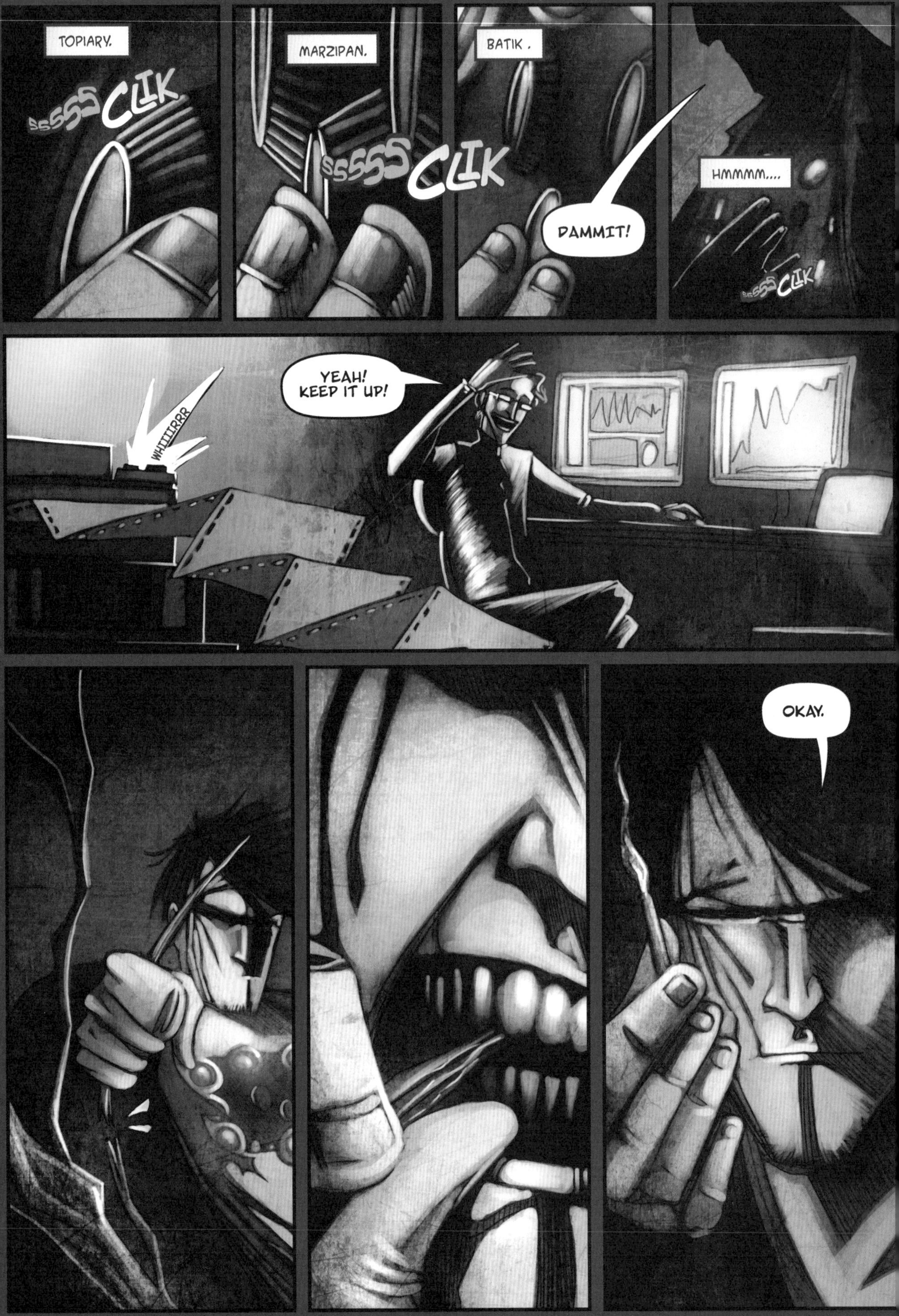
TOPIARY.
SSSSS CLIK
MARZIPAN.
SSSSS CLIK
BATIK.
DAMMIT!
HMMMM....
SSSSS CLIK
WHIIIIRRR
YEAH! KEEP IT UP!
OKAY.

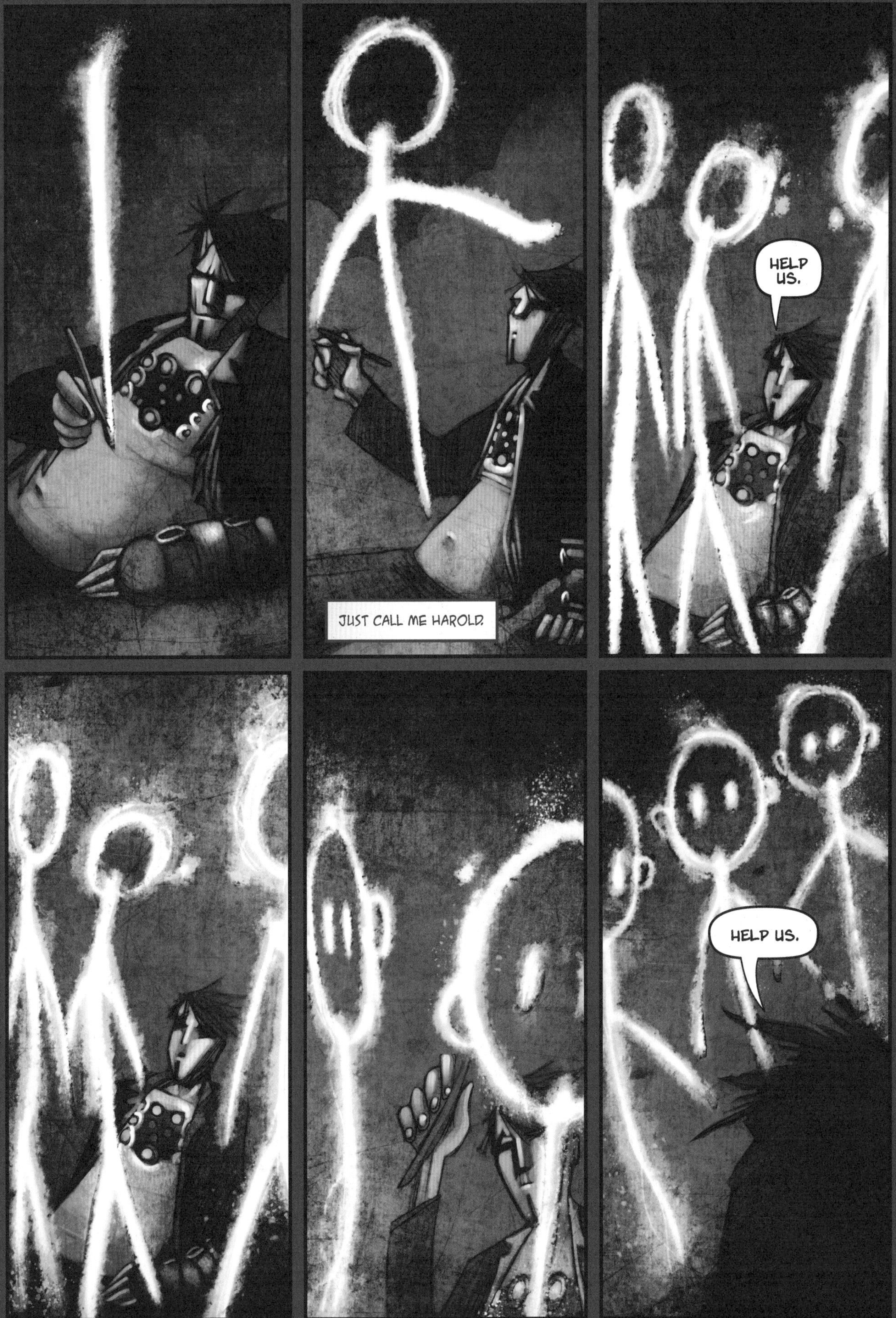
JUST CALL ME HAROLD.
HELP US.
HELP US.

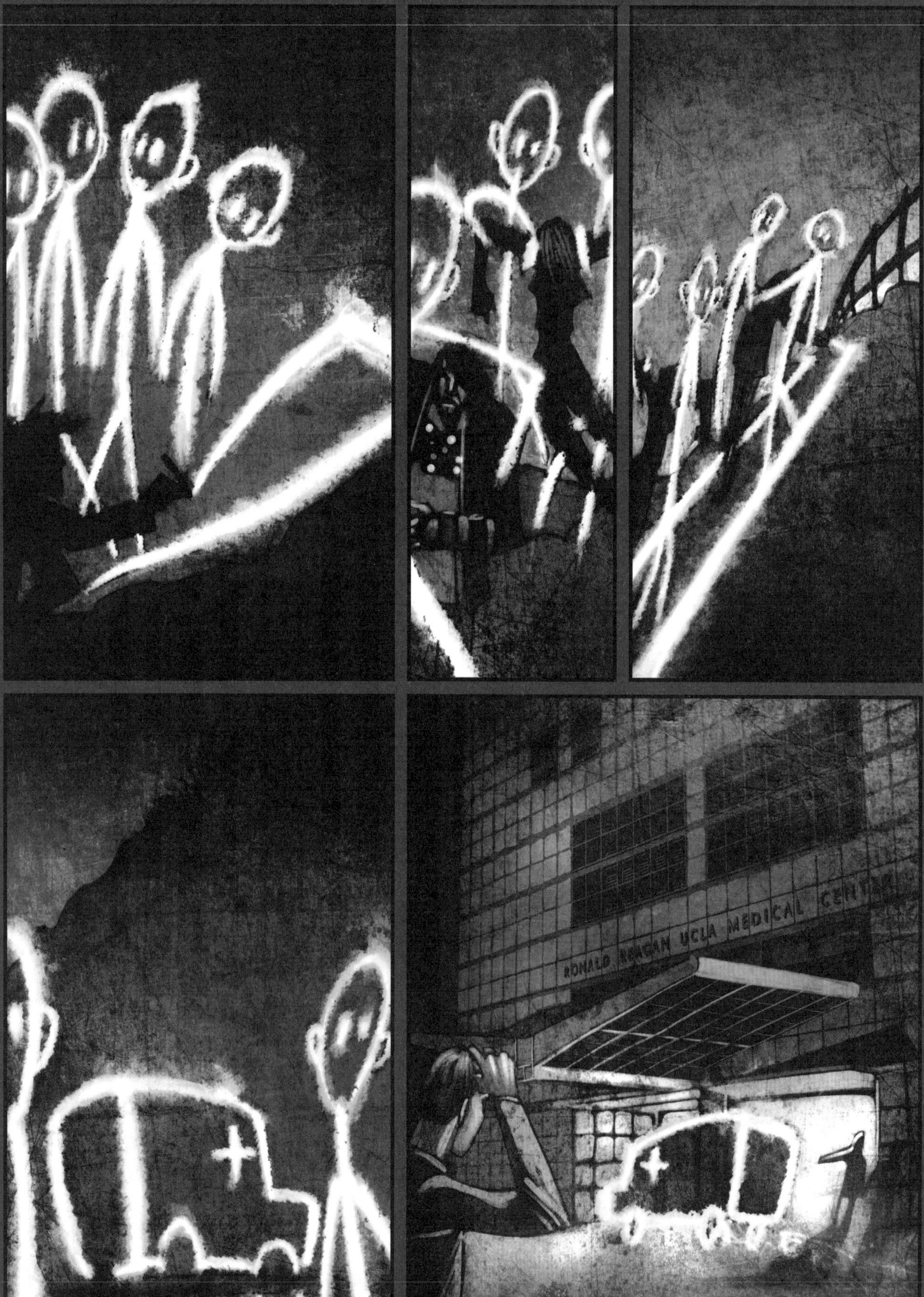
RONALD REAGAN UCLA MEDICAL

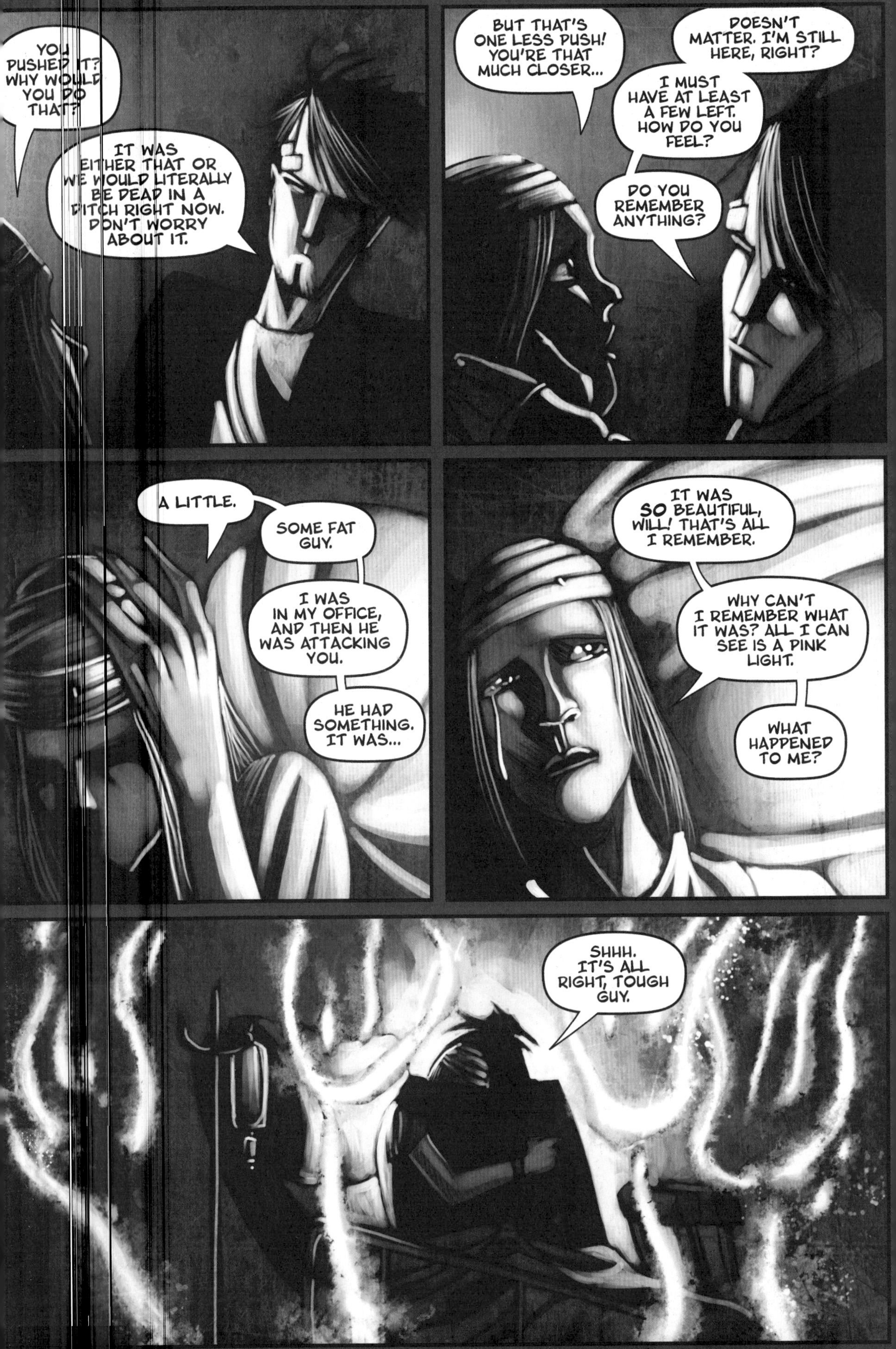
YOU PUSHED IT? WHY WOULD YOU DO THAT?
IT WAS EITHER THAT OR WE WOULD LITERALLY BE DEAD IN A DITCH RIGHT NOW. DON'T WORRY ABOUT IT.
BUT THAT'S ONE LESS PUSH! YOU'RE THAT MUCH CLOSER...
DOESN'T MATTER. I'M STILL HERE, RIGHT?
I MUST HAVE AT LEAST A FEW LEFT. HOW DO YOU FEEL?
DO YOU REMEMBER ANYTHING?
A LITTLE.
SOME FAT GUY.
I WAS IN MY OFFICE, AND THEN HE WAS ATTACKING YOU.
HE HAD SOMETHING. IT WAS...
IT WAS SO BEAUTIFUL, WILL! THAT'S ALL I REMEMBER.
WHY CAN'T I REMEMBER WHAT IT WAS? ALL I CAN SEE IS A PINK LIGHT.
WHAT HAPPENED TO ME?
SHHH. IT'S ALL RIGHT, TOUGH GUY.

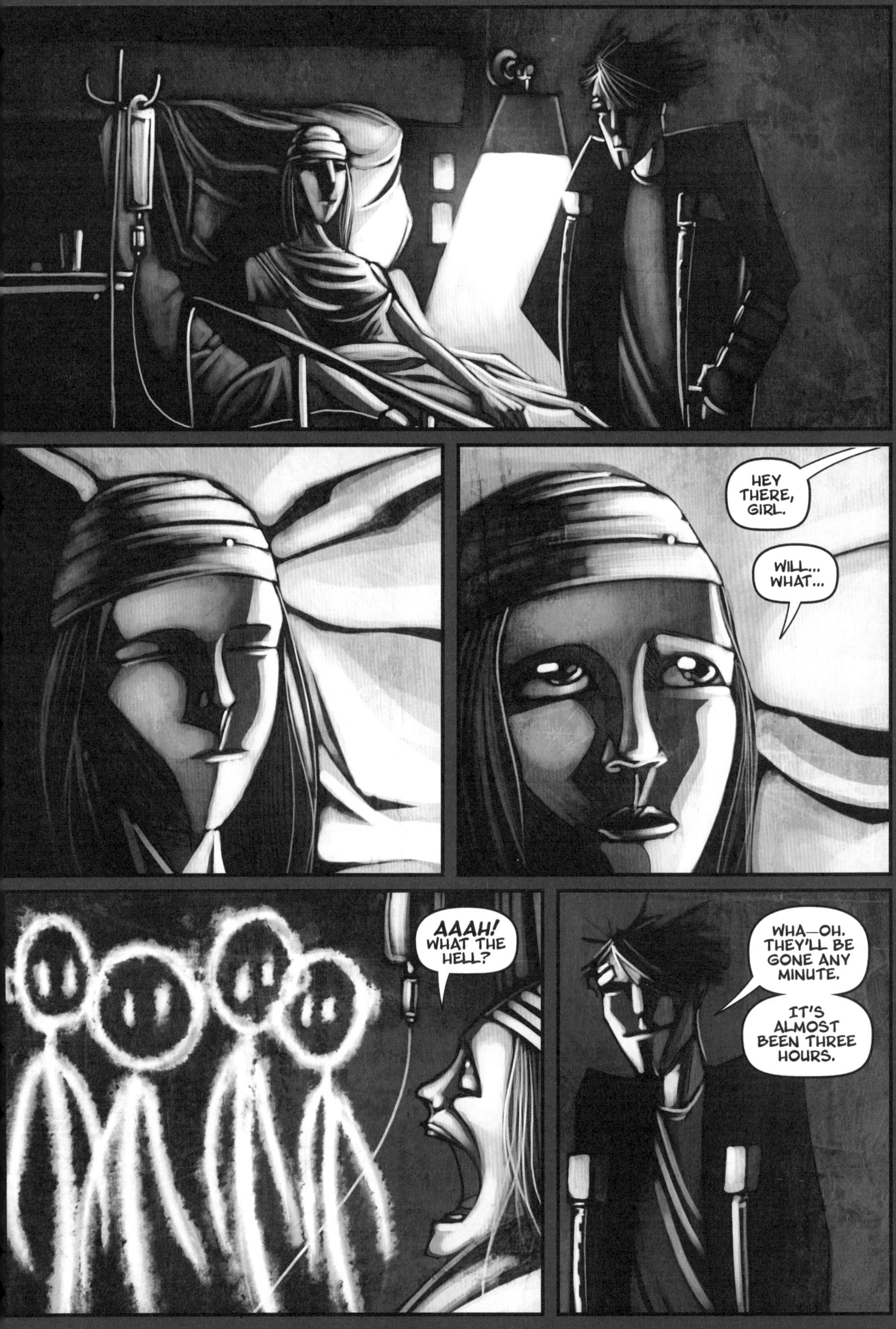
HEY THERE, GIRL.
WILL... WHAT...
AAAH! WHAT THE HELL?
WHA—OH. THEY'LL BE GONE ANY MINUTE.
IT'S ALMOST BEEN THREE HOURS.

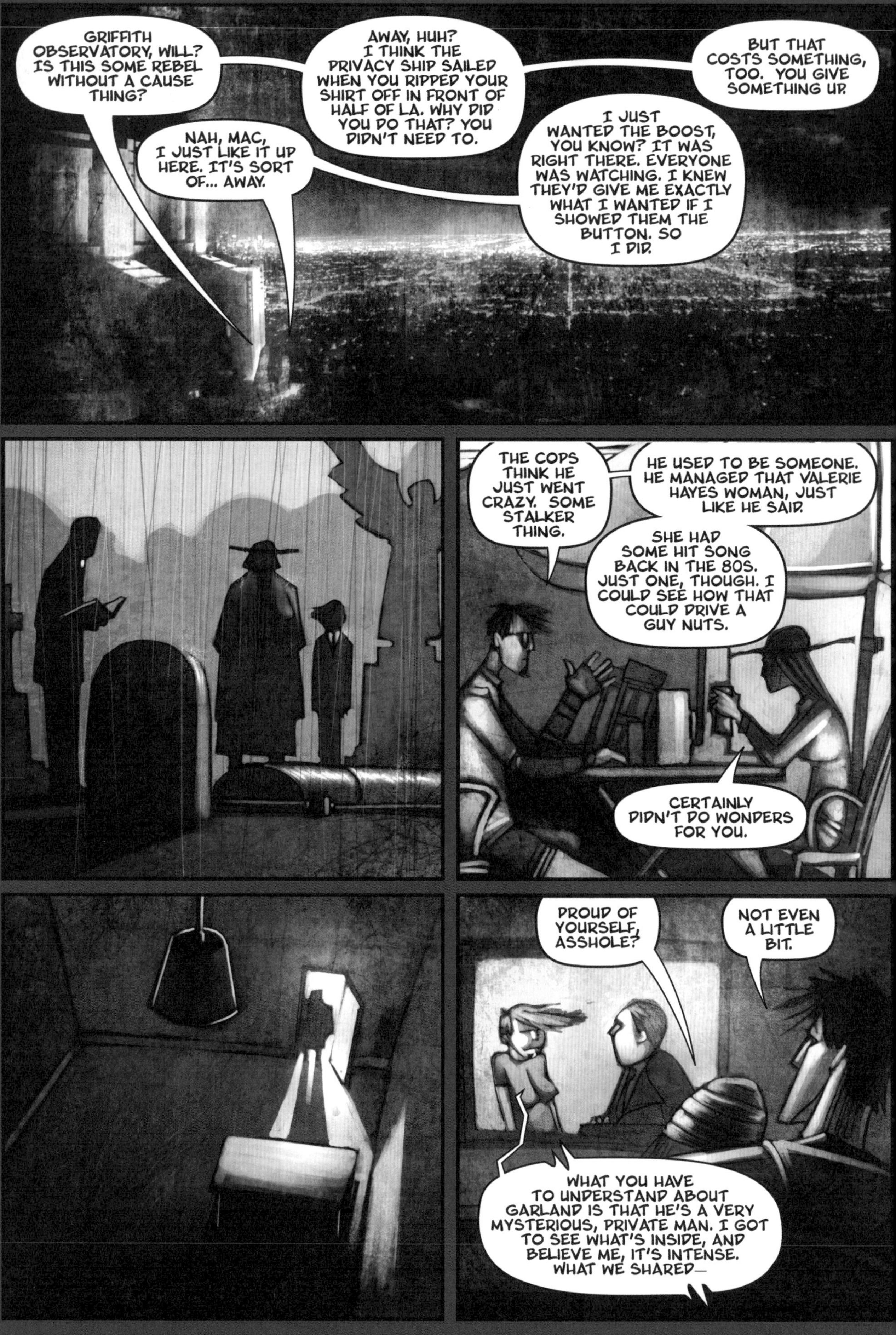
GRIFFITH OBSERVATORY, WILL? IS THIS SOME REBEL WITHOUT A CAUSE THING?
NAH, MAC, I JUST LIKE IT UP HERE. IT'S SORT OF... AWAY.
AWAY, HUH? I THINK THE PRIVACY SHIP SAILED WHEN YOU RIPPED YOUR SHIRT OFF IN FRONT OF HALF OF LA. WHY DID YOU DO THAT? YOU DIDN'T NEED TO.
I JUST WANTED THE BOOST, YOU KNOW? IT WAS RIGHT THERE. EVERYONE WAS WATCHING. I KNEW THEY'D GIVE ME EXACTLY WHAT I WANTED IF I SHOWED THEM THE BUTTON. SO I DID.
BUT THAT COSTS SOMETHING, TOO. YOU GIVE SOMETHING UP.
THE COPS THINK HE JUST WENT CRAZY. SOME STALKER THING.
HE USED TO BE SOMEONE. HE MANAGED THAT VALERIE HAYES WOMAN, JUST LIKE HE SAID.
SHE HAD SOME HIT SONG BACK IN THE 80S. JUST ONE, THOUGH. I COULD SEE HOW THAT COULD DRIVE A GUY NUTS.
CERTAINLY DIDN'T DO WONDERS FOR YOU.
PROUD OF YOURSELF, ASSHOLE?
NOT EVEN A LITTLE BIT.
WHAT YOU HAVE TO UNDERSTAND ABOUT GARLAND IS THAT HE'S A VERY MYSTERIOUS, PRIVATE MAN. I GOT TO SEE WHAT'S INSIDE, AND BELIEVE ME, IT'S INTENSE. WHAT WE SHARED—

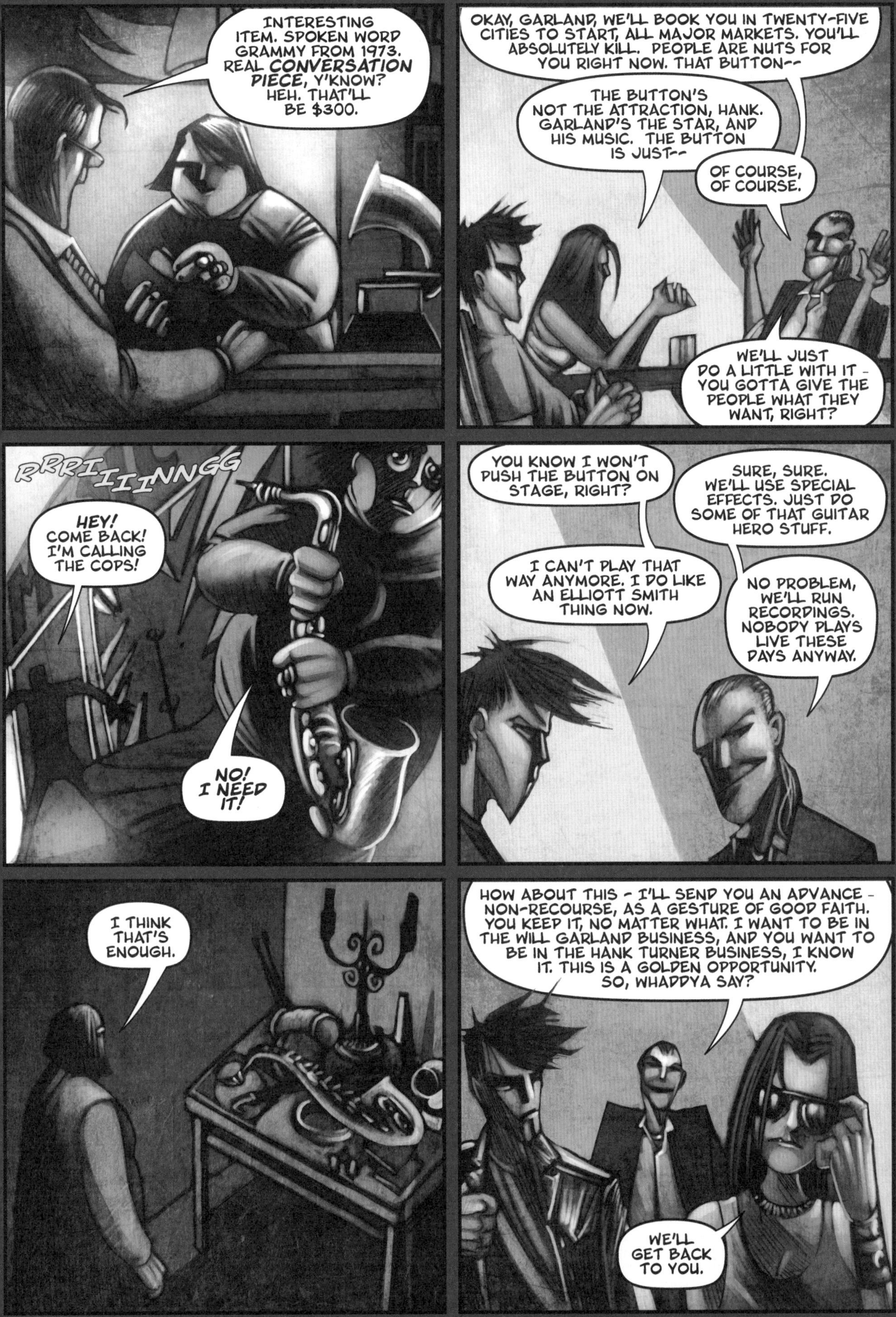
INTERESTING ITEM. SPOKEN WORD GRAMMY FROM 1973. REAL CONVERSATION PIECE, Y'KNOW? HEH. THAT'LL BE $300.
OKAY, GARLAND, WE'LL BOOK YOU IN TWENTY-FIVE CITIES TO START, ALL MAJOR MARKETS. YOU'LL ABSOLUTELY KILL. PEOPLE ARE NUTS FOR YOU RIGHT NOW. THAT BUTTON--
THE BUTTON'S NOT THE ATTRACTION, HANK. GARLAND'S THE STAR, AND HIS MUSIC. THE BUTTON IS JUST--
OF COURSE, OF COURSE.
WE'LL JUST DO A LITTLE WITH IT - YOU GOTTA GIVE THE PEOPLE WHAT THEY WANT, RIGHT?
RRRIIIINNGG
HEY! COME BACK! I'M CALLING THE COPS!
NO! I NEED IT!
YOU KNOW I WON'T PUSH THE BUTTON ON STAGE, RIGHT?
SURE, SURE. WE'LL USE SPECIAL EFFECTS. JUST DO SOME OF THAT GUITAR HERO STUFF.
I CAN'T PLAY THAT WAY ANYMORE. I DO LIKE AN ELLIOTT SMITH THING NOW.
NO PROBLEM, WE'LL RUN RECORDINGS. NOBODY PLAYS LIVE THESE DAYS ANYWAY.
I THINK THAT'S ENOUGH.
HOW ABOUT THIS - I'LL SEND YOU AN ADVANCE - NON-RECOURSE, AS A GESTURE OF GOOD FAITH. YOU KEEP IT, NO MATTER WHAT. I WANT TO BE IN THE WILL GARLAND BUSINESS, AND YOU WANT TO BE IN THE HANK TURNER BUSINESS, I KNOW IT. THIS IS A GOLDEN OPPORTUNITY. SO, WHADDYA SAY?
WE'LL GET BACK TO YOU.

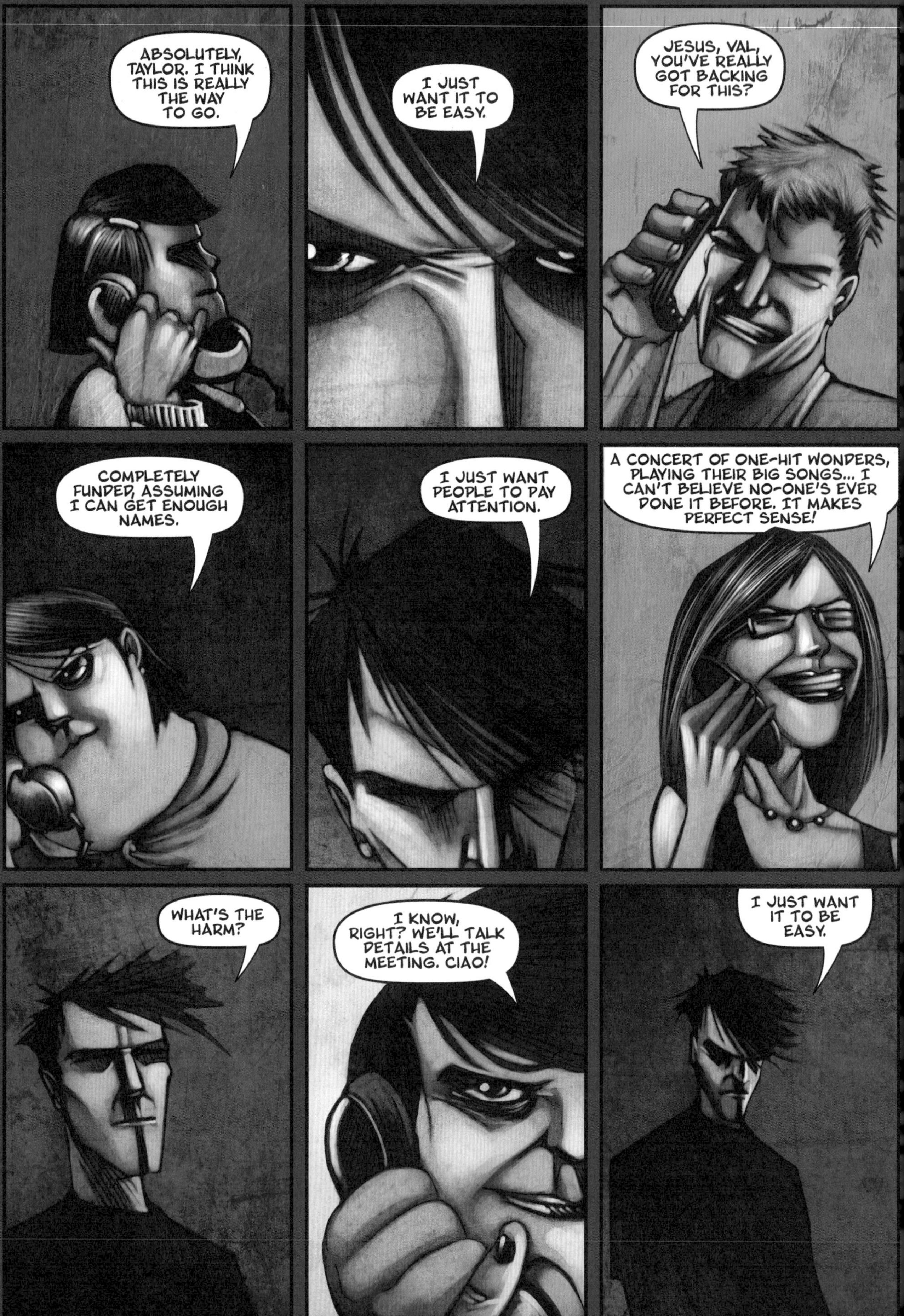
ABSOLUTELY, TAYLOR. I THINK THIS IS REALLY THE WAY TO GO.
I JUST WANT IT TO BE EASY.
JESUS, VAL, YOU'VE REALLY GOT BACKING FOR THIS?
COMPLETELY FUNDED, ASSUMING I CAN GET ENOUGH NAMES.
I JUST WANT PEOPLE TO PAY ATTENTION.
A CONCERT OF ONE-HIT WONDERS, PLAYING THEIR BIG SONGS... I CAN'T BELIEVE NO-ONE'S EVER DONE IT BEFORE. IT MAKES PERFECT SENSE!
WHAT'S THE HARM?
I KNOW, RIGHT? WE'LL TALK DETAILS AT THE MEETING. CIAO!
I JUST WANT IT TO BE EASY.

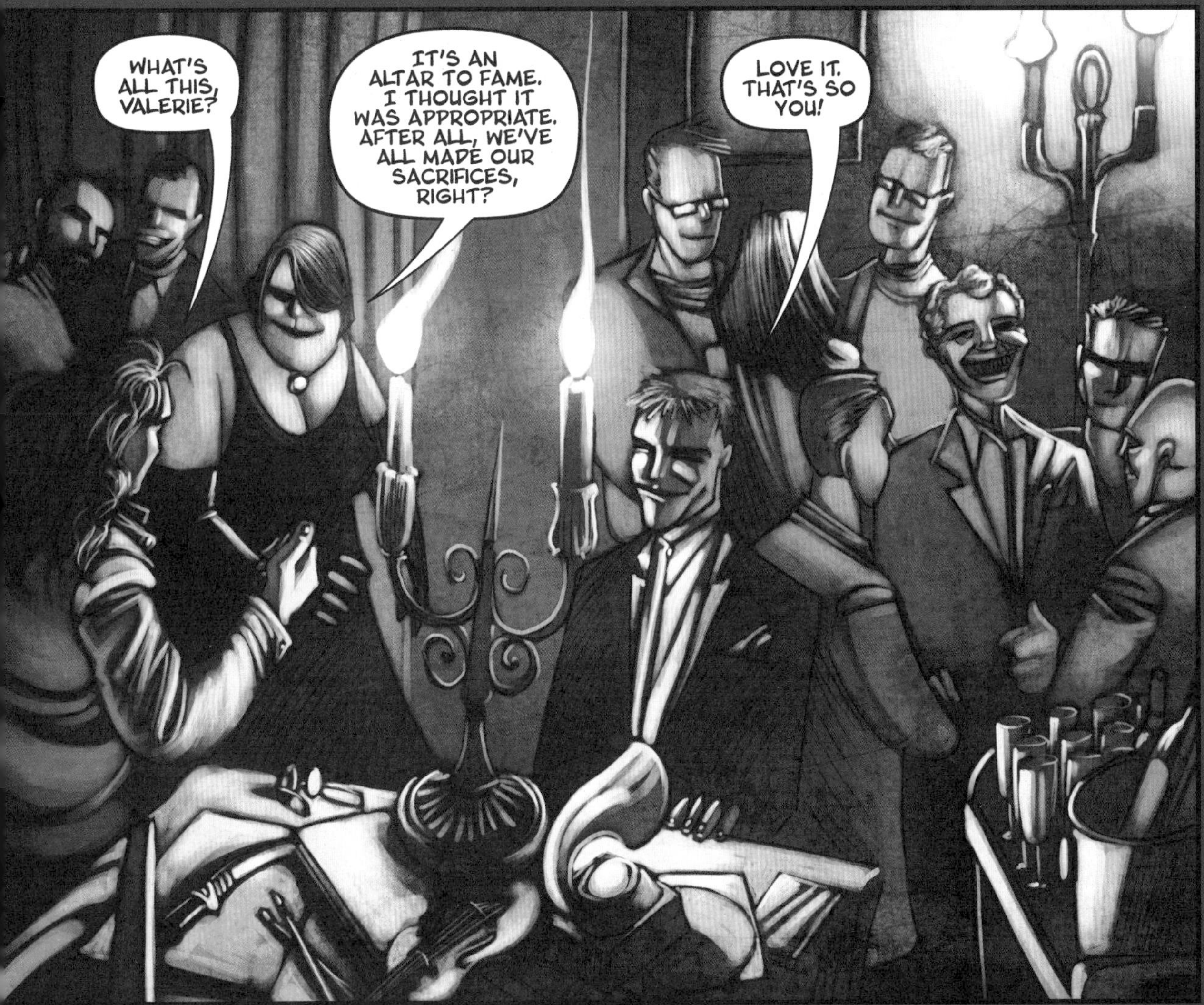
WHAT'S ALL THIS, VALERIE?
IT'S AN ALTAR TO FAME. I THOUGHT IT WAS APPROPRIATE. AFTER ALL, WE'VE ALL MADE OUR SACRIFICES, RIGHT?
LOVE IT. THAT'S SO YOU!

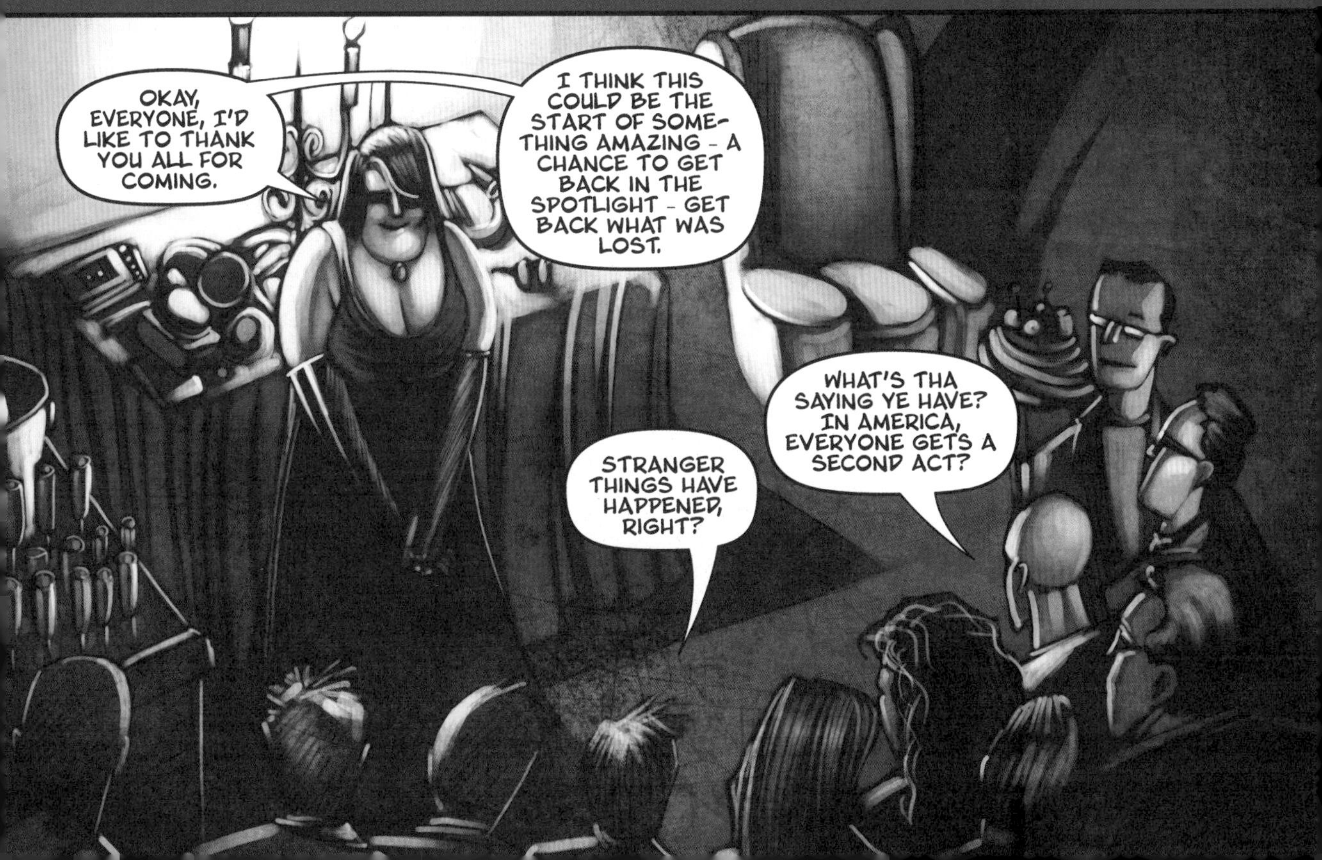
OKAY, EVERYONE, I'D LIKE TO THANK YOU ALL FOR COMING.
I THINK THIS COULD BE THE START OF SOME-THING AMAZING - A CHANCE TO GET BACK IN THE SPOTLIGHT - GET BACK WHAT WAS LOST.
WHAT'S THA SAYING YE HAVE? IN AMERICA, EVERYONE GETS A SECOND ACT?
STRANGER THINGS HAVE HAPPENED, RIGHT?

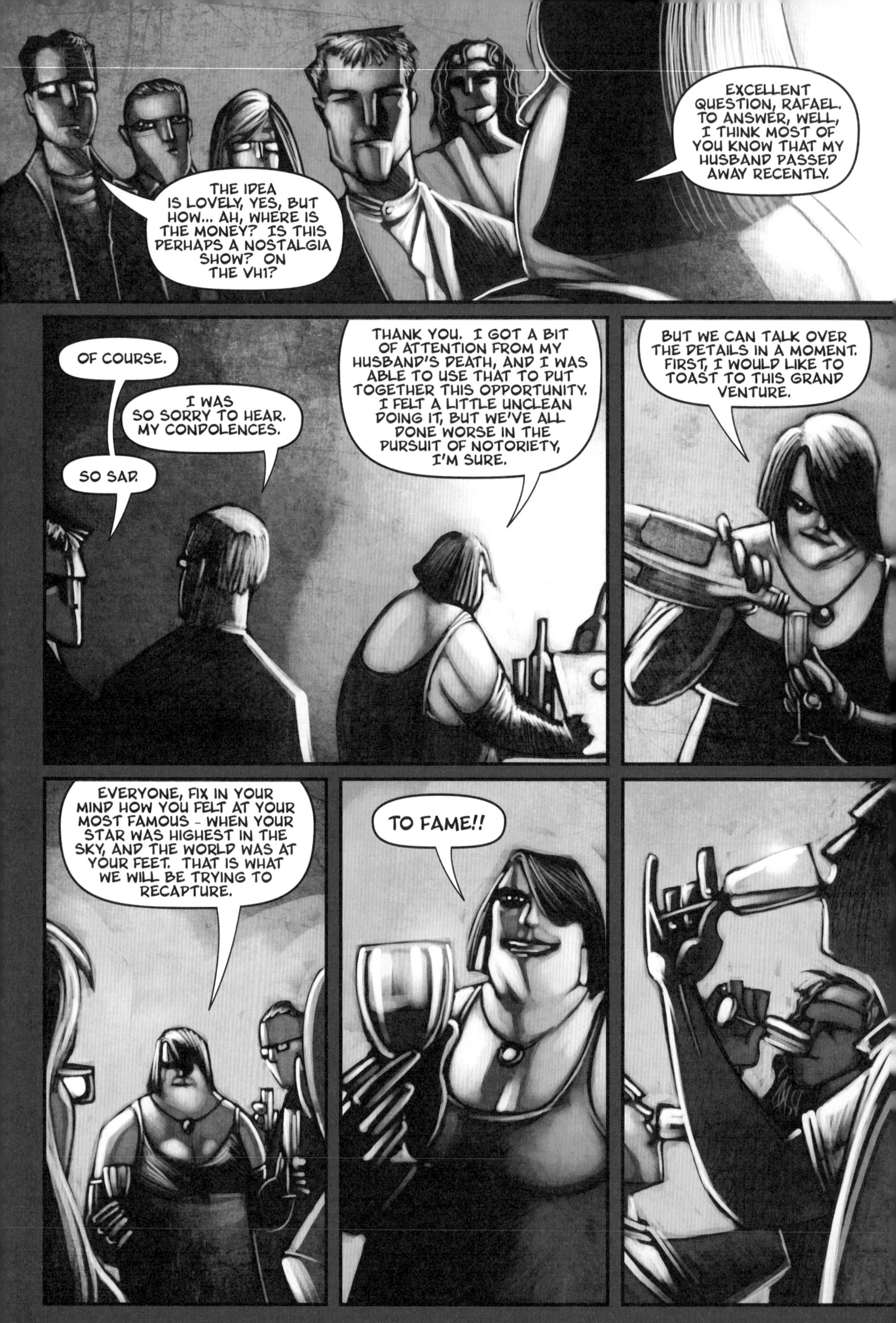
THE IDEA IS LOVELY, YES, BUT HOW... AH, WHERE IS THE MONEY? IS THIS PERHAPS A NOSTALGIA SHOW? ON THE VH1?
EXCELLENT QUESTION, RAFAEL. TO ANSWER, WELL, I THINK MOST OF YOU KNOW THAT MY HUSBAND PASSED AWAY RECENTLY.
OF COURSE.
I WAS SO SORRY TO HEAR. MY CONDOLENCES.
SO SAD.
THANK YOU. I GOT A BIT OF ATTENTION FROM MY HUSBAND'S DEATH, AND I WAS ABLE TO USE THAT TO PUT TOGETHER THIS OPPORTUNITY. I FELT A LITTLE UNCLEAN DOING IT, BUT WE'VE ALL DONE WORSE IN THE PURSUIT OF NOTORIETY, I'M SURE.
BUT WE CAN TALK OVER THE DETAILS IN A MOMENT. FIRST, I WOULD LIKE TO TOAST TO THIS GRAND VENTURE.
EVERYONE, FIX IN YOUR MIND HOW YOU FELT AT YOUR MOST FAMOUS - WHEN YOUR STAR WAS HIGHEST IN THE SKY, AND THE WORLD WAS AT YOUR FEET. THAT IS WHAT WE WILL BE TRYING TO RECAPTURE.
TO FAME!!

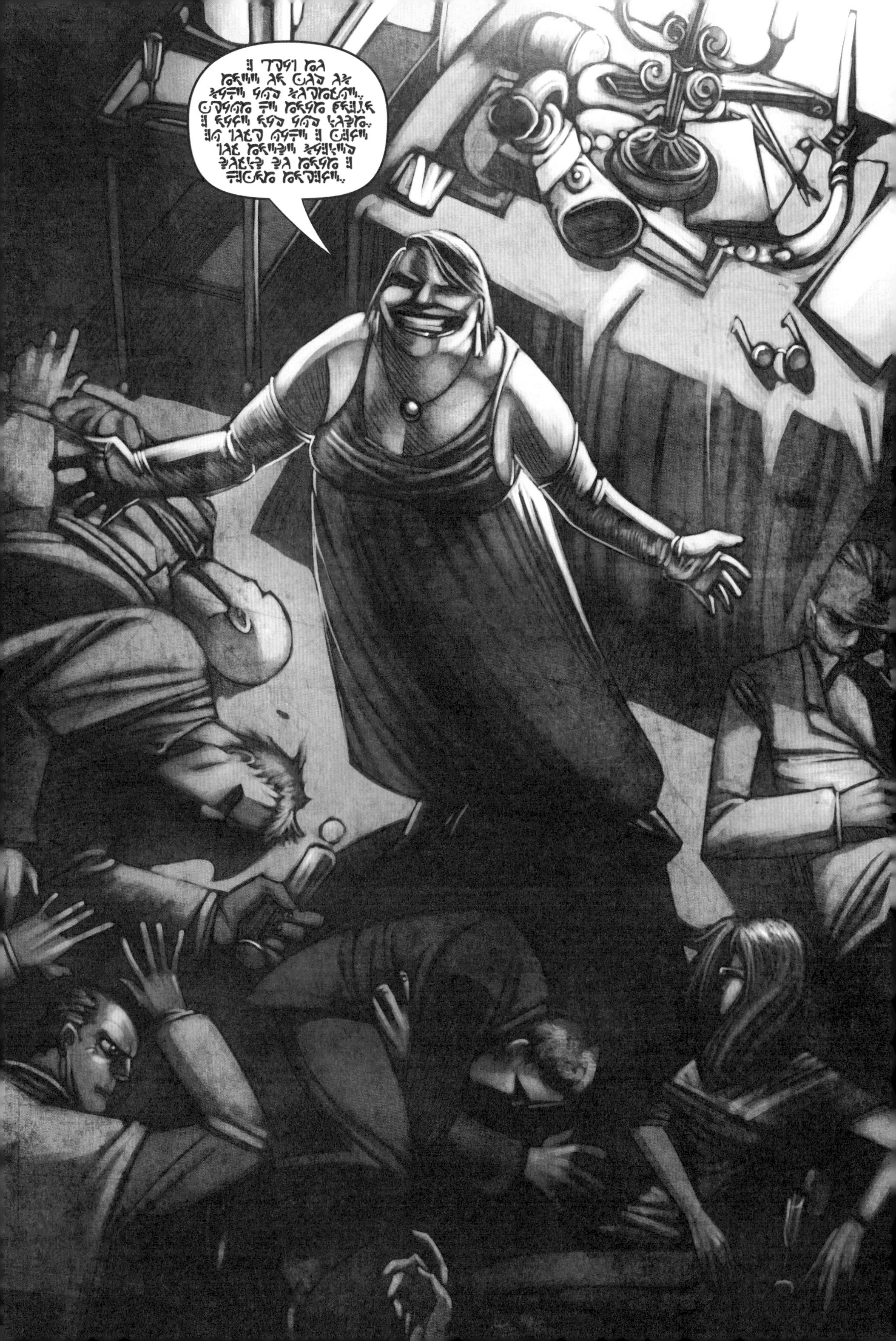

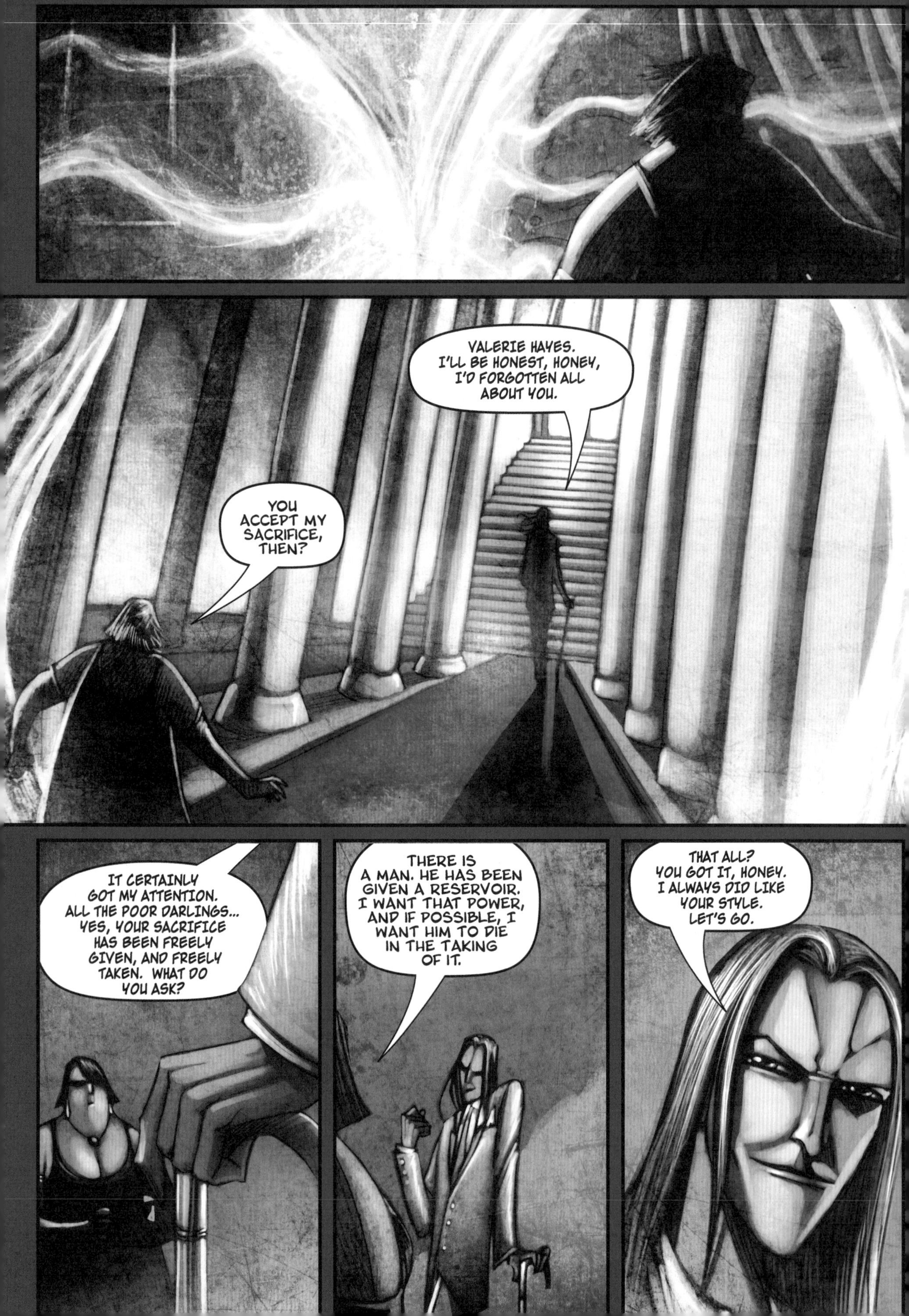

YOU ACCEPT MY SACRIFICE, THEN?
VALERIE HAYES. I'LL BE HONEST, HONEY, I'D FORGOTTEN ALL ABOUT YOU.
IT CERTAINLY GOT MY ATTENTION. ALL THE POOR DARLINGS... YES, YOUR SACRIFICE HAS BEEN FREELY GIVEN, AND FREELY TAKEN. WHAT DO YOU ASK?
THERE IS A MAN. HE HAS BEEN GIVEN A RESERVOIR. I WANT THAT POWER, AND IF POSSIBLE, I WANT HIM TO DIE IN THE TAKING OF IT.
THAT ALL? YOU GOT IT, HONEY. I ALWAYS DID LIKE YOUR STYLE. LET'S GO.

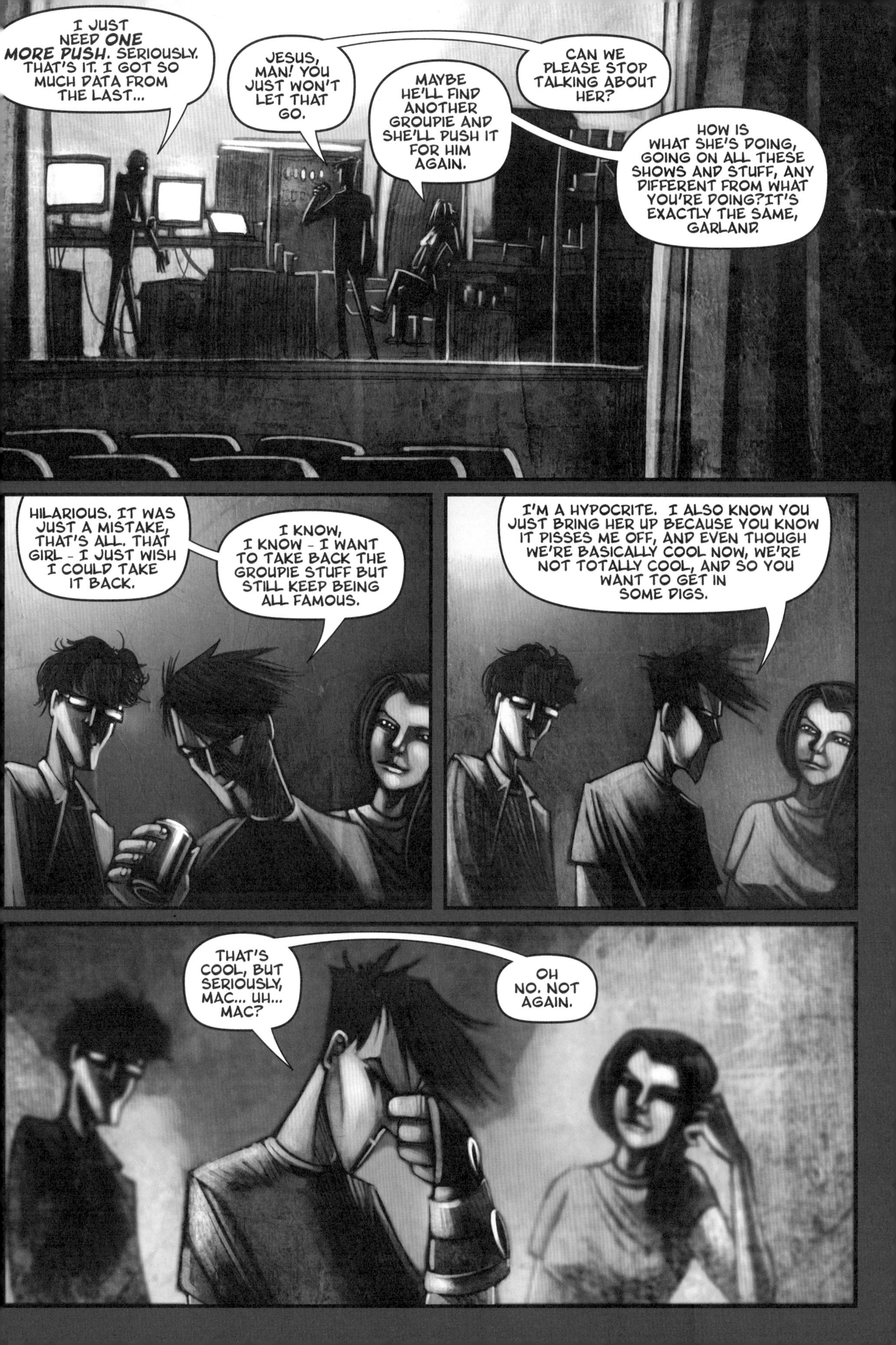
I JUST NEED ONE MORE PUSH. SERIOUSLY. THAT'S IT. I GOT SO MUCH DATA FROM THE LAST...
JESUS, MAN! YOU JUST WON'T LET THAT GO.
MAYBE HE'LL FIND ANOTHER GROUPIE AND SHE'LL PUSH IT FOR HIM AGAIN.
CAN WE PLEASE STOP TALKING ABOUT HER?
HOW IS WHAT SHE'S DOING, GOING ON ALL THESE SHOWS AND STUFF, ANY DIFFERENT FROM WHAT YOU'RE DOING? IT'S EXACTLY THE SAME, GARLAND.
HILARIOUS. IT WAS JUST A MISTAKE, THAT'S ALL. THAT GIRL - I JUST WISH I COULD TAKE IT BACK.
I KNOW, I KNOW - I WANT TO TAKE BACK THE GROUPIE STUFF BUT STILL KEEP BEING ALL FAMOUS.
I'M A HYPOCRITE. I ALSO KNOW YOU JUST BRING HER UP BECAUSE YOU KNOW IT PISSES ME OFF, AND EVEN THOUGH WE'RE BASICALLY COOL NOW, WE'RE NOT TOTALLY COOL, AND SO YOU WANT TO GET IN SOME DIGS.
THAT'S COOL, BUT SERIOUSLY, MAC... UH... MAC?
OH NO. NOT AGAIN.

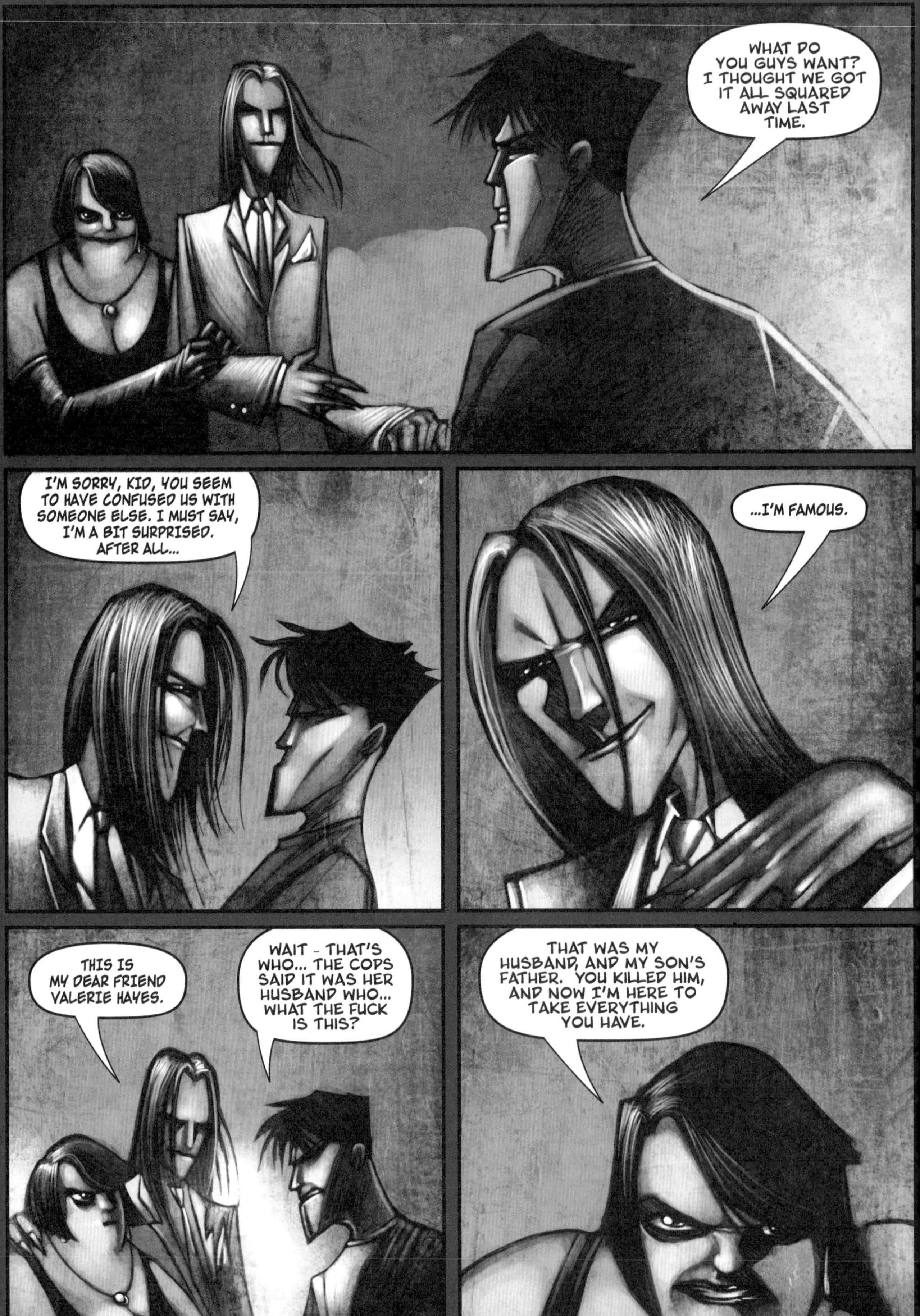
WHAT DO YOU GUYS WANT? I THOUGHT WE GOT IT ALL SQUARED AWAY LAST TIME.
I'M SORRY, KID, YOU SEEM TO HAVE CONFUSED US WITH SOMEONE ELSE. I MUST SAY, I'M A BIT SURPRISED. AFTER ALL...
...I'M FAMOUS.
THIS IS MY DEAR FRIEND VALERIE HAYES.
WAIT - THAT'S WHO... THE COPS SAID IT WAS HER HUSBAND WHO... WHAT THE FUCK IS THIS?
THAT WAS MY HUSBAND, AND MY SON'S FATHER. YOU KILLED HIM, AND NOW I'M HERE TO TAKE EVERYTHING YOU HAVE.

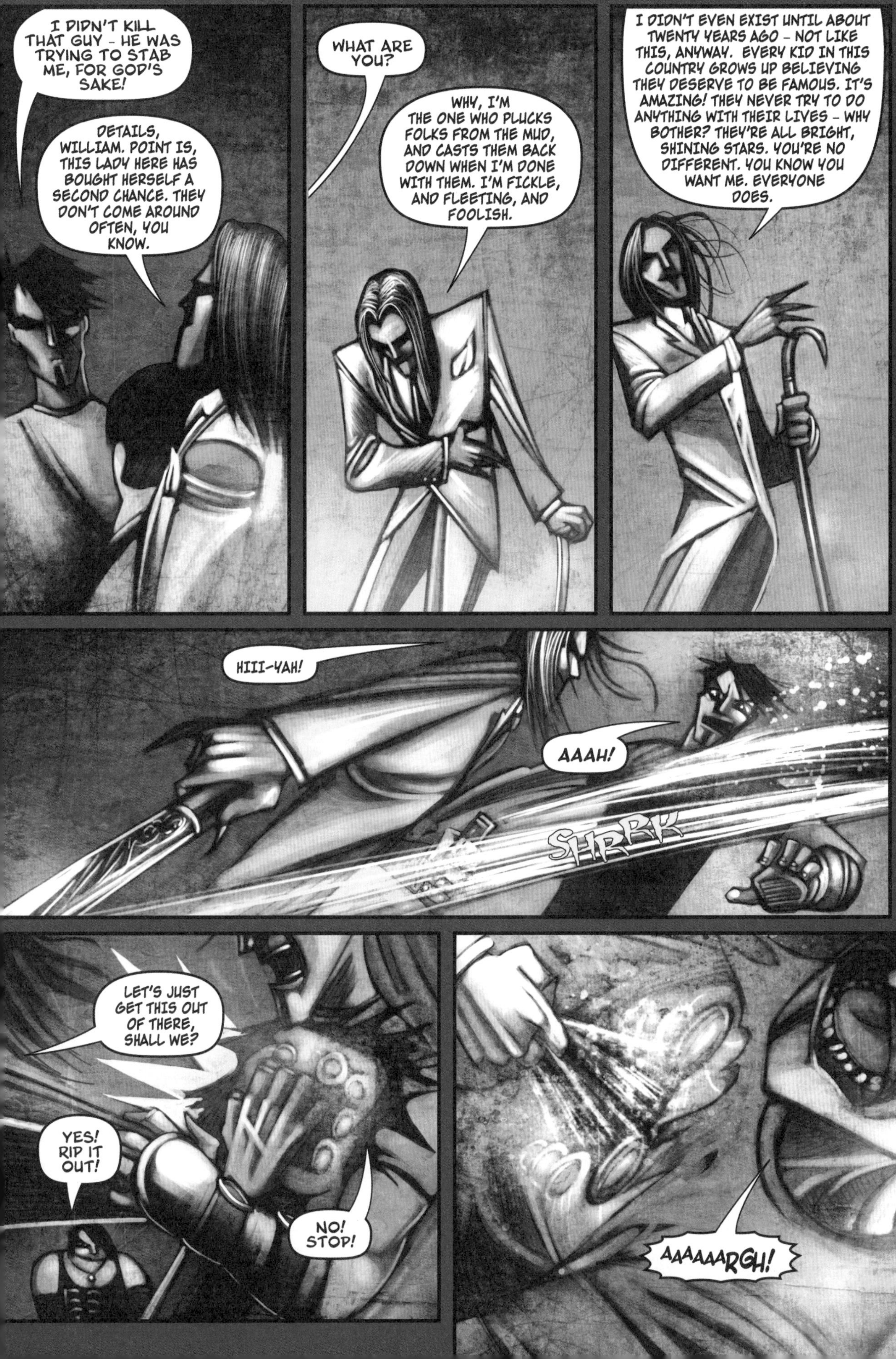
I DIDN'T KILL THAT GUY - HE WAS TRYING TO STAB ME, FOR GOD'S SAKE!
DETAILS, WILLIAM. POINT IS, THIS LADY HERE HAS BOUGHT HERSELF A SECOND CHANCE. THEY DON'T COME AROUND OFTEN, YOU KNOW.
WHAT ARE YOU?
WHY, I'M THE ONE WHO PLUCKS FOLKS FROM THE MUD, AND CASTS THEM BACK DOWN WHEN I'M DONE WITH THEM. I'M FICKLE, AND FLEETING, AND FOOLISH.
I DIDN'T EVEN EXIST UNTIL ABOUT TWENTY YEARS AGO - NOT LIKE THIS, ANYWAY. EVERY KID IN THIS COUNTRY GROWS UP BELIEVING THEY DESERVE TO BE FAMOUS. IT'S AMAZING! THEY NEVER TRY TO DO ANYTHING WITH THEIR LIVES - WHY BOTHER? THEY'RE ALL BRIGHT, SHINING STARS. YOU'RE NO DIFFERENT. YOU KNOW YOU WANT ME. EVERYONE DOES.
HIII-YAH!
AAAH!
SHRRK
LET'S JUST GET THIS OUT OF THERE, SHALL WE?
YES! RIP IT OUT!
NO! STOP!
AAAAAARGH!

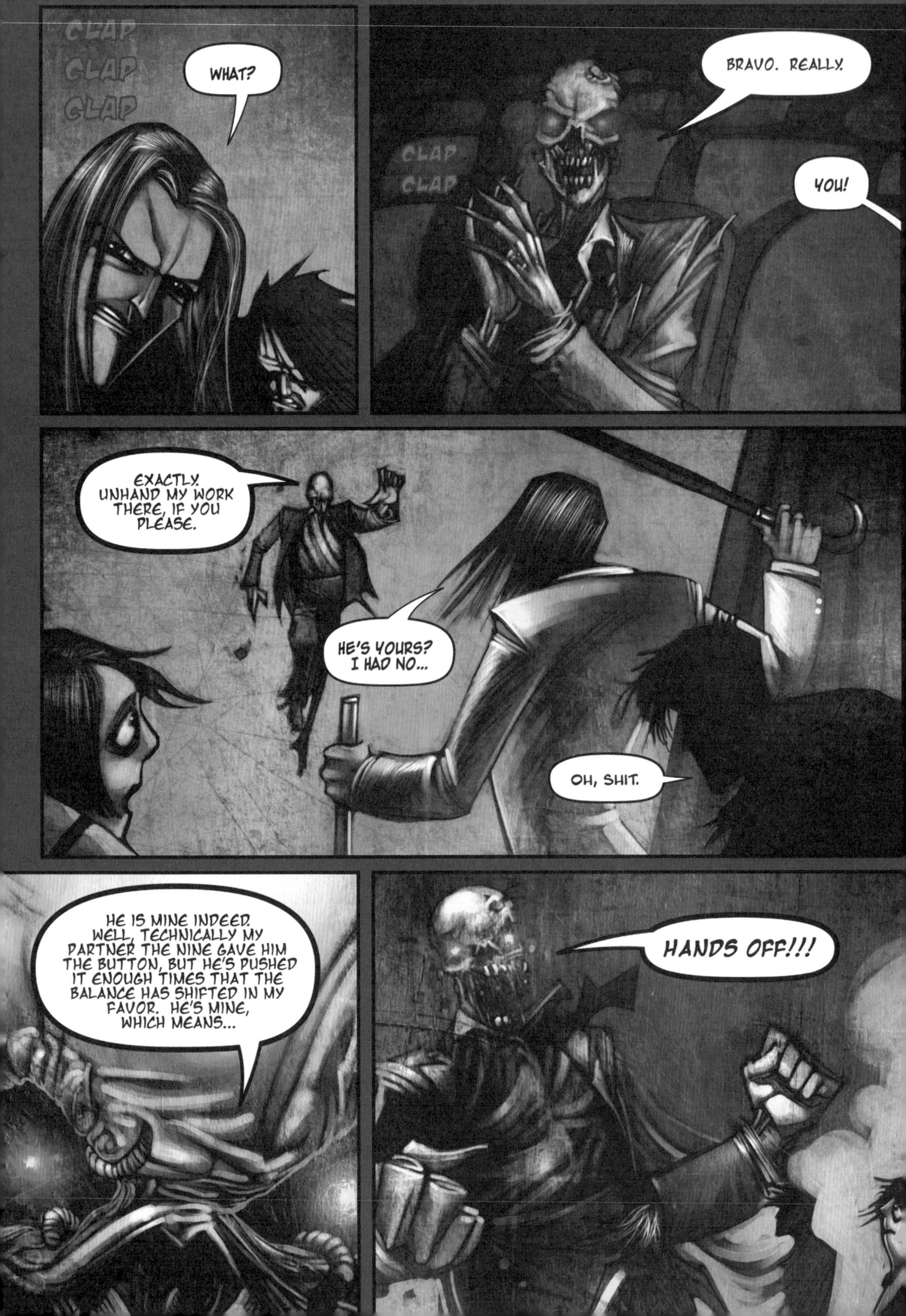
CLAP
CLAP
CLAP
WHAT?
BRAVO. REALLY.
CLAP
CLAP
YOU!
EXACTLY. UNHAND MY WORK THERE, IF YOU PLEASE.
HE'S YOURS? I HAD NO...
OH, SHIT.
HE IS MINE INDEED. WELL, TECHNICALLY MY PARTNER THE NINE GAVE HIM THE BUTTON, BUT HE'S PUSHED IT ENOUGH TIMES THAT THE BALANCE HAS SHIFTED IN MY FAVOR. HE'S MINE, WHICH MEANS...
HANDS OFF!!!

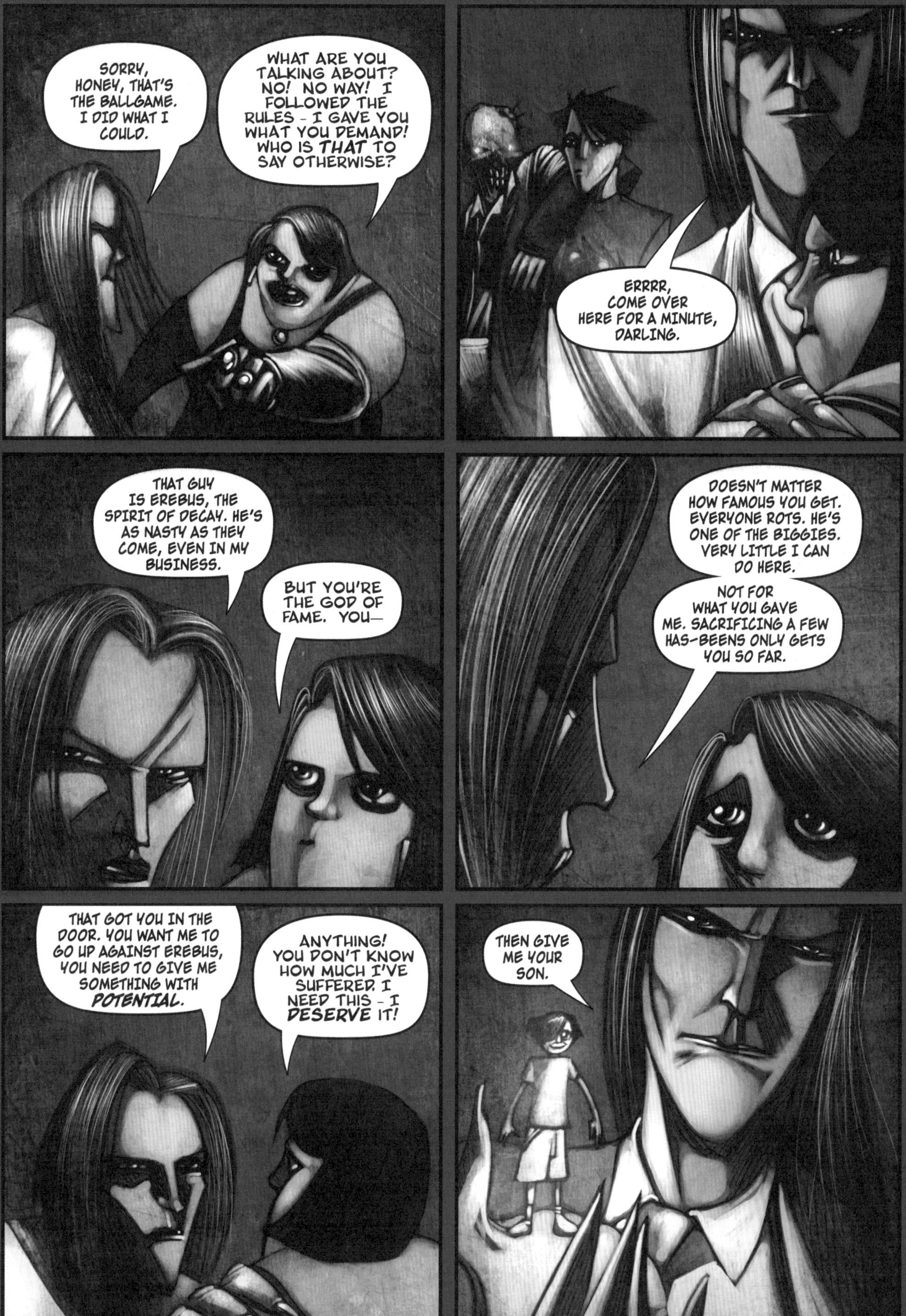
SORRY, HONEY, THAT'S THE BALLGAME. I DID WHAT I COULD.
WHAT ARE YOU TALKING ABOUT? NO! NO WAY! I FOLLOWED THE RULES - I GAVE YOU WHAT YOU DEMAND! WHO IS THAT TO SAY OTHERWISE?
ERRRR, COME OVER HERE FOR A MINUTE, DARLING.
THAT GUY IS EREBUS, THE SPIRIT OF DECAY. HE'S AS NASTY AS THEY COME, EVEN IN MY BUSINESS.
BUT YOU'RE THE GOD OF FAME. YOU—
DOESN'T MATTER HOW FAMOUS YOU GET. EVERYONE ROTS. HE'S ONE OF THE BIGGIES. VERY LITTLE I CAN DO HERE.
NOT FOR WHAT YOU GAVE ME. SACRIFICING A FEW HAS-BEENS ONLY GETS YOU SO FAR.
THAT GOT YOU IN THE DOOR. YOU WANT ME TO GO UP AGAINST EREBUS, YOU NEED TO GIVE ME SOMETHING WITH POTENTIAL.
ANYTHING! YOU DON'T KNOW HOW MUCH I'VE SUFFERED. I NEED THIS - I DESERVE IT!
THEN GIVE ME YOUR SON.

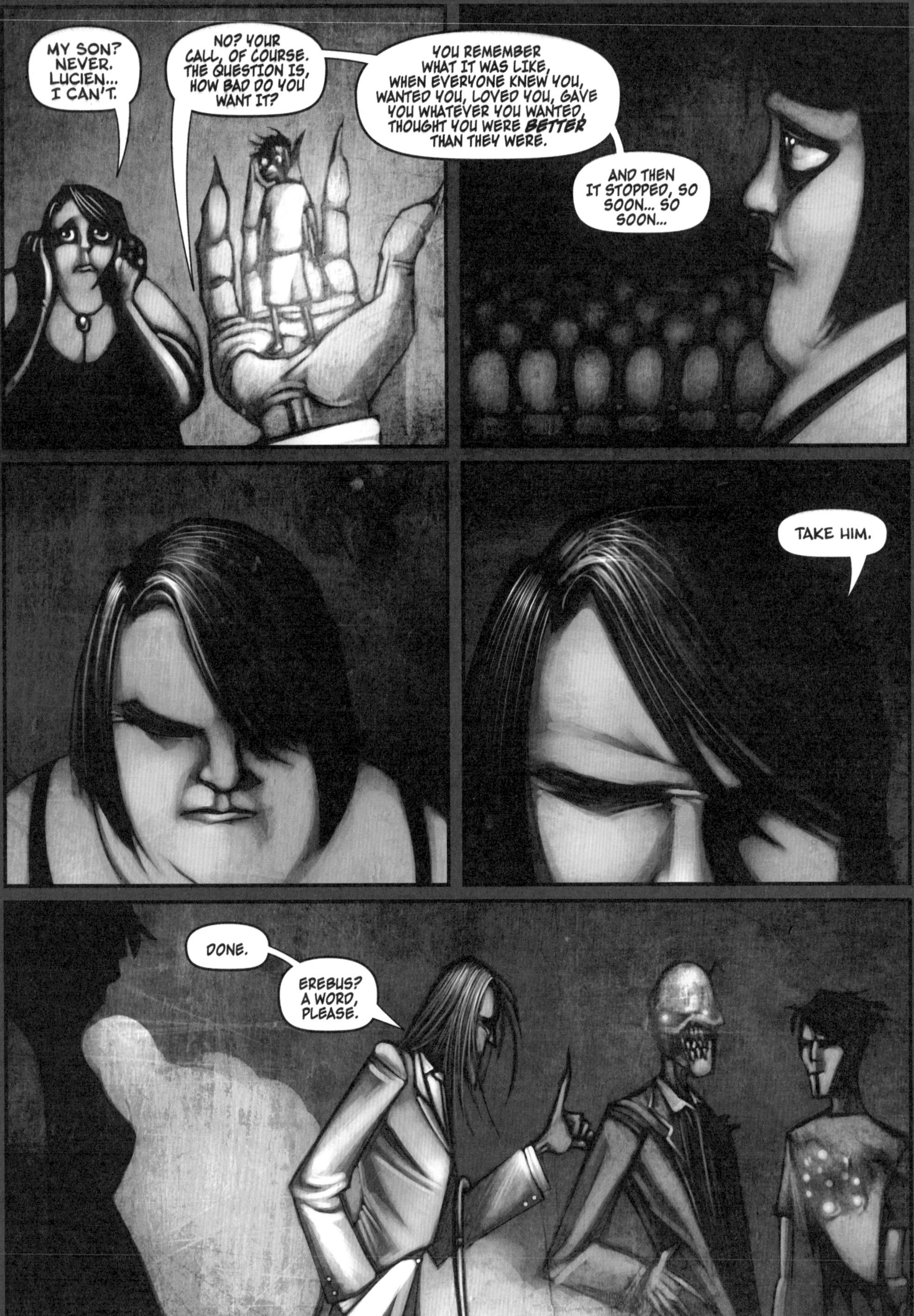
MY SON? NEVER. LUCIEN... I CAN'T.
NO? YOUR CALL, OF COURSE. THE QUESTION IS, HOW BAD DO YOU WANT IT?
YOU REMEMBER WHAT IT WAS LIKE, WHEN EVERYONE KNEW YOU, WANTED YOU, LOVED YOU, GAVE YOU WHATEVER YOU WANTED, THOUGHT YOU WERE *BETTER* THAN THEY WERE.
AND THEN IT STOPPED, SO SOON... SO SOON...
TAKE HIM.
DONE.
EREBUS? A WORD, PLEASE.

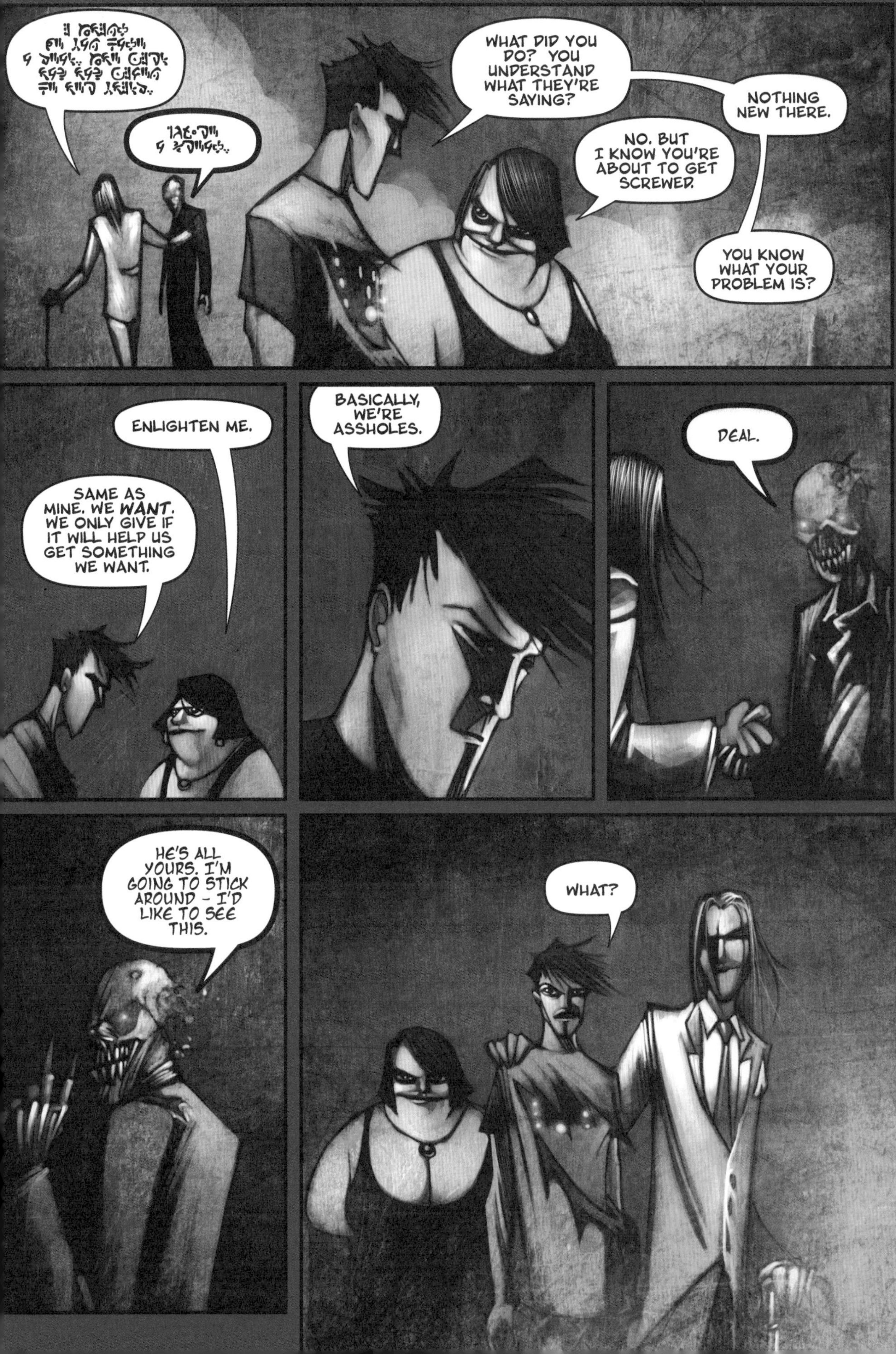
WHAT DID YOU DO? YOU UNDERSTAND WHAT THEY'RE SAYING?
NO. BUT I KNOW YOU'RE ABOUT TO GET SCREWED.
NOTHING NEW THERE.
YOU KNOW WHAT YOUR PROBLEM IS?
ENLIGHTEN ME.
SAME AS MINE. WE *WANT*. WE ONLY GIVE IF IT WILL HELP US GET SOMETHING WE WANT.
BASICALLY, WE'RE ASSHOLES.
DEAL.
HE'S ALL YOURS. I'M GOING TO STICK AROUND – I'D LIKE TO SEE THIS.
WHAT?

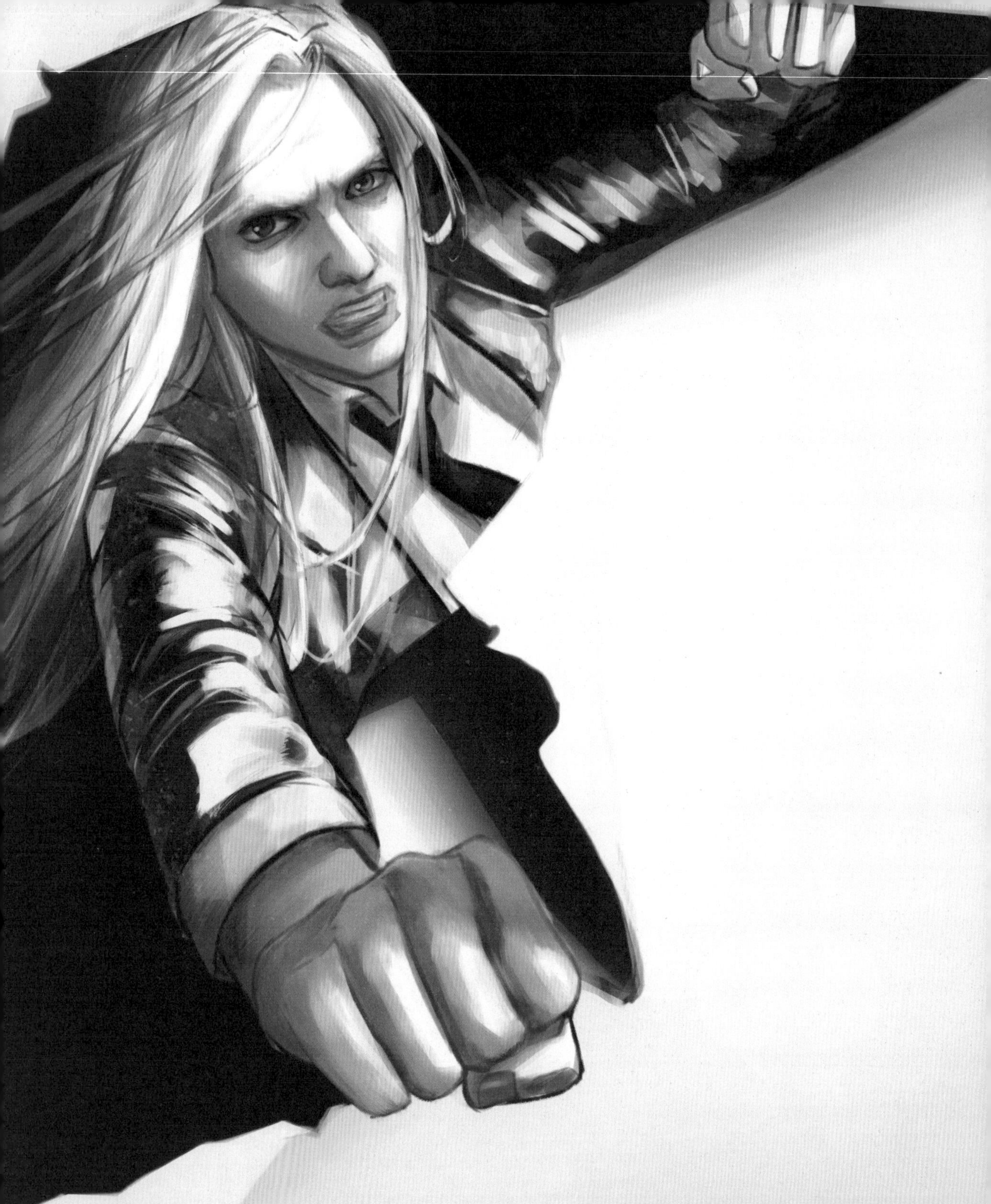

27 SECOND SET #4 cover by W. SCOTT FORBES
Based on "Kung-Fu Fighting" by Carl Douglas

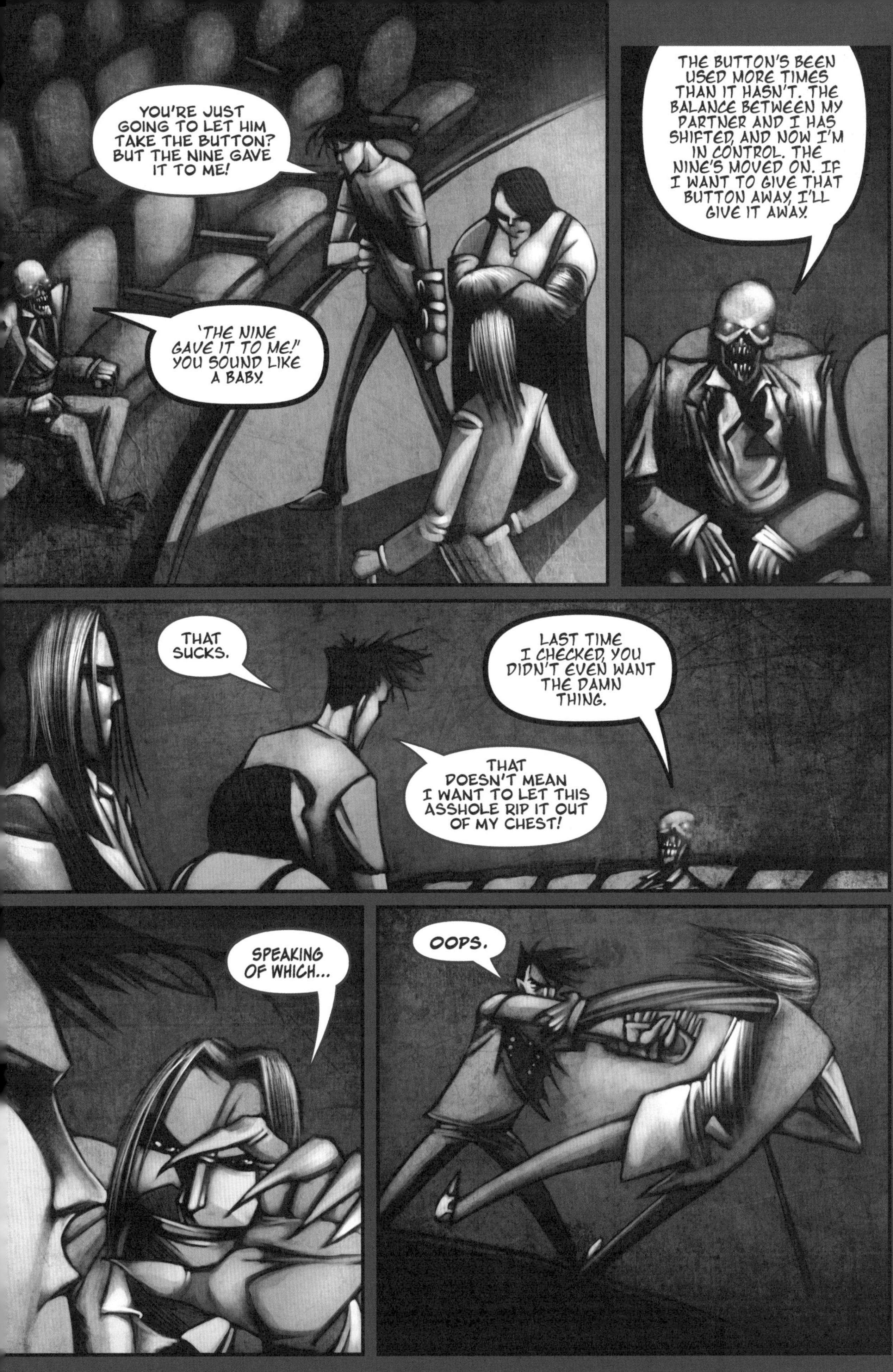
YOU'RE JUST GOING TO LET HIM TAKE THE BUTTON? BUT THE NINE GAVE IT TO ME!
'THE NINE GAVE IT TO ME!' YOU SOUND LIKE A BABY.
THE BUTTON'S BEEN USED MORE TIMES THAN IT HASN'T. THE BALANCE BETWEEN MY PARTNER AND I HAS SHIFTED, AND NOW I'M IN CONTROL. THE NINE'S MOVED ON. IF I WANT TO GIVE THAT BUTTON AWAY, I'LL GIVE IT AWAY.
THAT SUCKS.
LAST TIME I CHECKED, YOU DIDN'T EVEN WANT THE DAMN THING.
THAT DOESN'T MEAN I WANT TO LET THIS ASSHOLE RIP IT OUT OF MY CHEST!
SPEAKING OF WHICH...
OOPS.

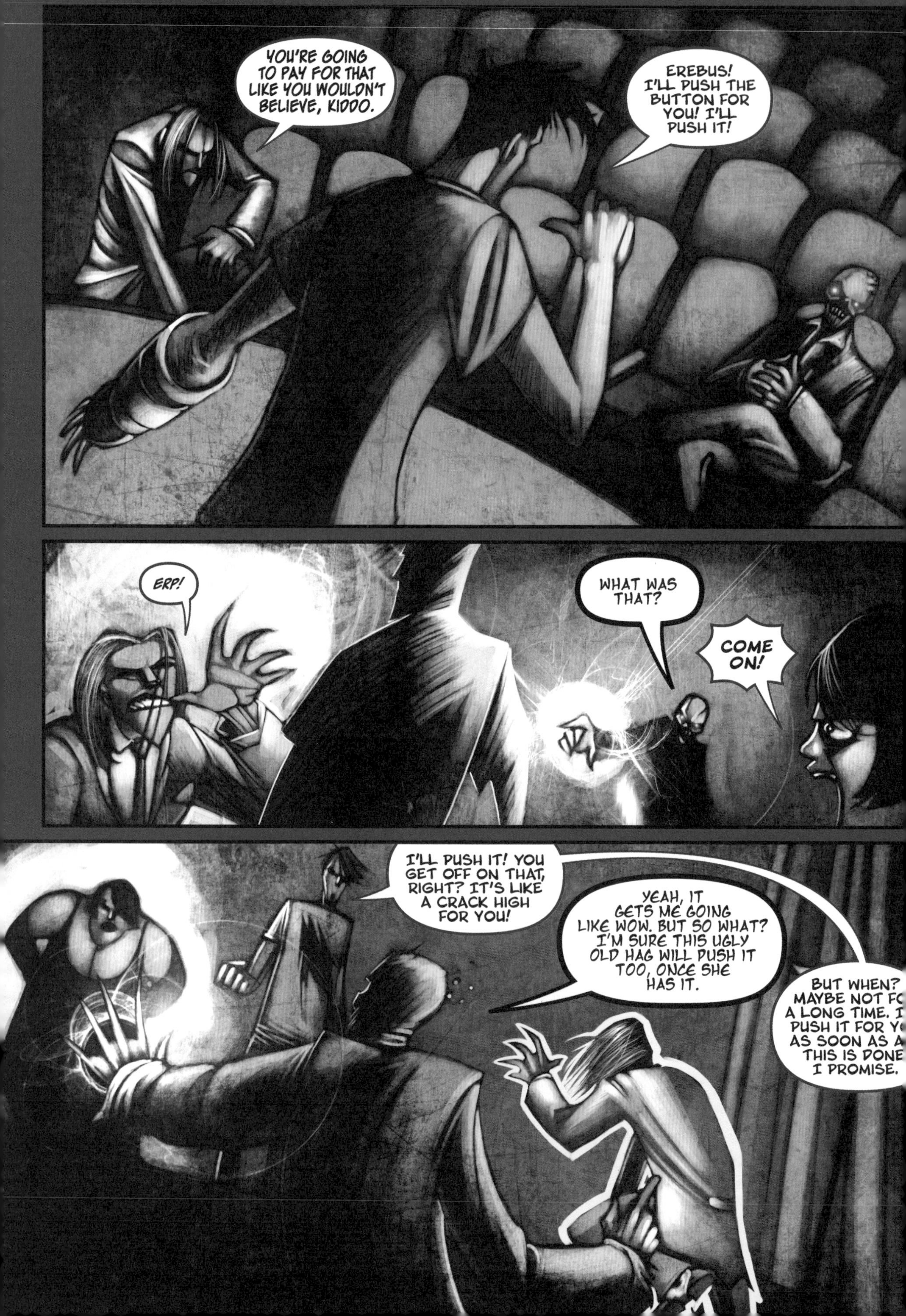

YOU'RE GOING TO PAY FOR THAT LIKE YOU WOULDN'T BELIEVE, KIDDO.
EREBUS! I'LL PUSH THE BUTTON FOR YOU! I'LL PUSH IT!
ERP!
WHAT WAS THAT?
COME ON!
I'LL PUSH IT! YOU GET OFF ON THAT, RIGHT? IT'S LIKE A CRACK HIGH FOR YOU!
YEAH, IT GETS ME GOING LIKE WOW. BUT SO WHAT? I'M SURE THIS UGLY OLD HAG WILL PUSH IT TOO, ONCE SHE HAS IT.
BUT WHEN? MAYBE NOT FO A LONG TIME. I PUSH IT FOR YO AS SOON AS A THIS IS DONE I PROMISE.

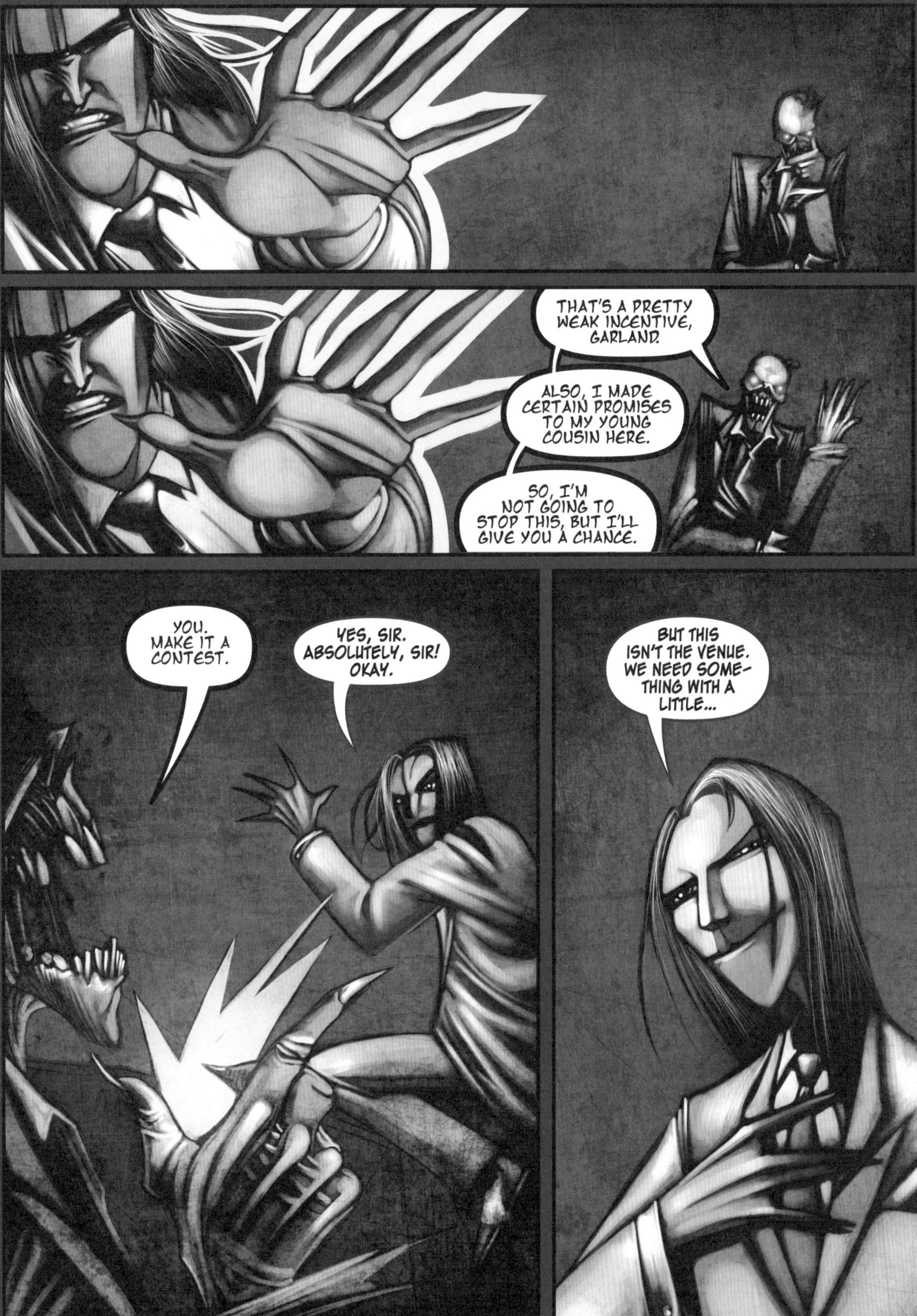
THAT'S A PRETTY WEAK INCENTIVE, GARLAND.
ALSO, I MADE CERTAIN PROMISES TO MY YOUNG COUSIN HERE.
SO, I'M NOT GOING TO STOP THIS, BUT I'LL GIVE YOU A CHANCE.
YOU. MAKE IT A CONTEST.
YES, SIR. ABSOLUTELY, SIR! OKAY.
BUT THIS ISN'T THE VENUE. WE NEED SOMETHING WITH A LITTLE...

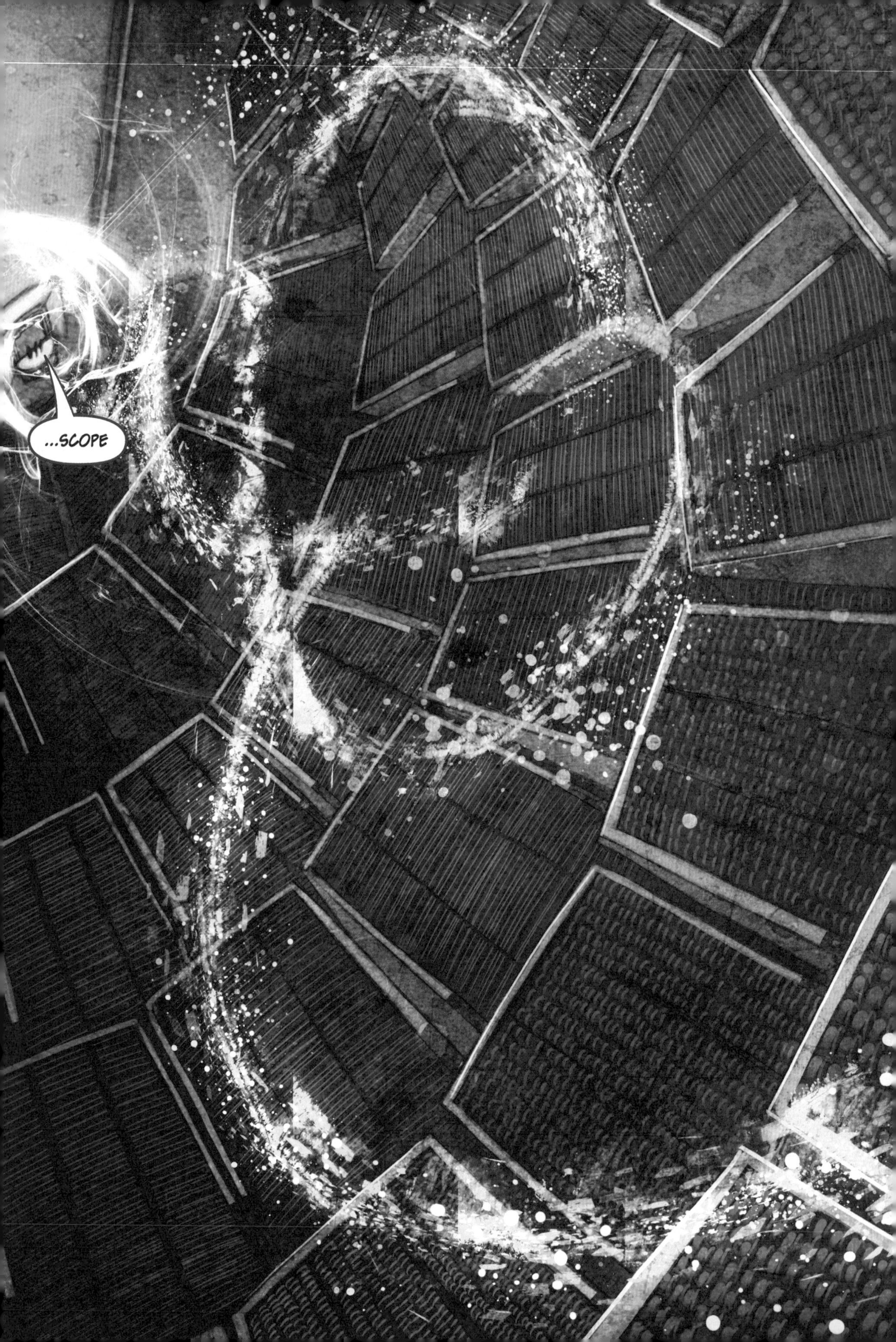
...SCOPE

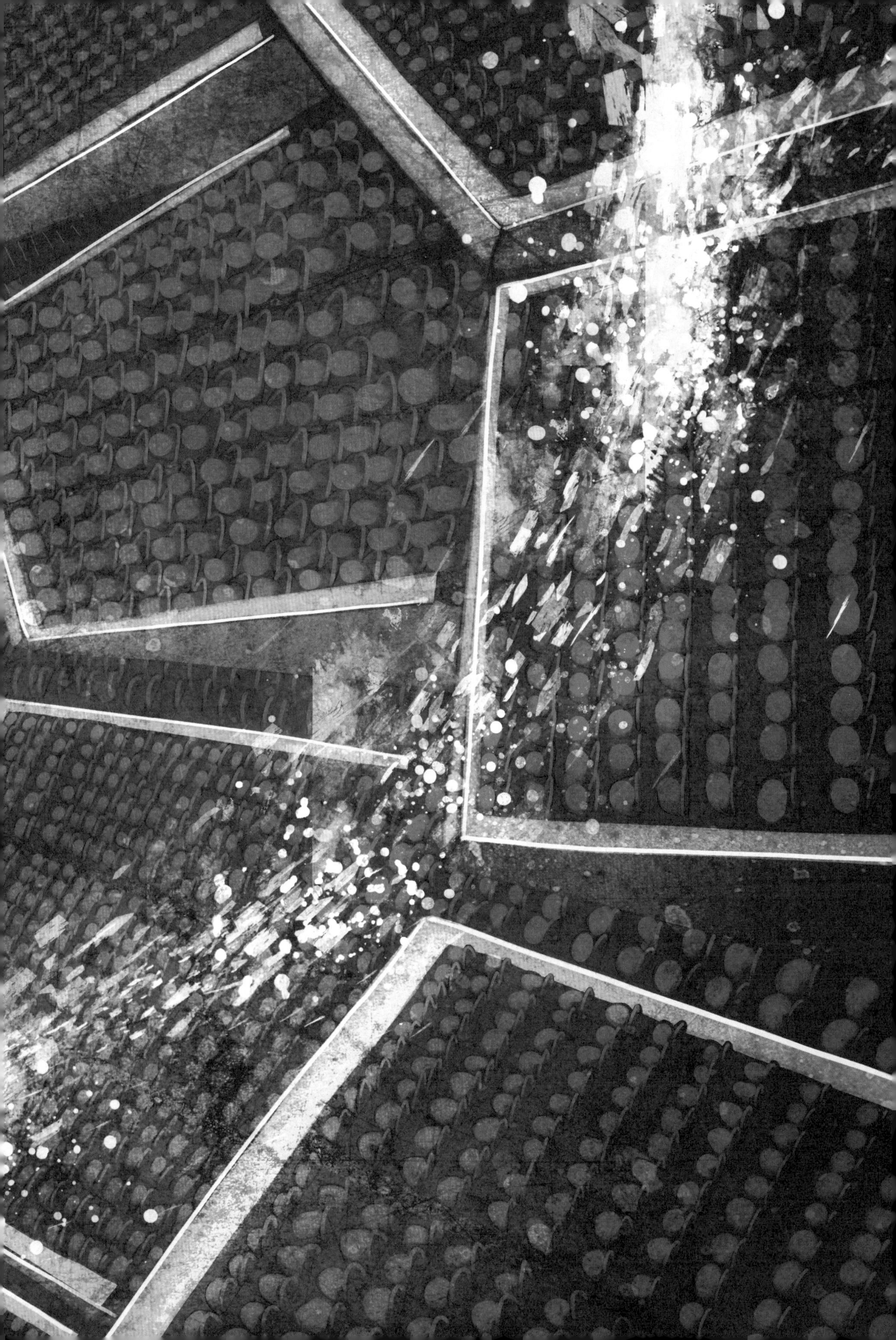

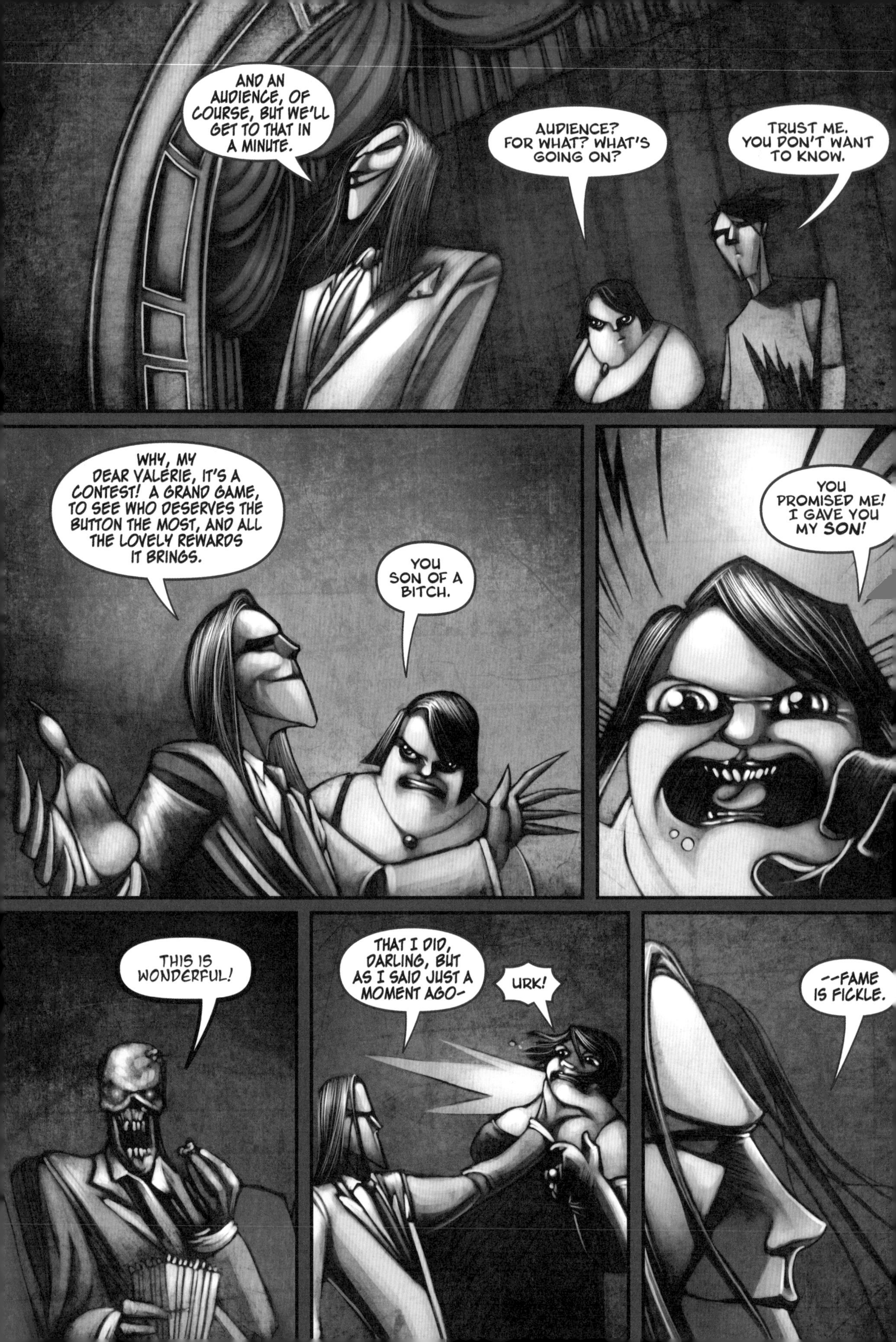
AND AN AUDIENCE, OF COURSE, BUT WE'LL GET TO THAT IN A MINUTE.
AUDIENCE? FOR WHAT? WHAT'S GOING ON?
TRUST ME. YOU DON'T WANT TO KNOW.
WHY, MY DEAR VALÉRIE, IT'S A CONTEST! A GRAND GAME, TO SEE WHO DESERVES THE BUTTON THE MOST, AND ALL THE LOVELY REWARDS IT BRINGS.
YOU SON OF A BITCH.
YOU PROMISED ME! I GAVE YOU MY **SON**!
THIS IS WONDERFUL!
THAT I DID, DARLING, BUT AS I SAID JUST A MOMENT AGO-
URK!
--FAME IS FICKLE.

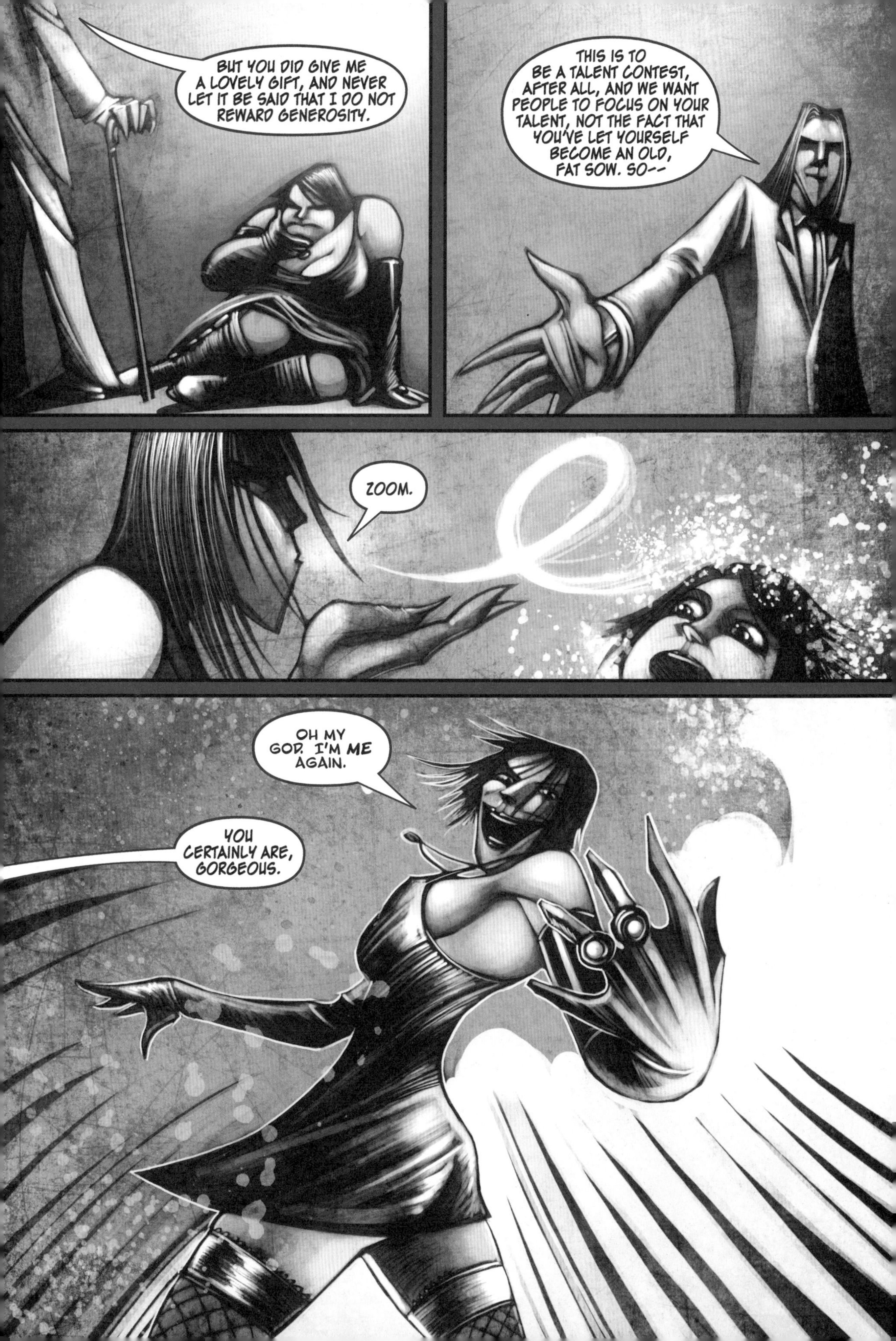
BUT YOU DID GIVE ME A LOVELY GIFT, AND NEVER LET IT BE SAID THAT I DO NOT REWARD GENEROSITY.
THIS IS TO BE A TALENT CONTEST, AFTER ALL, AND WE WANT PEOPLE TO FOCUS ON YOUR TALENT, NOT THE FACT THAT YOU'VE LET YOURSELF BECOME AN OLD, FAT SOW. SO--
ZOOM.
OH MY GOD. I'M ME AGAIN.
YOU CERTAINLY ARE, GORGEOUS.

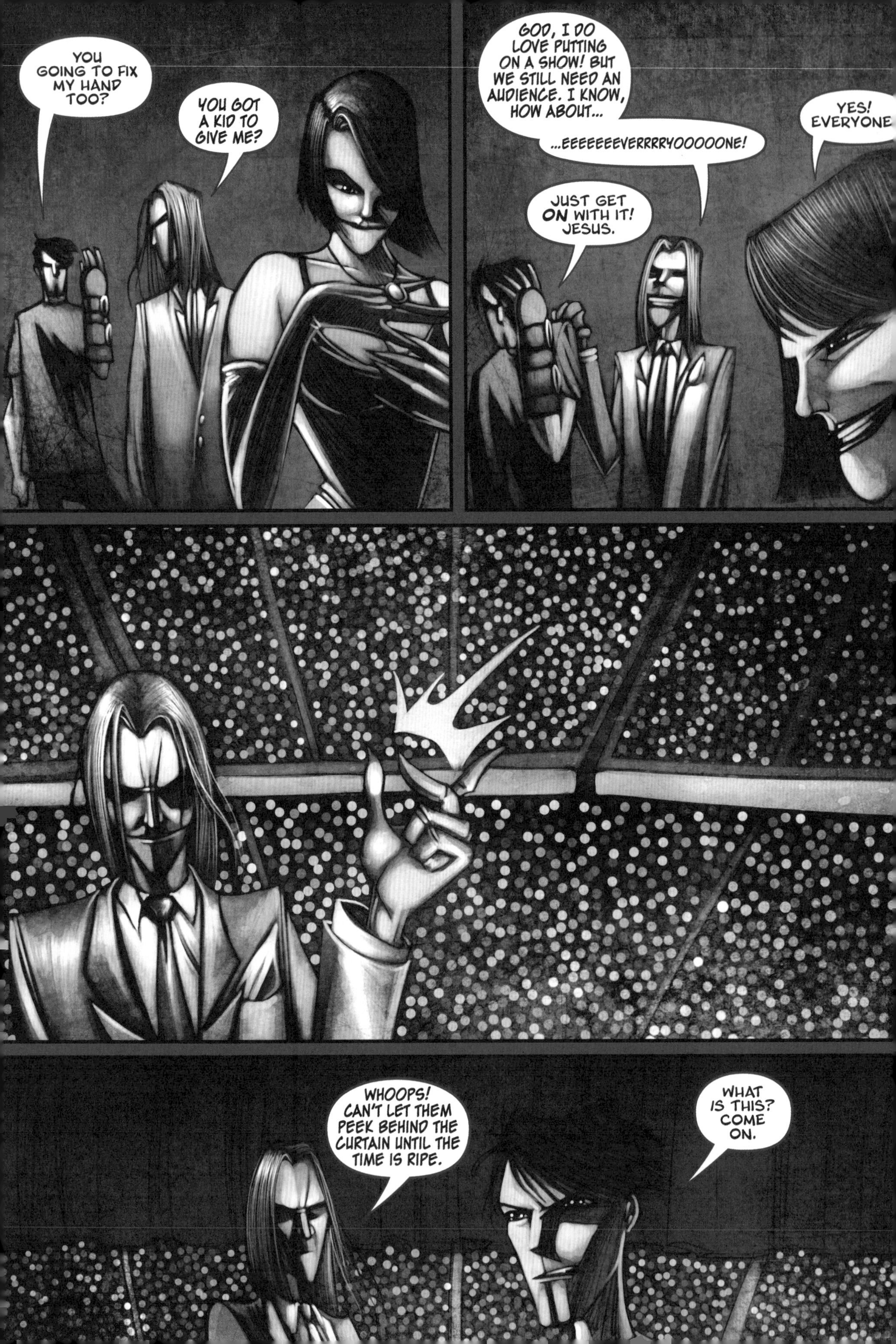
YOU GOING TO FIX MY HAND TOO?
YOU GOT A KID TO GIVE ME?
GOD, I DO LOVE PUTTING ON A SHOW! BUT WE STILL NEED AN AUDIENCE. I KNOW, HOW ABOUT...
...EEEEEEEVERRRRYOOOOONE!
YES! EVERYONE
JUST GET ON WITH IT! JESUS.
WHOOPS! CAN'T LET THEM PEEK BEHIND THE CURTAIN UNTIL THE TIME IS RIPE.
WHAT IS THIS? COME ON.

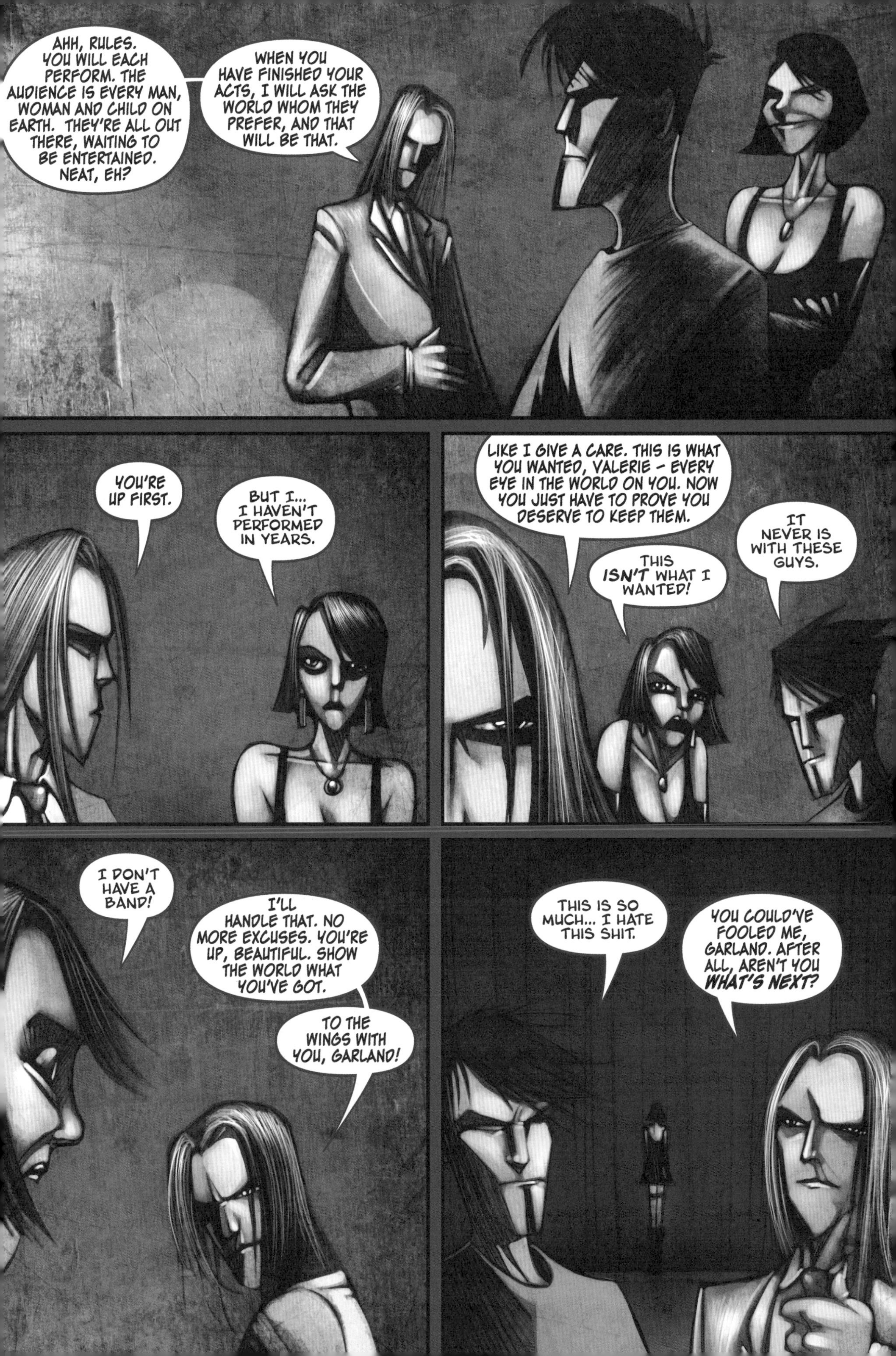

AHH, RULES. YOU WILL EACH PERFORM. THE AUDIENCE IS EVERY MAN, WOMAN AND CHILD ON EARTH. THEY'RE ALL OUT THERE, WAITING TO BE ENTERTAINED. NEAT, EH?
WHEN YOU HAVE FINISHED YOUR ACTS, I WILL ASK THE WORLD WHOM THEY PREFER, AND THAT WILL BE THAT.
YOU'RE UP FIRST.
BUT I... I HAVEN'T PERFORMED IN YEARS.
LIKE I GIVE A CARE. THIS IS WHAT YOU WANTED, VALERIE – EVERY EYE IN THE WORLD ON YOU. NOW YOU JUST HAVE TO PROVE YOU DESERVE TO KEEP THEM.
THIS ISN'T WHAT I WANTED!
IT NEVER IS WITH THESE GUYS.
I DON'T HAVE A BAND!
I'LL HANDLE THAT. NO MORE EXCUSES. YOU'RE UP, BEAUTIFUL. SHOW THE WORLD WHAT YOU'VE GOT.
TO THE WINGS WITH YOU, GARLAND!
THIS IS SO MUCH... I HATE THIS SHIT.
YOU COULD'VE FOOLED ME, GARLAND. AFTER ALL, AREN'T YOU WHAT'S NEXT?

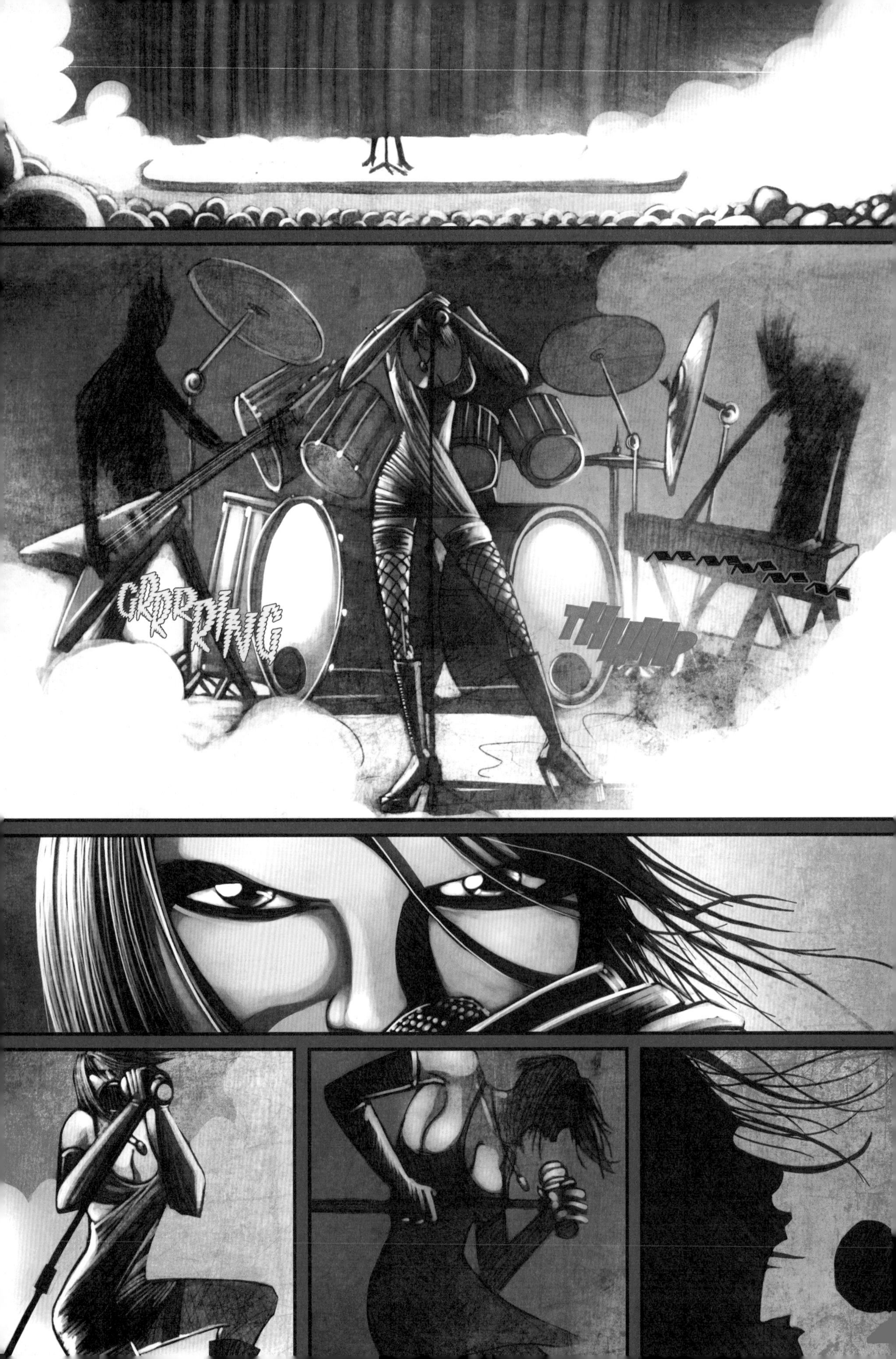
GRRRRING
THUMP

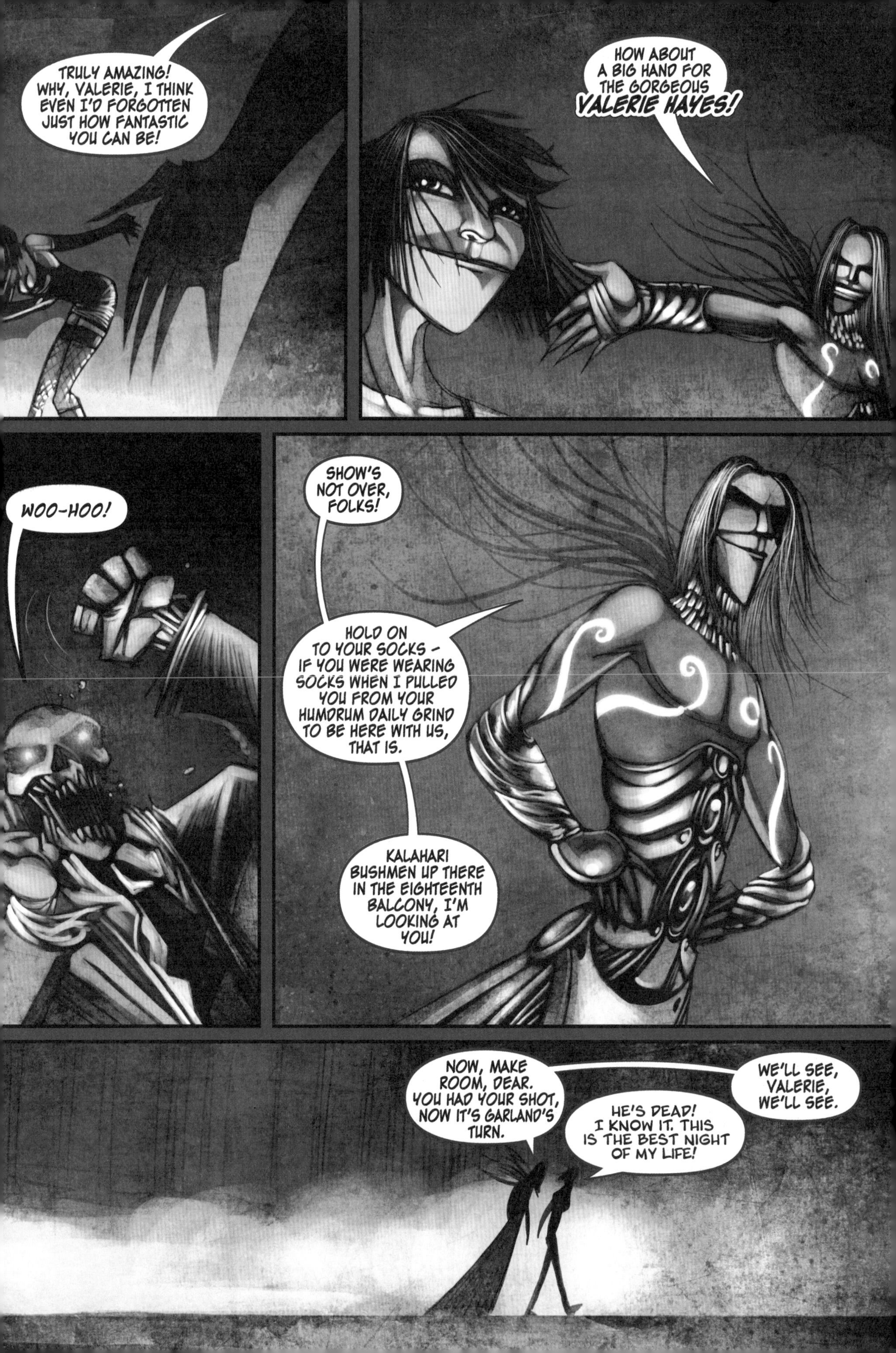
TRULY AMAZING! WHY, VALERIE, I THINK EVEN I'D FORGOTTEN JUST HOW FANTASTIC YOU CAN BE!
HOW ABOUT A BIG HAND FOR THE GORGEOUS VALERIE HAYES!
WOO-HOO!
SHOW'S NOT OVER, FOLKS!
HOLD ON TO YOUR SOCKS - IF YOU WERE WEARING SOCKS WHEN I PULLED YOU FROM YOUR HUMDRUM DAILY GRIND TO BE HERE WITH US, THAT IS.
KALAHARI BUSHMEN UP THERE IN THE EIGHTEENTH BALCONY, I'M LOOKING AT YOU!
NOW, MAKE ROOM, DEAR. YOU HAD YOUR SHOT, NOW IT'S GARLAND'S TURN.
WE'LL SEE, VALERIE, WE'LL SEE.
HE'S DEAD! I KNOW IT. THIS IS THE BEST NIGHT OF MY LIFE!

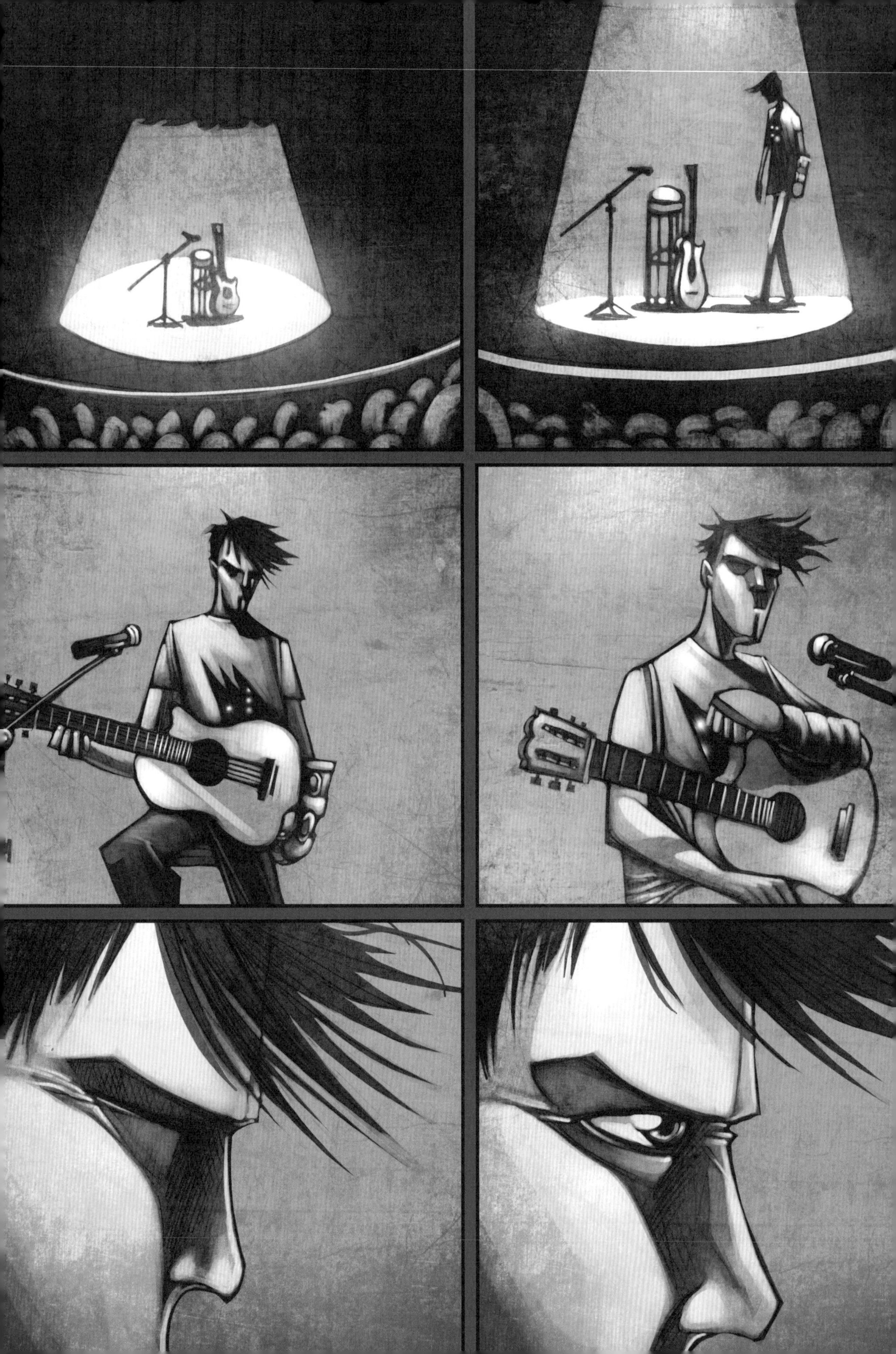

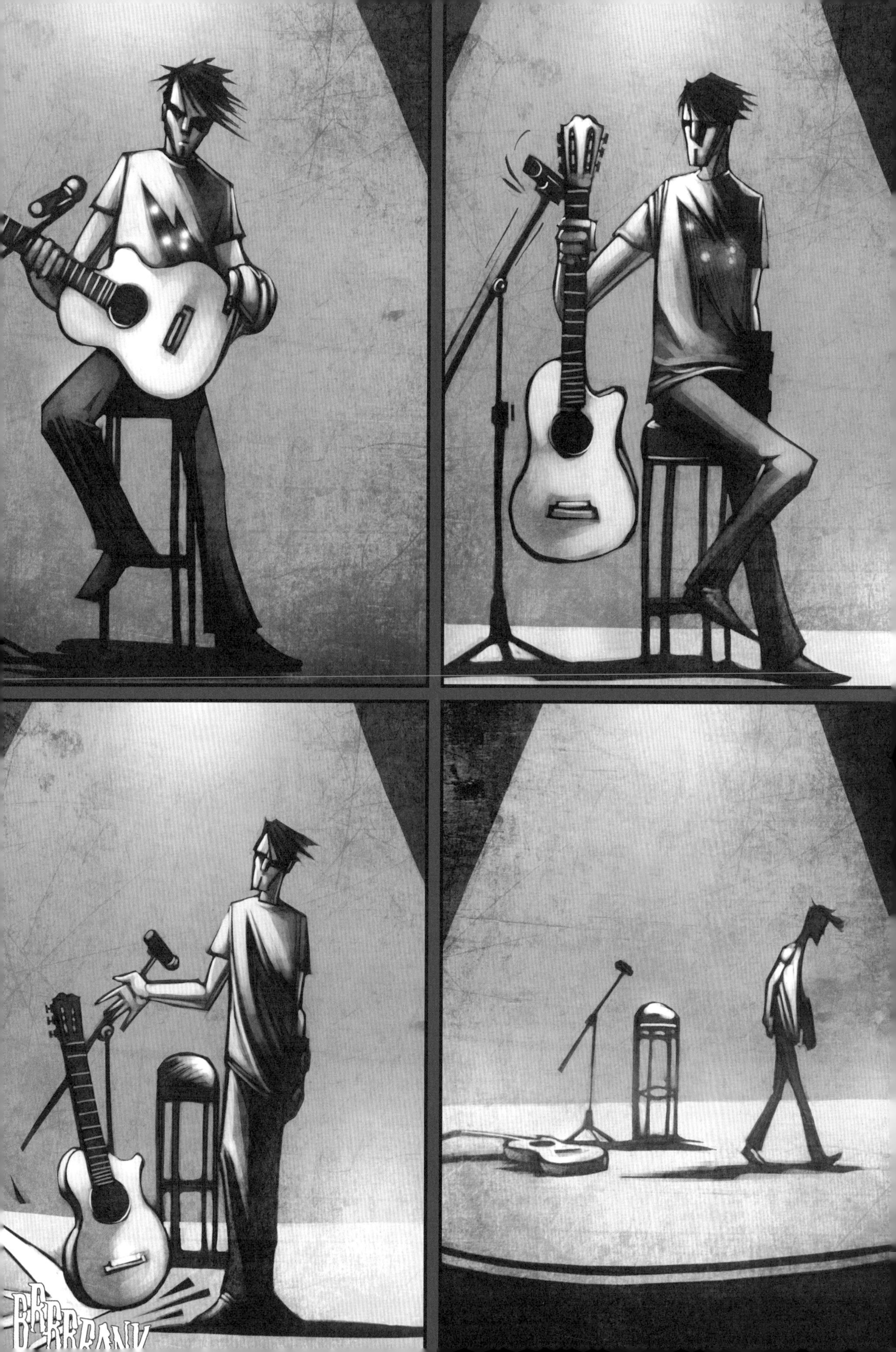
BRRRRANK

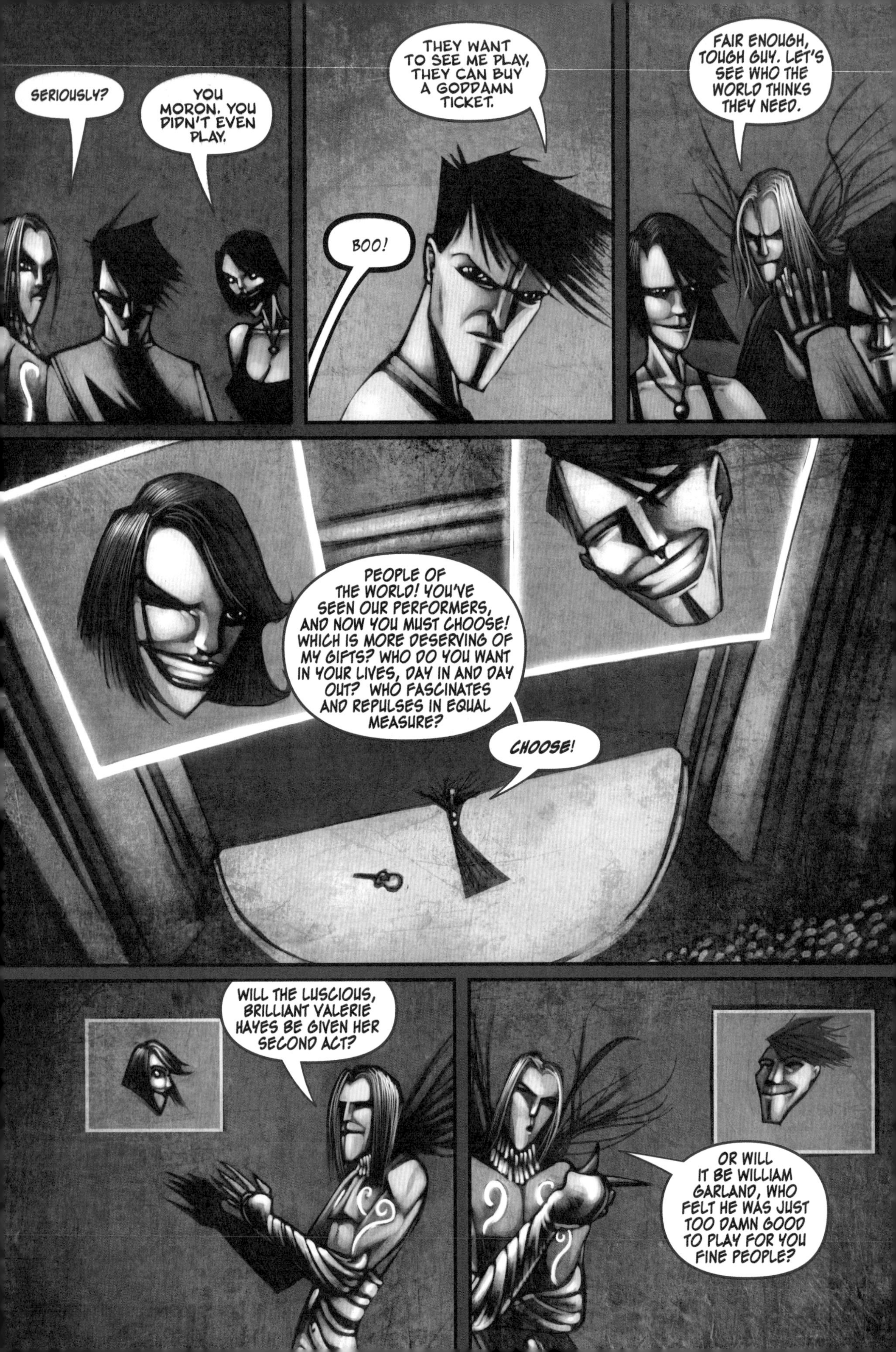
SERIOUSLY?
YOU MORON. YOU DIDN'T EVEN PLAY.
THEY WANT TO SEE ME PLAY, THEY CAN BUY A GODDAMN TICKET.
BOO!
FAIR ENOUGH, TOUGH GUY. LET'S SEE WHO THE WORLD THINKS THEY NEED.
PEOPLE OF THE WORLD! YOU'VE SEEN OUR PERFORMERS, AND NOW YOU MUST CHOOSE! WHICH IS MORE DESERVING OF MY GIFTS? WHO DO YOU WANT IN YOUR LIVES, DAY IN AND DAY OUT? WHO FASCINATES AND REPULSES IN EQUAL MEASURE?
CHOOSE!
WILL THE LUSCIOUS, BRILLIANT VALERIE HAYES BE GIVEN HER SECOND ACT?
OR WILL IT BE WILLIAM GARLAND, WHO FELT HE WAS JUST TOO DAMN GOOD TO PLAY FOR YOU FINE PEOPLE?

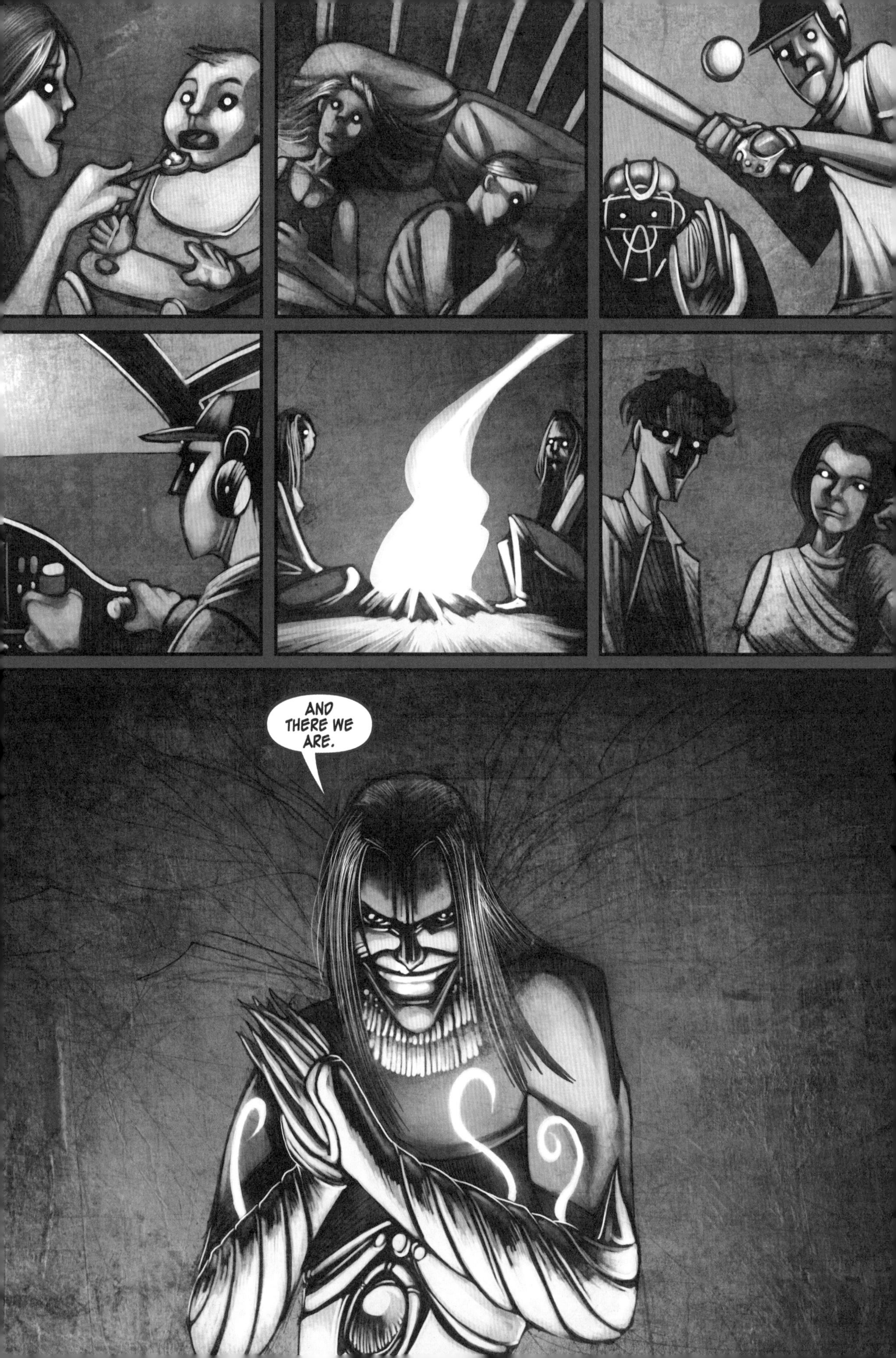
AND THERE WE ARE.

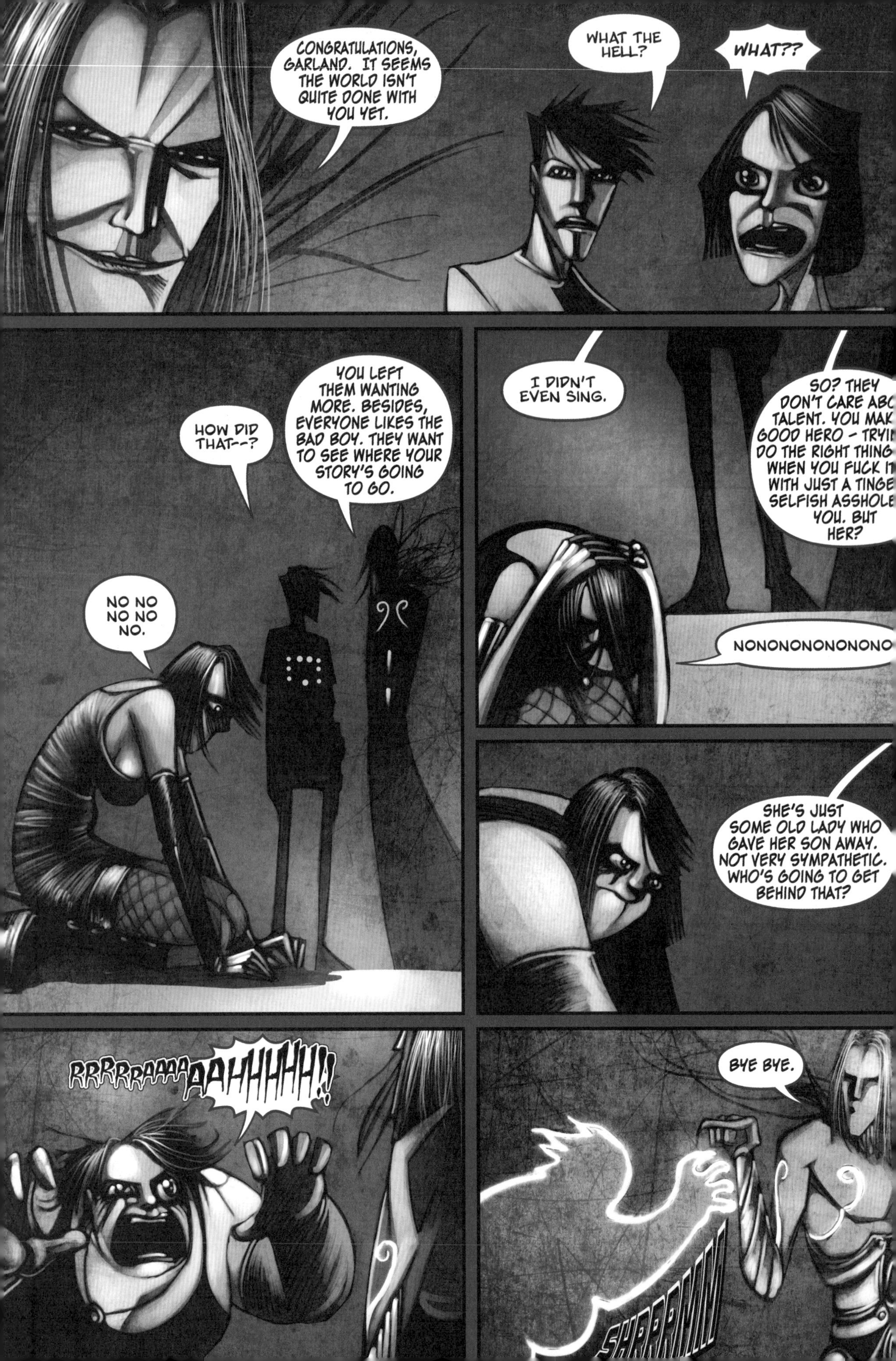
CONGRATULATIONS, GARLAND. IT SEEMS THE WORLD ISN'T QUITE DONE WITH YOU YET.
WHAT THE HELL?
WHAT??
HOW DID THAT--?
YOU LEFT THEM WANTING MORE. BESIDES, EVERYONE LIKES THE BAD BOY. THEY WANT TO SEE WHERE YOUR STORY'S GOING TO GO.
NO NO NO NO NO.
I DIDN'T EVEN SING.
SO? THEY DON'T CARE ABO TALENT. YOU MAK GOOD HERO - TRYI DO THE RIGHT THING WHEN YOU FUCK I WITH JUST A TINGE SELFISH ASSHOLE YOU. BUT HER?
NONONONONONONO
SHE'S JUST SOME OLD LADY WHO GAVE HER SON AWAY. NOT VERY SYMPATHETIC. WHO'S GOING TO GET BEHIND THAT?
RRRRRAAAAAAHHHHHH!!
BYE BYE.
SHRRRMM

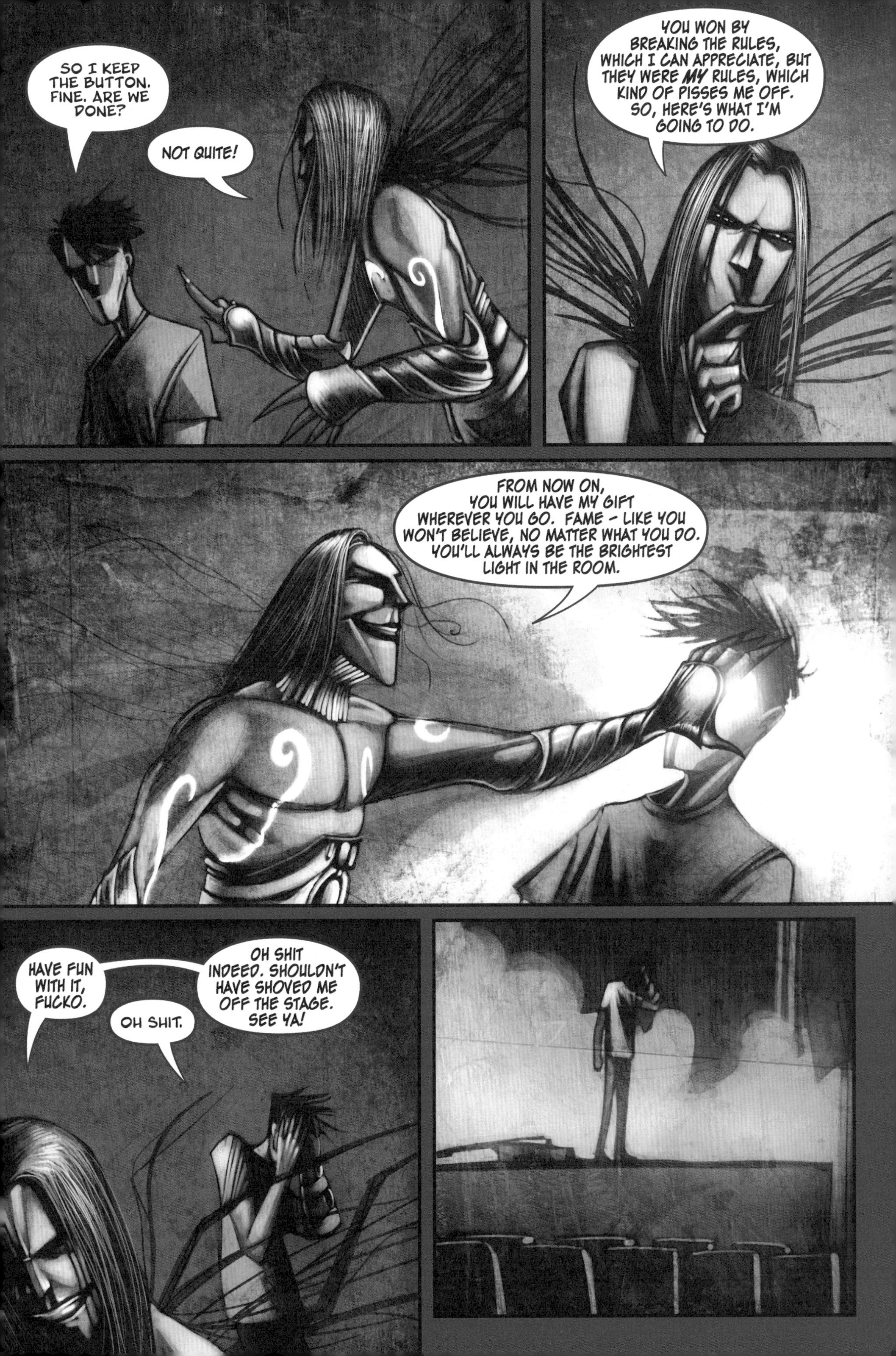
SO I KEEP THE BUTTON. FINE. ARE WE DONE?
NOT QUITE!
YOU WON BY BREAKING THE RULES, WHICH I CAN APPRECIATE, BUT THEY WERE MY RULES, WHICH KIND OF PISSES ME OFF. SO, HERE'S WHAT I'M GOING TO DO.
FROM NOW ON, YOU WILL HAVE MY GIFT WHEREVER YOU GO. FAME - LIKE YOU WON'T BELIEVE, NO MATTER WHAT YOU DO. YOU'LL ALWAYS BE THE BRIGHTEST LIGHT IN THE ROOM.
HAVE FUN WITH IT, FUCKO.
OH SHIT.
OH SHIT INDEED. SHOULDN'T HAVE SHOVED ME OFF THE STAGE. SEE YA!

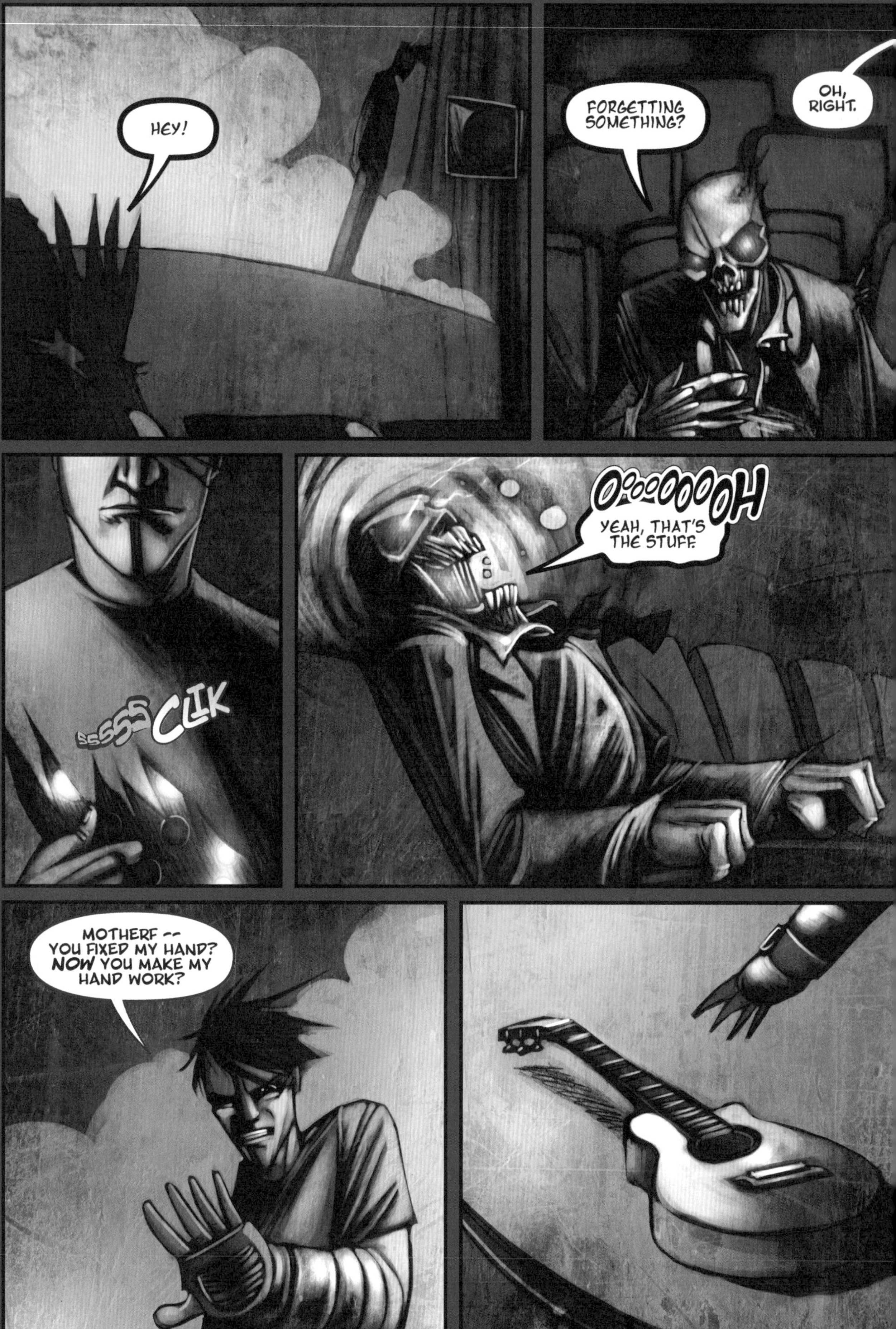
HEY!
FORGETTING SOMETHING?
OH, RIGHT.
SSSSSCLIK
OOOOOOOOOH
YEAH, THAT'S THE STUFF.
MOTHERF --
YOU FIXED MY HAND? NOW YOU MAKE MY HAND WORK?

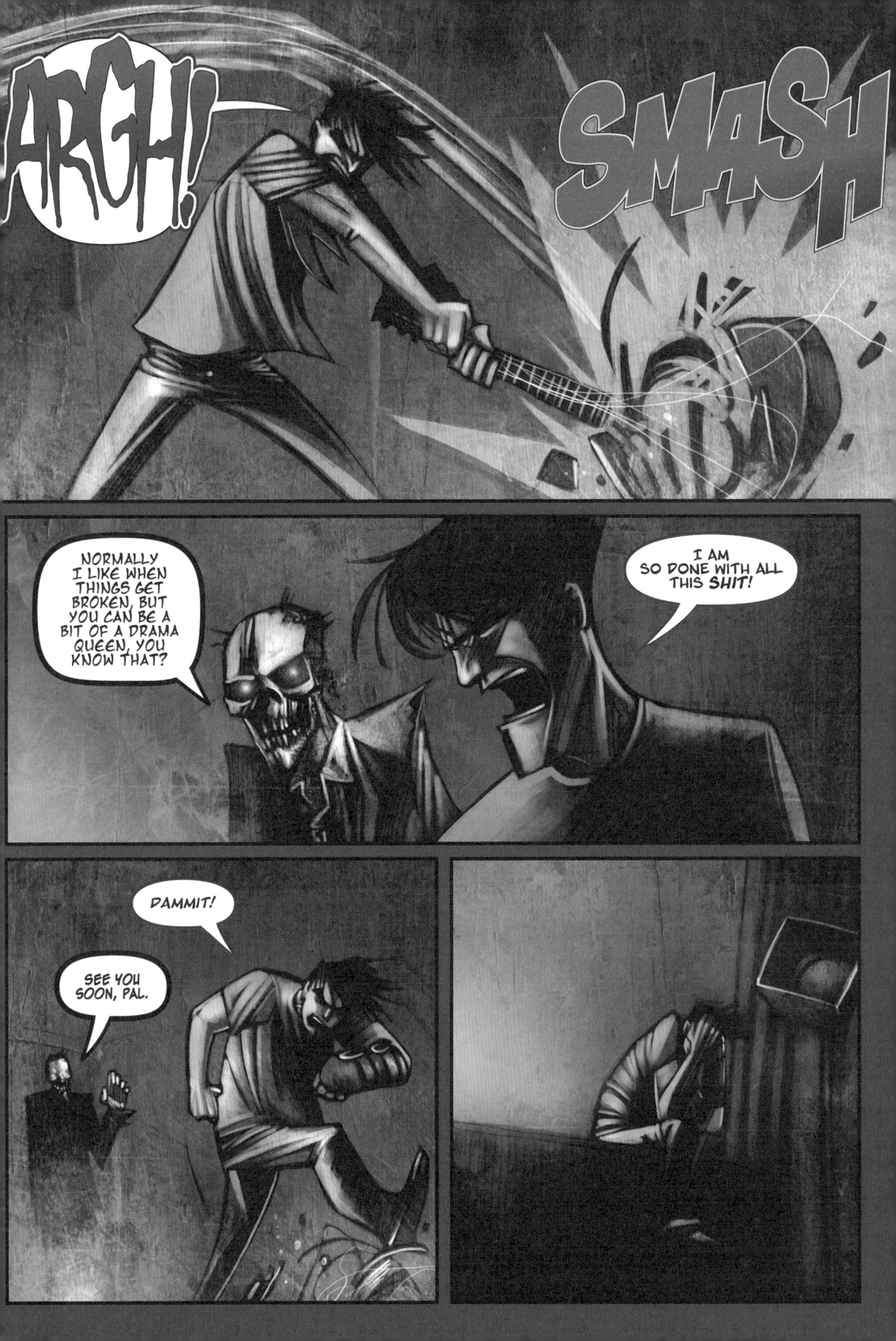
ARGH!
SMASH
NORMALLY I LIKE WHEN THINGS GET BROKEN, BUT YOU CAN BE A BIT OF A DRAMA QUEEN, YOU KNOW THAT?
I AM SO DONE WITH ALL THIS SHIT!
DAMMIT!
SEE YOU SOON, PAL.

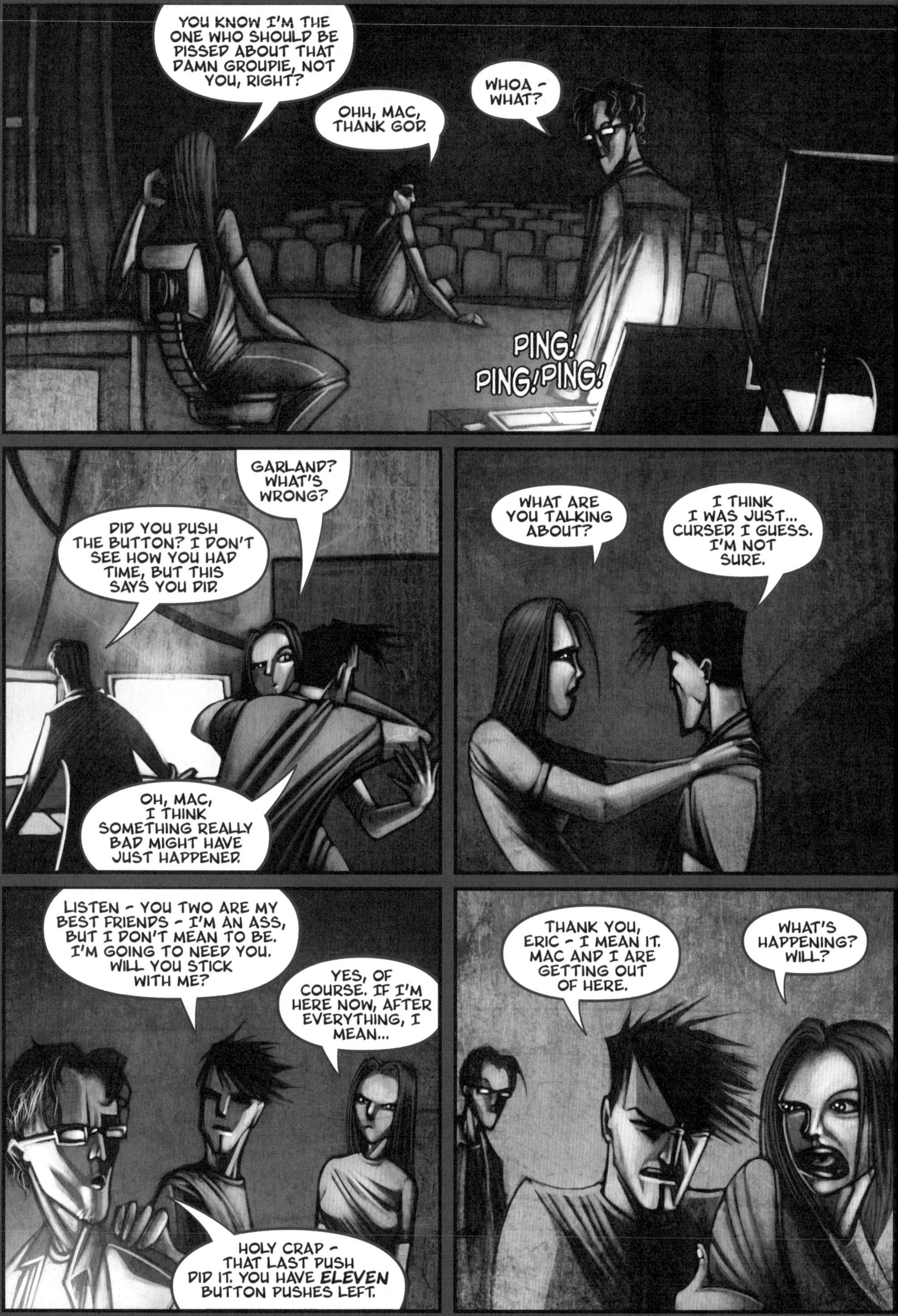
YOU KNOW I'M THE ONE WHO SHOULD BE PISSED ABOUT THAT DAMN GROUPIE, NOT YOU, RIGHT?
OHH, MAC, THANK GOD.
WHOA - WHAT?
PING! PING! PING!
GARLAND? WHAT'S WRONG?
DID YOU PUSH THE BUTTON? I DON'T SEE HOW YOU HAD TIME, BUT THIS SAYS YOU DID.
OH, MAC, I THINK SOMETHING REALLY BAD MIGHT HAVE JUST HAPPENED.
WHAT ARE YOU TALKING ABOUT?
I THINK I WAS JUST... CURSED. I GUESS. I'M NOT SURE.
LISTEN - YOU TWO ARE MY BEST FRIENDS - I'M AN ASS, BUT I DON'T MEAN TO BE. I'M GOING TO NEED YOU. WILL YOU STICK WITH ME?
YES, OF COURSE. IF I'M HERE NOW, AFTER EVERYTHING, I MEAN...
HOLY CRAP - THAT LAST PUSH DID IT. YOU HAVE ELEVEN BUTTON PUSHES LEFT.
THANK YOU, ERIC - I MEAN IT. MAC AND I ARE GETTING OUT OF HERE.
WHAT'S HAPPENING? WILL?

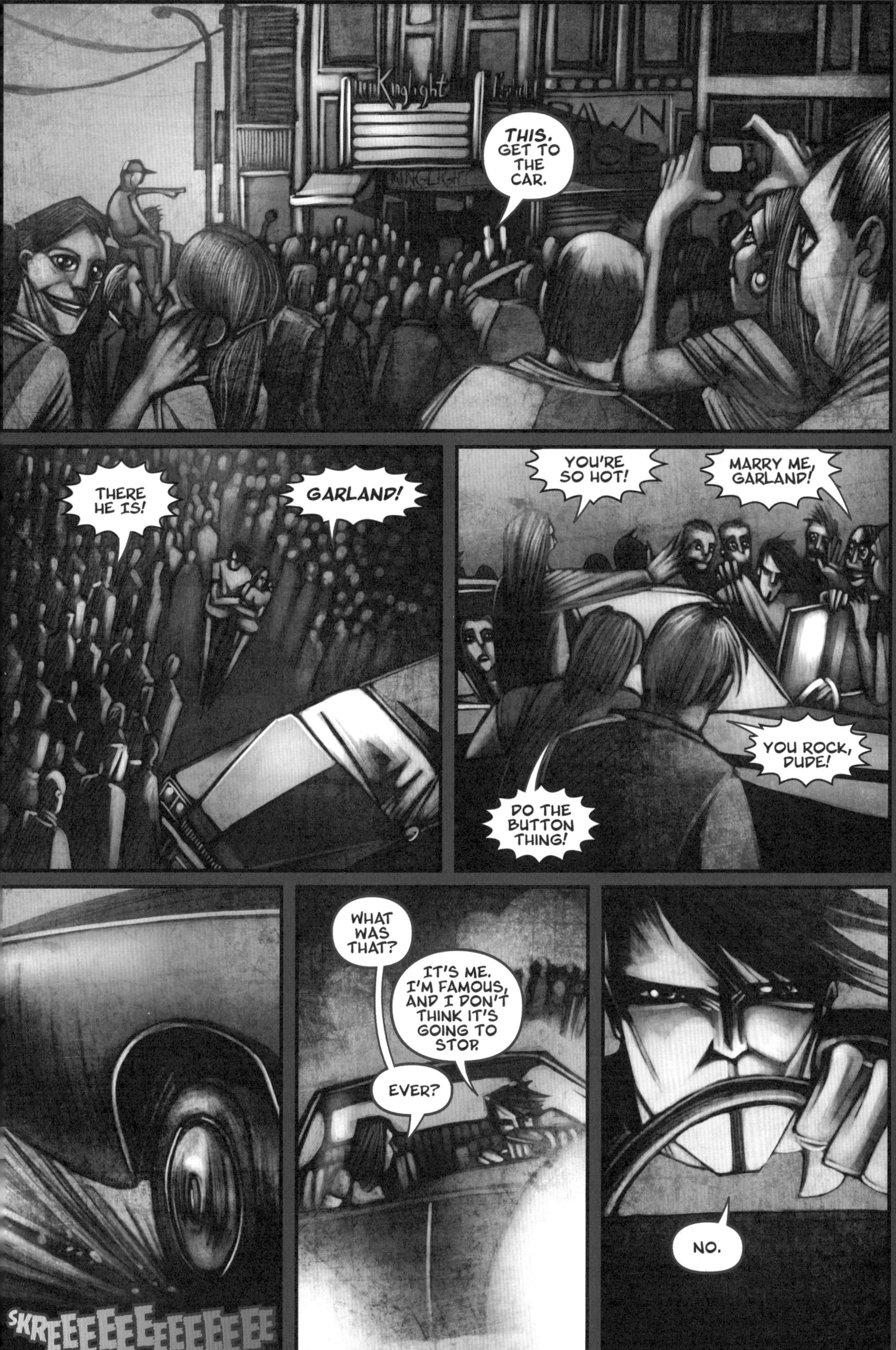
THIS. GET TO THE CAR.
THERE HE IS!
GARLAND!
YOU'RE SO HOT!
MARRY ME, GARLAND!
YOU ROCK, DUDE!
DO THE BUTTON THING!
SKREEEEEEEEEEEEEE
WHAT WAS THAT?
IT'S ME. I'M FAMOUS, AND I DON'T THINK IT'S GOING TO STOP.
EVER?
NO.

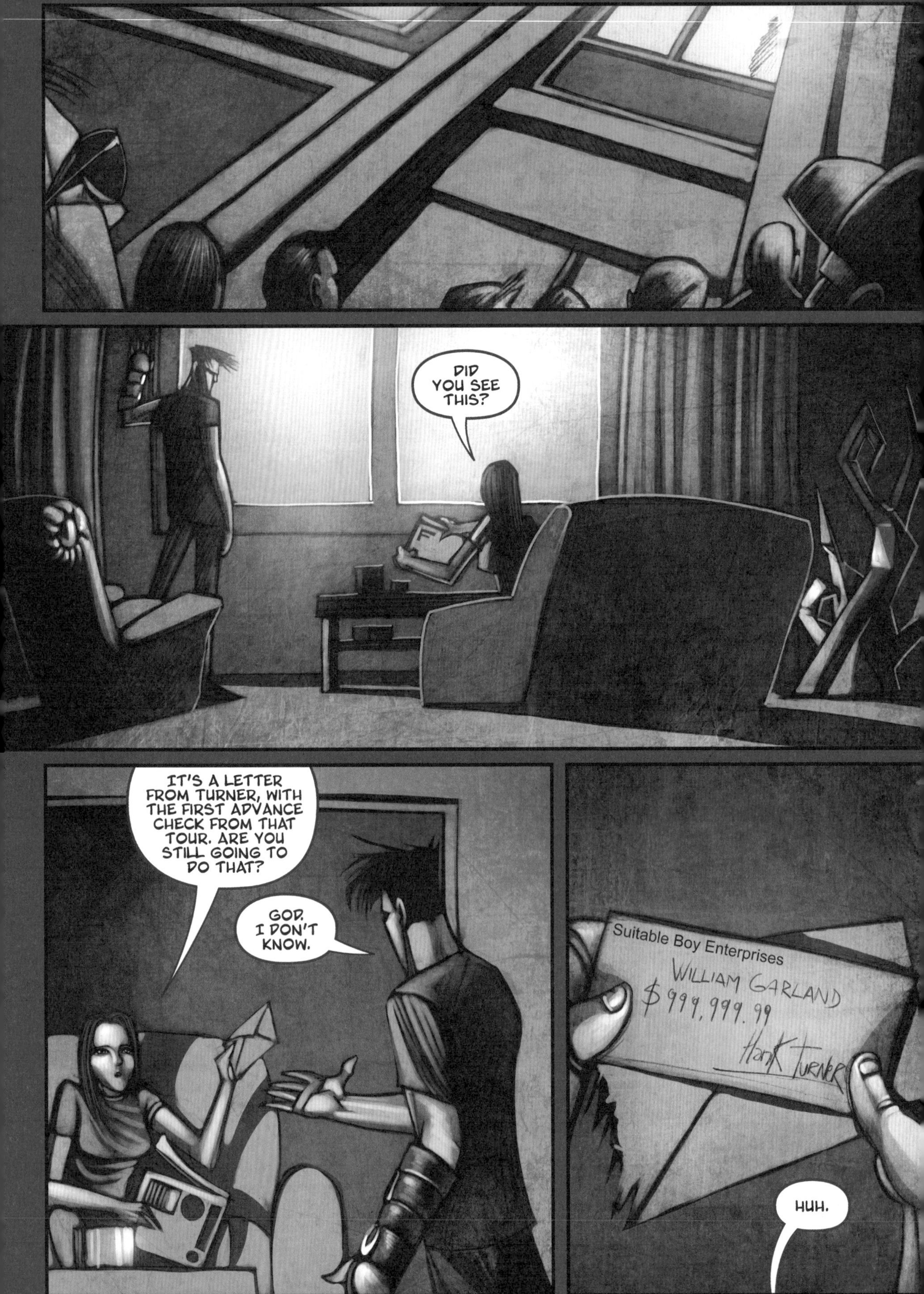
DID YOU SEE THIS?
IT'S A LETTER FROM TURNER, WITH THE FIRST ADVANCE CHECK FROM THAT TOUR. ARE YOU STILL GOING TO DO THAT?
GOD. I DON'T KNOW.
Suitable Boy Enterprises
WILLIAM GARLAND
$999,999.99
Hank Turner
HUH.

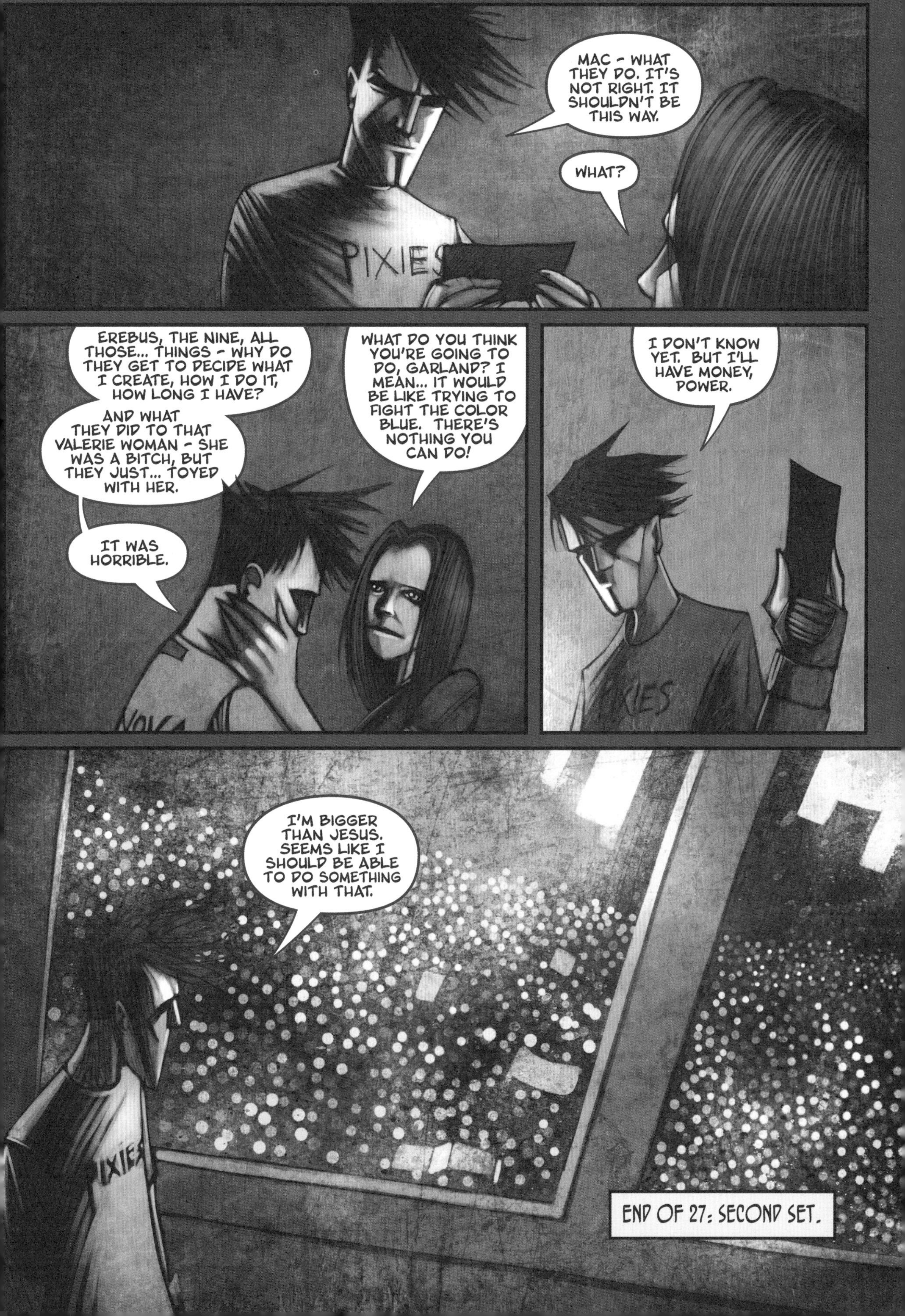
MAC - WHAT THEY DO. IT'S NOT RIGHT. IT SHOULDN'T BE THIS WAY.
WHAT?
PIXIES
EREBUS, THE NINE, ALL THOSE... THINGS - WHY DO THEY GET TO DECIDE WHAT I CREATE, HOW I DO IT, HOW LONG I HAVE?
AND WHAT THEY DID TO THAT VALERIE WOMAN - SHE WAS A BITCH, BUT THEY JUST... TOYED WITH HER.
IT WAS HORRIBLE.
WHAT DO YOU THINK YOU'RE GOING TO DO, GARLAND? I MEAN... IT WOULD BE LIKE TRYING TO FIGHT THE COLOR BLUE. THERE'S NOTHING YOU CAN DO!
I DON'T KNOW YET. BUT I'LL HAVE MONEY, POWER.
I'M BIGGER THAN JESUS. SEEMS LIKE I SHOULD BE ABLE TO DO SOMETHING WITH THAT.
END OF 27: SECOND SET.

extras

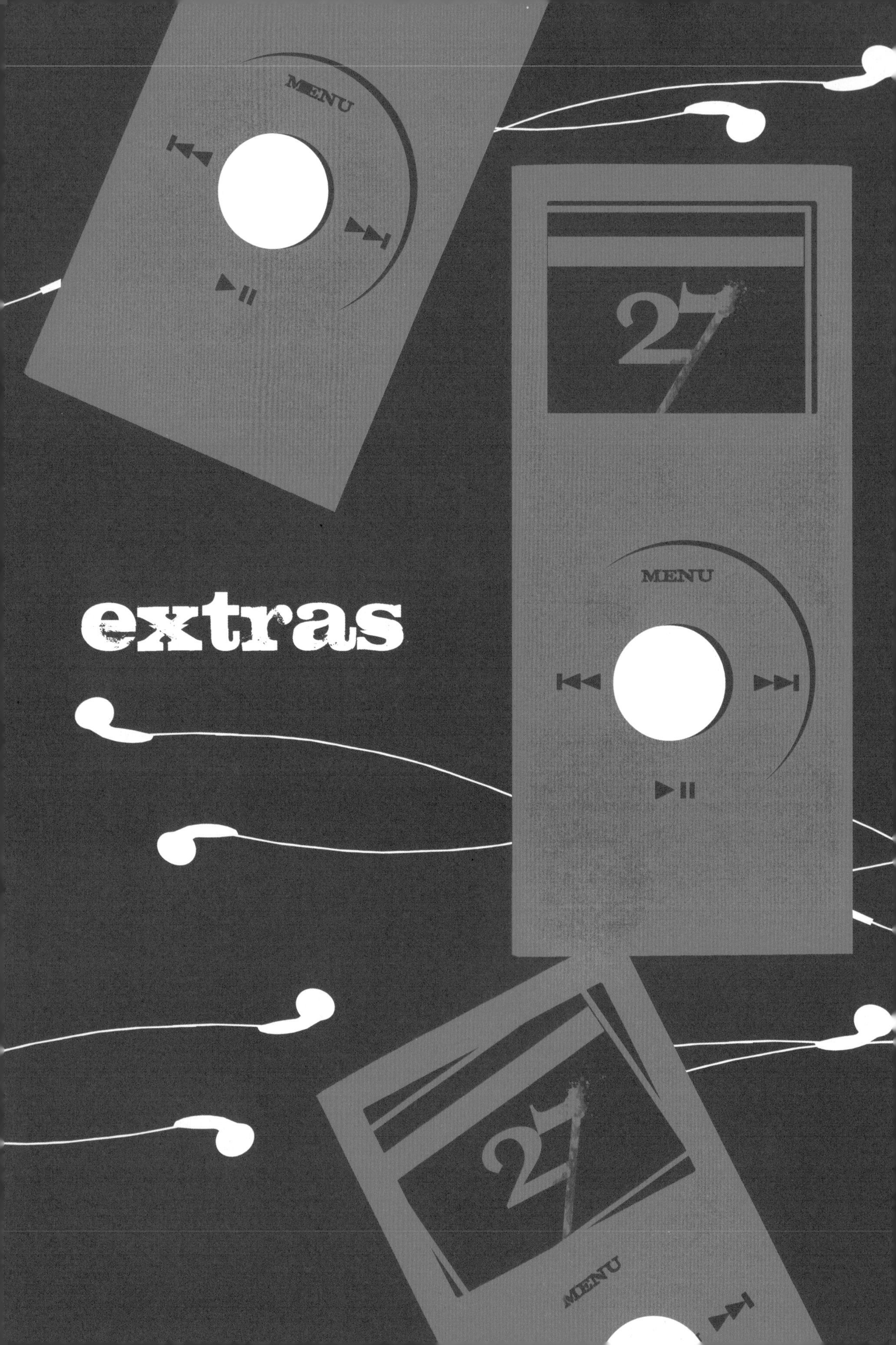
MENU
27
MENU
27
MENU

pin-up// renzo podesta

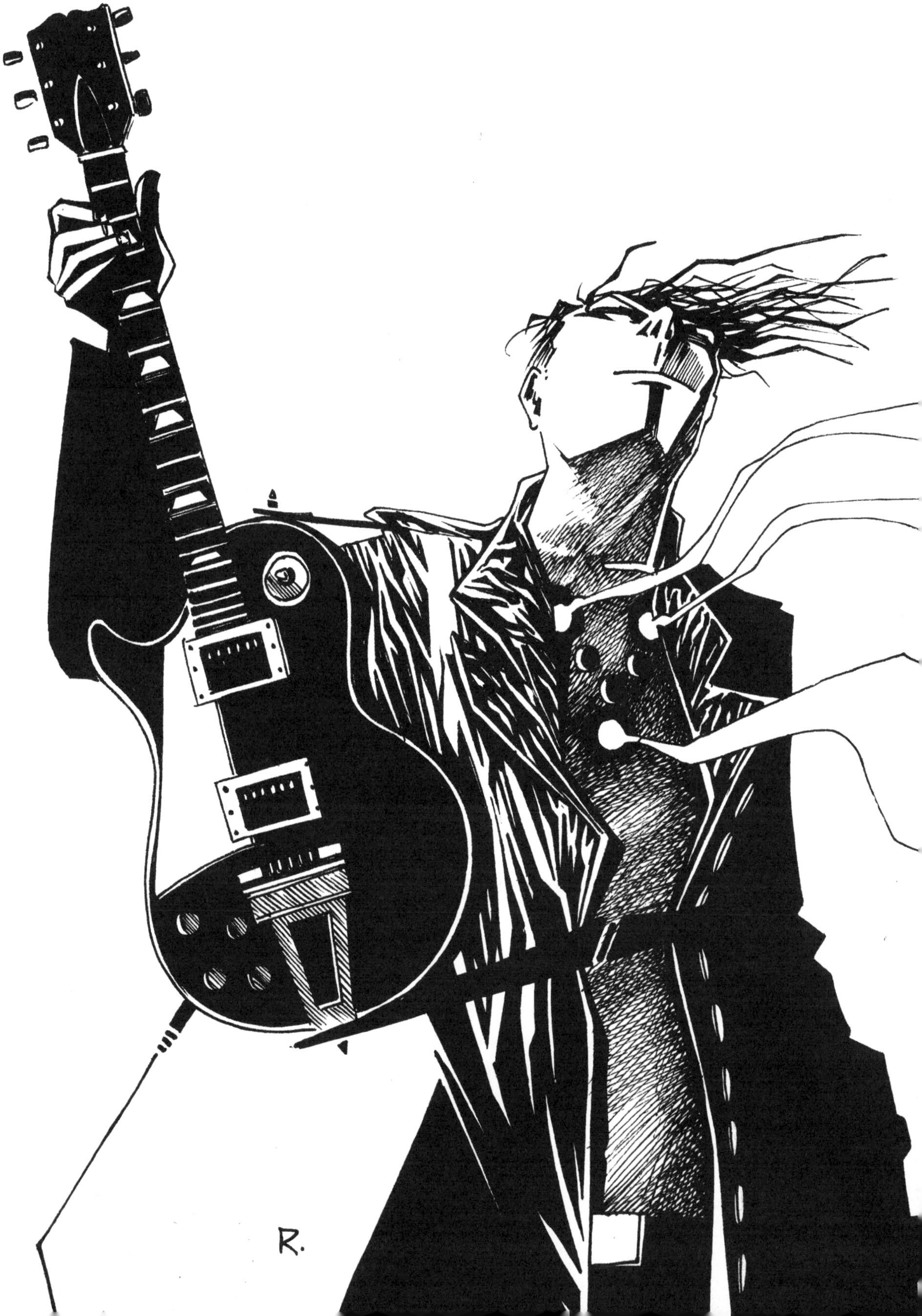
R.

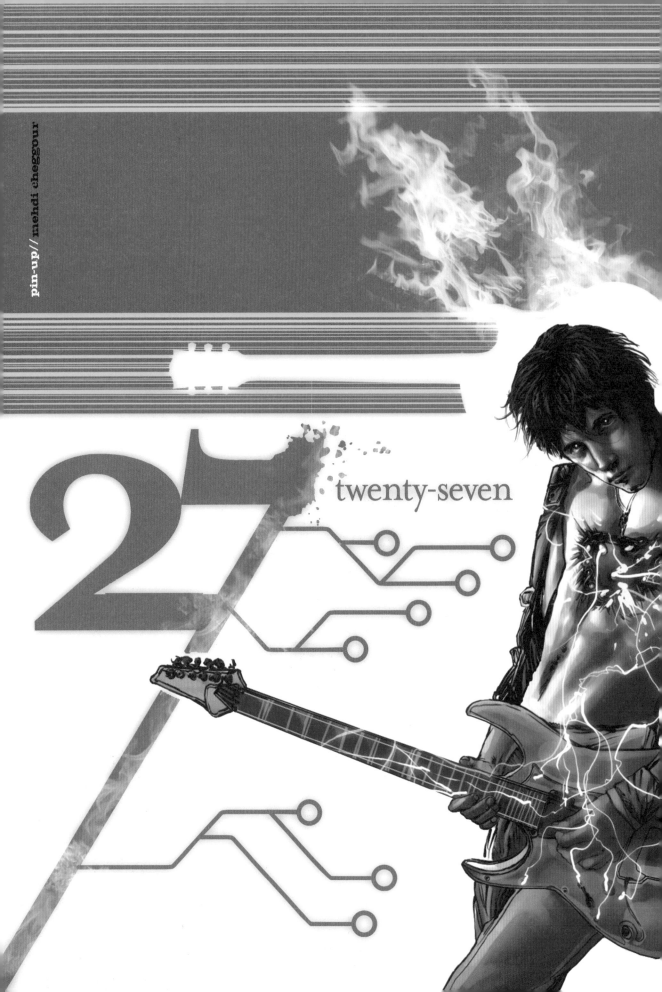

pin-up// mehdi cheggour

27
twenty-seven

1. Issue 1 included two references to Amy Winehouse, who passed away tragically at age 27 shortly before the issue went to press. One can be seen in the form of a Winehouse tribute album referenced on the "After the Nine" album review page, and the other is hidden in the dialogue. We decided that we wanted to acknowledge what had happened in some fashion, but it had to be subtle.

2. The first panel of Issue 1 is designed to mirror the first panel of Issue 1 of First Set.

3. The Sting, the club seen in Issue 1, is the same club Garland visits in First Set, where his band The Fizz originally got it's start. If you look closely, you can see the red velvet rope marking off Garland's favorite barstool, which is left that way permanently in case he decides to swing by on any given night.

4. The "KingLight" theater in Issue 1 is based on the old Palace theater in Los Angeles.

5. The original cover for Issue 2 was planned to reference Chumbawumba's Tubthumper record, but the draft cover was too terrifying, and was swapped out in favor of the gorgeous Buggles homage we actually used. I think we're all better off.

6. Many albums were considered for the Second Set homage covers. Just a few: the Divynlys, Right Said Fred, Sugarhill Gang, Devo, Deee-lite, Dexy's Midnight Runners and many more. Most were rejected because while the songs were instantly recognizable, the album covers were not. The Divynyls were negged because doing that cover properly would get us too much heat from Tipper Gore and the PMRC.

7. Issue 3 includes a meeting between Valerie Hayes and a bunch of one-hit wonders that she subsequently poisons. In tribute to their sacrifice at the altar of fame, here are the names of the real artists who inspired Valerie's guests: Taylor Hicks, Lisa Loeb, Gerardo, the Proclaimers and the Macarena guys (Los Del Rio). Raise a glass in their memory, won't you?

8. The God of Fame has one blue eye and one green eye, a la David Bowie (who might actually be the God of Fame).

9. The name of Hank Turner's production company (seen on the $999,999.99 check at the end of Issue 4) is Suitable Boy Enterprises. The Suitable Boys were yet another of Charles' college bands (he had more than a few).

27 second set

10. The actual 1973 Grammy for Best Spoken Word Performance, as purchased by Valerie Hayes in Issue 3, was won by Bruce Botnick, the producer of Lenny on Broadway. So there's that.

11. Comic book covers need to be complete much earlier than the pages, for solicitation purposes. So, Scott Forbes needed to prepare the cover for Issue 4 before Renzo had designed the God of Fame. We asked Renzo to do a quick sketch. The script called for a slim, ivory-skinned man in a gold suit and tie, elegant and imposing. Renzo came back with this (right). Unexpected, but so cool that the script for Issue 4 was revised so Renzo's design could be the "stage outfit" for the God of Fame.

one eye is blue, the other is green (Bowie style!)
blond hair
Painted lips (androgynous look)
Golden plates (think Xerxes!)
golden and glowing tatoos (think Tron!)
EVERYTHING (the whole costume and accesories) is gold!
feathers (NOT wings!)
long nails
the skirt ends on the floor (we never see his feet)
GOD OF FAME

GOD of FAME

12. The http://onehitwonderz.wordpress.com website that provides the writeup on Valerie Hayes you see earlier in the trade is an actual, registered domain, with the post about Valerie there for everyone to see. (Go ahead and check, kids, we'll wait.)

13. Garland primarily plays his cutaway Taylor acoustic in Second Set, except for his appearance on the Damon O'Bairn show in Issue 2. There, he's playing a Les Paul Custom. All guitars are, of course, strung lefty.

14. The comedian Garland meets in the green room in Issue 2 is named TJ, after an actor on an NBC sitcom whose EGOT-winning character is known for appearing in the film "Honky Grandma Be Trippin'".

15. Valerie Hayes learned most of her magical abilities from Screamin' Jay Hawkins.

16. Original plans for Issue 4 would have included a showbill with the following fine print:

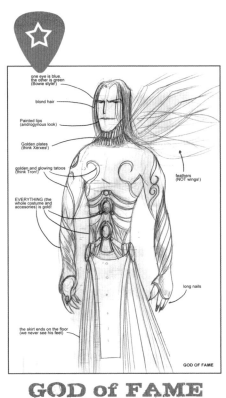

WILLIAM GARLAND AND VALERIE HAYES
TOGETHER FOR THE FIRST TIME, FOR ONE NIGHT ONLY!
THE WANNA-BE AND THE HAS-BEEN IN AN EPIC FIGHT TO THE FINISH!
A night of chills, thrills, spills, pills and skills, arranged exclusively for your entertainment.
Two enter, one leaves, etc. etc.
NO ONE WILL BE ADMITTED ONCE THE SHOW BEGINS.
Please silence your cell phones. No smoking allowed inside the theater.
You attend this performance at your own risk. Management cannot be held responsible for injuries caused in connection with poorly thought-out bargains with pan-dimensional personifications of abstract concepts.
AND HAVE FUN!

17. An epilogue for Second Set was written, but not drawn (yet) featuring the Groupie and Erebus.

18. Kings of Rain, Garland's biggest single with The Fizz, was performed live at the release party for the 27: First Set trade.

19. The last panel of Issue 4 has Garland in exactly the same place as the last panel of Issue 4 of First Set, doing more or less the same thing. Just like a good pop song, 27 keeps cycling back to reprise the cool parts.

20. To celebrate and promote the release of 27: Second Set #1, Charles arranged and recorded solo acoustic versions of nine famous one-hit wonders and posted them online. You can find them at http://www.youtube.com/cdsoule, if you're so inclined.

21. The puzzle placed in the four original issues of First Set was never officially solved prior to the release of its solution in the trade for the first arc.

22. Four different versions of 27-logo guitar picks have been created for the series and handed out at cons and in-store signings. Here's every one we've done so far:

23. Renzo Podesta has yet to meet any of the other members of the 27 team in person.

24. Renzo did all of his incredible work in Issue 4 under an incredibly tight deadline, producing thumbnails, pencils and full-color finals for twenty-three pages in four weeks.

25. Batik, referenced in Issue 3 as Garland is running through the list of useless creative powers the button gives him while he's stuck at the bottom of the cliff, is a type of Indonesian fabric art, reminiscent of tye-dying. It is almost unfortunate that Garland was not in a position to create a few batik masterpieces – that's what people really want to see in today's comics.

26. The total number of pages of artwork produced by the 27 creators to date is two hundred and seven. 207. 2+0+7 = 9.

27. As of this writing, Scott Forbes, cover artist for the entire series, still has not beaten the 27 Club curse. We're pulling for him.

27 After The Nine

Metronome.tv

in tune and on time.

reviews | news | features | nomenculture | downloads | videos

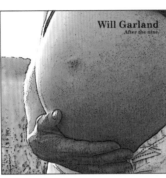

Will Garland
After the nine.

Will Garland
After The Nine

[shadowlinerecords 2011]

2.0

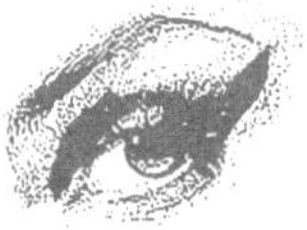

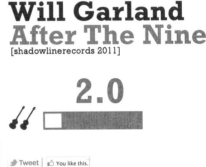

Tweet | You like this.

In The Vein, but not On The Level

It is clear that William Garland has been through a great deal. He disappeared from the scene at a moment when his band, The Fizz, was poised to capitalize on the immense success of their first record and take their place among the greats. He returned a year later with some sort of medical brace on his left hand and a radically different playing style, which is evidenced on his first solo effort, 'After the Nine.' Gone are the fretboard pyrotechnics that brought him fame, replaced by a gentler sound reminiscent of latter-day folk balladeers like Andrew Bird and Bon Iver. Garland's guitar work with The Fizz was clearly influenced by muscular, involved players like Hendrix, Van Halen and Prince, but on 'After the Nine' a new reflectiveness has entered his songwriting style. A verse here, a chorus there, and you might think you're listening to something in the vein of John Prine or even the hard-drinking truths of Tom Waits. Unfortunately, 'in the vein of' does not equate with 'on the level of.'

From a certain perspective, it is admirable to see a musician so true to his artistic compass that he rejected everything that went before to strike out in a new direction. Still, this reviewer is not tasked to evaluate artistic integrity, just whether or not the album is any good. 'After the Nine' has its moments, particularly 'Dark, Faceless Man' and 'Saving the Children,' but in this case, it is impossible to ignore the Garland that came before the cocksure guitar hero. The album is not a success, but it is also not a total failure. The guitar work, while nowhere near as complex as in Garland's previous incarnation, is still appealing, and Garland's singing voice maintains a resonant power on these more subdued numbers that is an unexpected pleasure after the pure rock stylings he used with The Fizz. It is not hard to imagine new fans latching on to Garland's reinvention, but he has certainly set himself on an uphill climb - it is almost as if 'After the Nine' is a calculated effort to alienate almost everyone who enjoyed The Fizz. What happened in the year Garland disappeared from the spotlight? Why the drastic, not entirely successful attempt to reinvent himself? For the moment, the answers remain obscured, leaving us with only the man's work to judge him by.

metronome ipad app

Comments

Bullshit. Bring back The Fizz. - heatseeker081467

Girly crap. - optimusprimus

More going on here than you think. It's a deeper listen than The Fizz ever was. Luv it. - tacotongue

That last comment = also girly crap. - anonymous

See More >

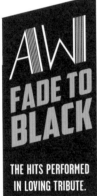

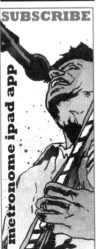

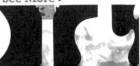

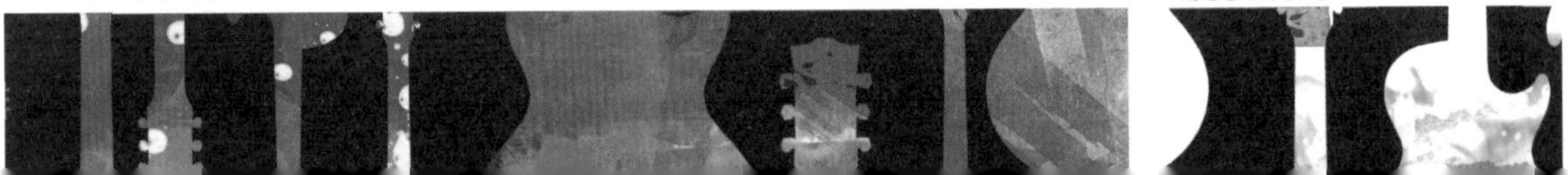

27 Onehitwonderz

http://onehitwonderz.com

onehitwonderz.com --wher..

onehitwonderz

The web's best Where Are They Now blog
for one-hit wonders!

The dark mistress of pop… Valerie Hayes!

Posted on August 23, 2002 by onehitwonderz

I know, I know, I haven't updated in a while. Sue me. To make up for that, I wanted to come back with a writeup on one of my personal favorite flash-in-the-pan artists, the mysterious Valerie Hayes.

Better known by her stage name Hei.se, Valerie Hayes was one of the biggest one-hit wonders of the mid-80s. Her single hit "Drink Me" was a phenomenon in 1986, its dark and gritty tone a stark alternative to the hair metal and electro-pop flooding the charts at the time.

The chorus, with its repeated refrain of 'Drink me, drink me, darling let's get kinky,' comes off as pure pop nonsense at the first listen, but an undeniable poetry eventually emerges in its repetition and variation, 'baby wants her binky' emerging as the shout-along line at live performances.

Somehow, Hayes seems a precursor both to the Nirvana-style alienation of the early 90s and the shock-rock tactics of Marilyn Manson a decade later. She presented herself as a goth bubblegum witch, and hinted at true connections to darker powers. Really, her vampire theatrics and feminist overtones wouldn't be out of place on a concert stage today.

Whether Valerie Hayes was ahead of her time or past it (after all, these sort of tricks go back to Alice Cooper in the 70s and Screamin' Jay Hawkins in the 50s), she did have her moment. Sadly, 'Drink Me' was the sole song Hayes was able to push forward into mainstream acceptance. No other singles from her album *Darkness in the Blood* charted, and her sophomore effort *Pu**y Envy* was deemed un-releasable by her label.

I did my usual thing and tried to follow up with Valerie to let you know what she's up to these days, but I couldn't track her down. Perhaps she worked a magic trick with her dark powers, because she certainly has managed to disappear.

'Drink Me' was all we really got from Ms. Hayes, better known to her public as Hei.se, but perhaps that's for the best. She achieved her own special sort of fame, as part of the potent, sad crew of one-hit wonders scattered throughout rock and pop history. Hell, that's more than most of us get.

Share this: Press This Twitter Facebook

Like this: Like Be the first to like this post.

Leave a comment

Posted in Uncategorized. Bookmark the permalink.

Previous Posts
The Proclaimers - Scottish nerd rock before it was cool.
Rico Suave - the other best oiled-up chest in music.
Right Said Fred - the best oiled-up chests in music.
Aqua - where are you, Barbie girl?
The Divinyls - when I think of you...
Sugar Hill Gang - de-lite-ful!

Search

SEARCH

Links

Discuss
Get Inspired
Get Polling
Get Support

TRIBUTE ALBUM
IN STORES NOW
AW
FADE TO BLACK
THE HITS PERFORMED IN LOVING TRIBUTE.

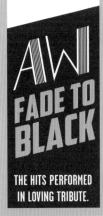

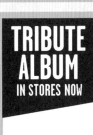

27 The Art of Renzo
second set

Will Garland
& The Chest Plate Designs

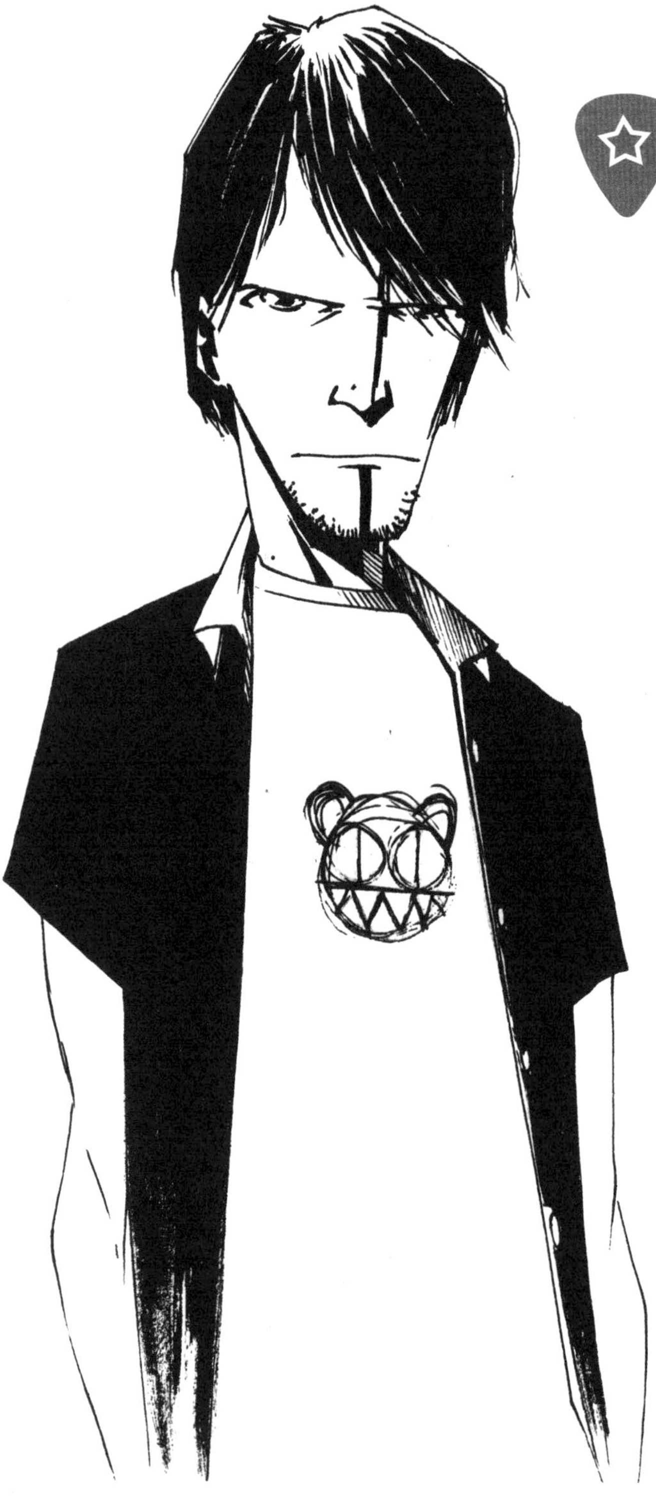

The very first sketch of Will Garland. Drawn around the end of 2008 and based on Radiohead guitarist Johnny Greenwood.

Steampunk radio receptor.

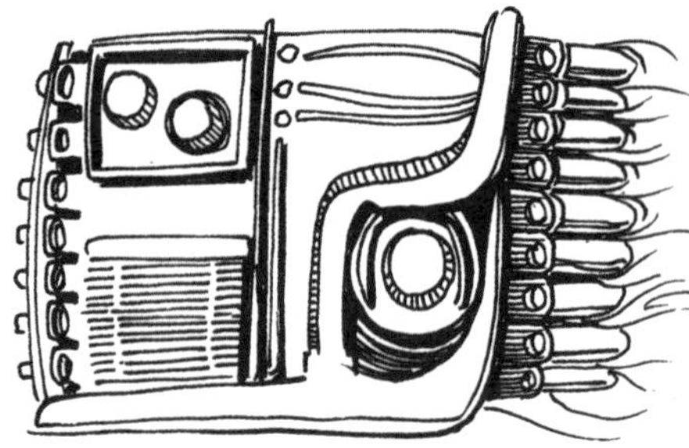

Something more industrial.

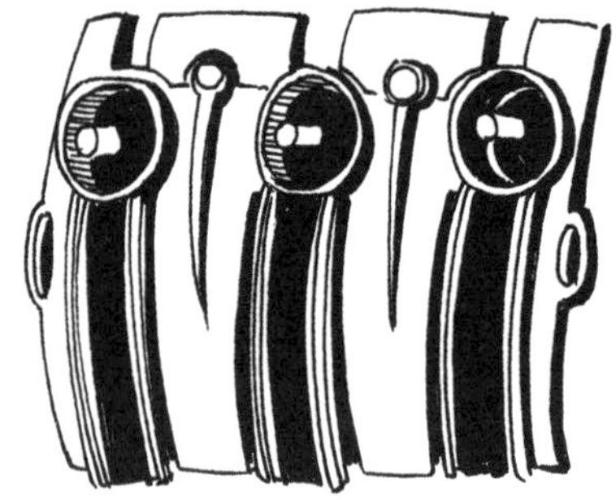

An HR Giger feel.

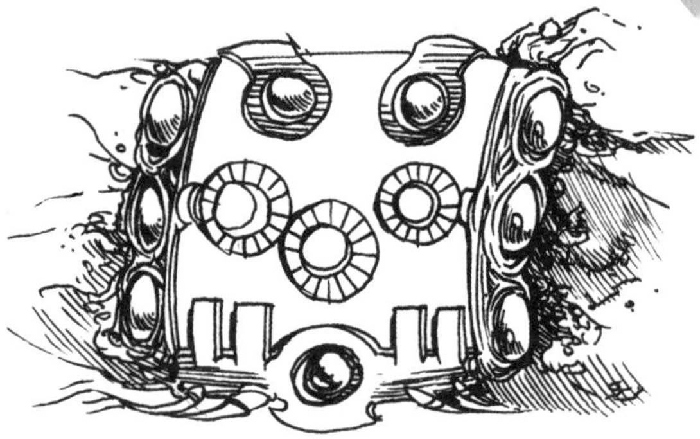

The final concept mixed in guitar amplifier buttons and then Renzo added the 9 green gems.

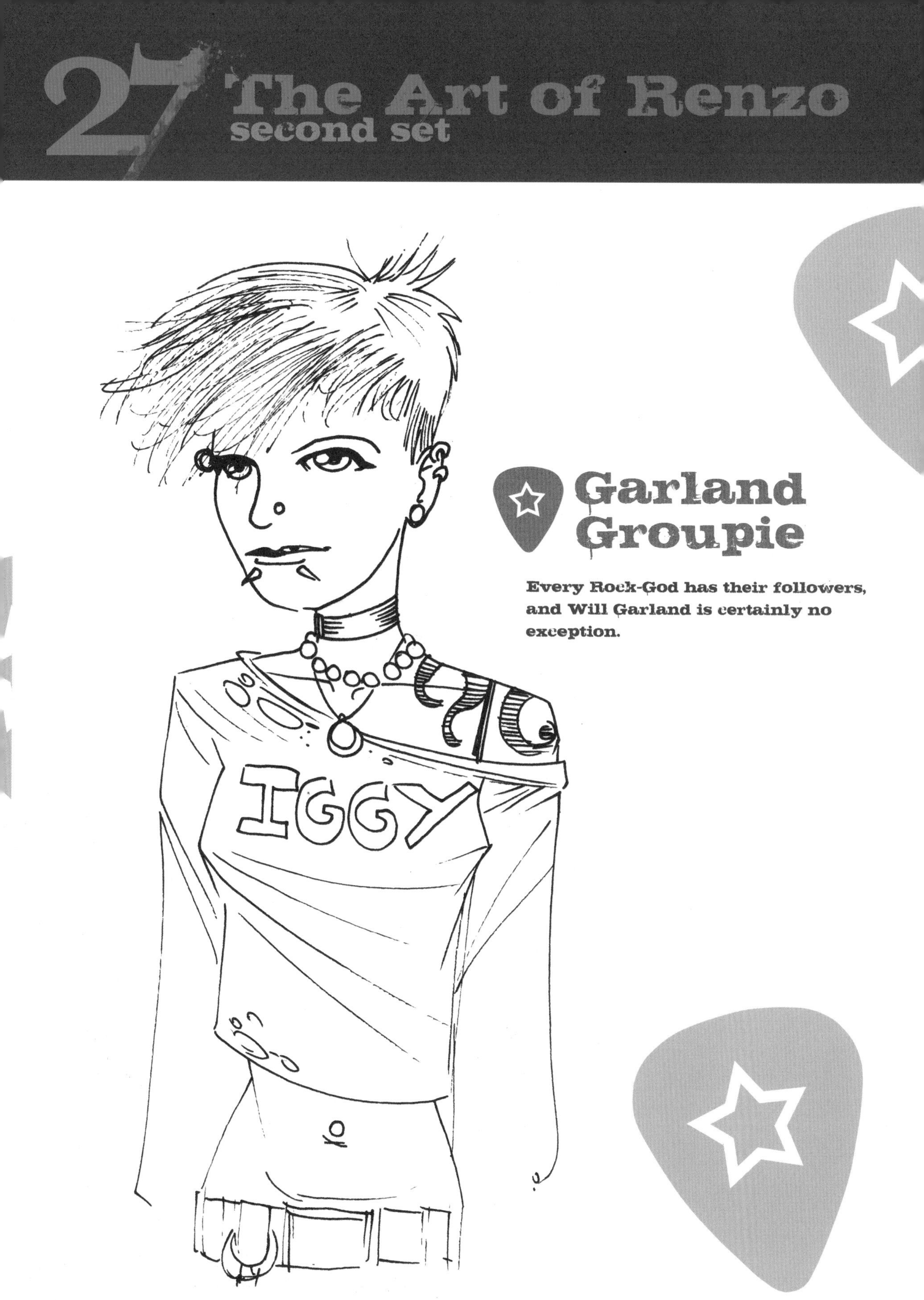
IGGY

Garland Groupie

Every Rock-God has their followers, and Will Garland is certainly no exception.

27 The Art of Renzo
second set

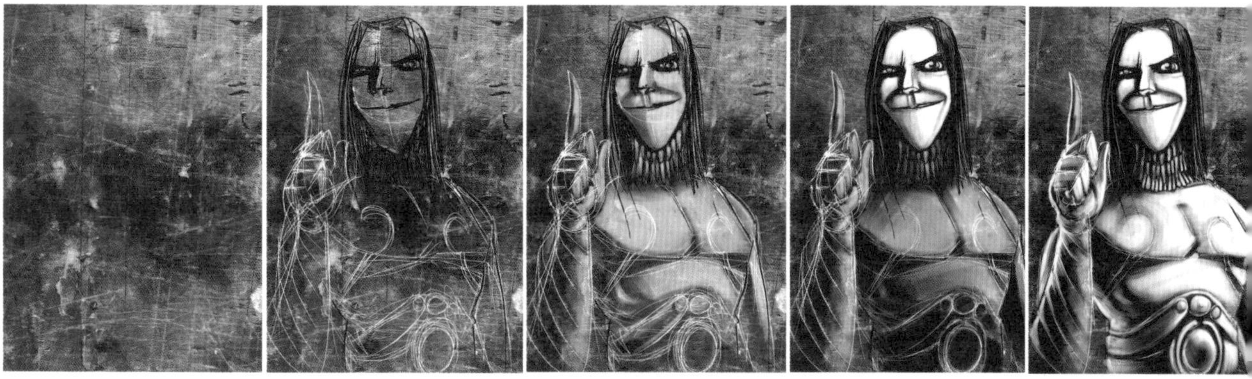

GOD of FAME

A step-by-step walkthrough of a God of Fame's digital pin-up.

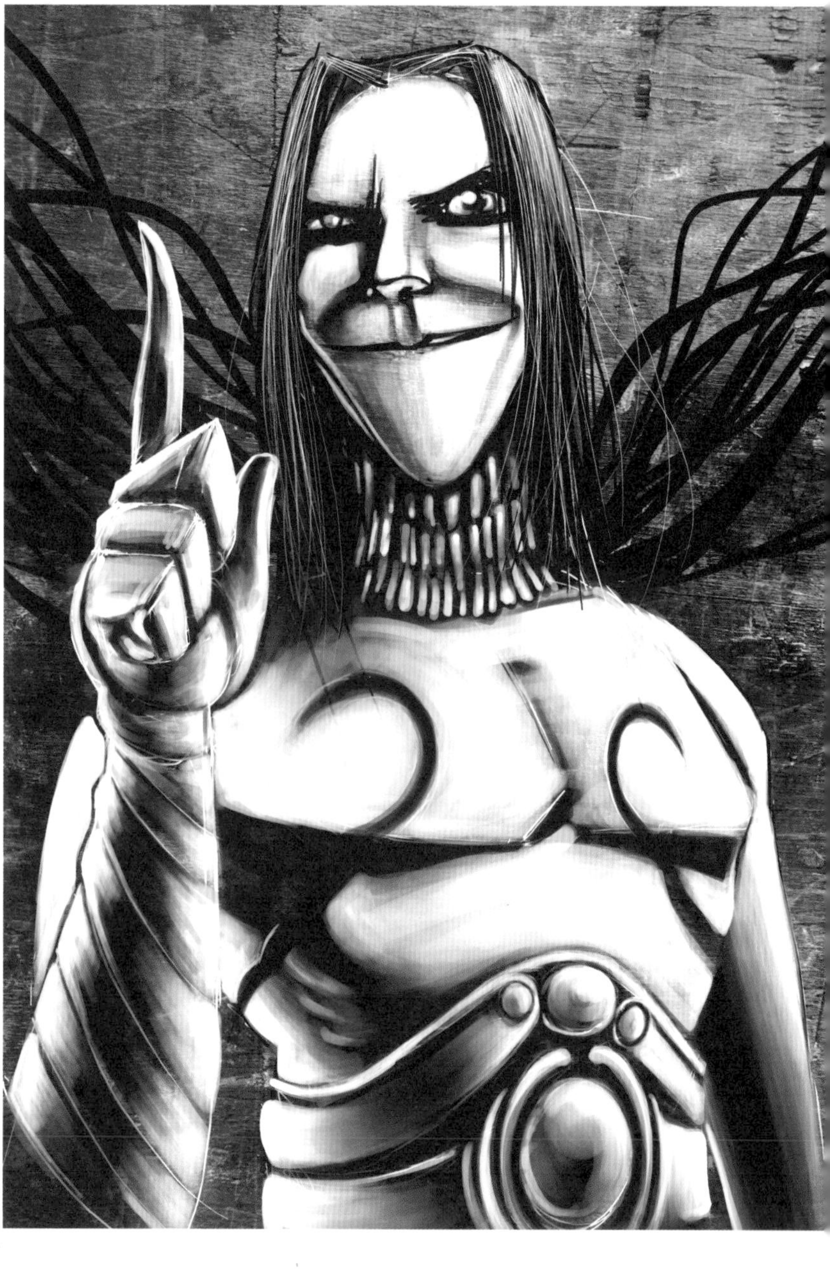

SET BREAK: FIRST, SECOND & BEYOND

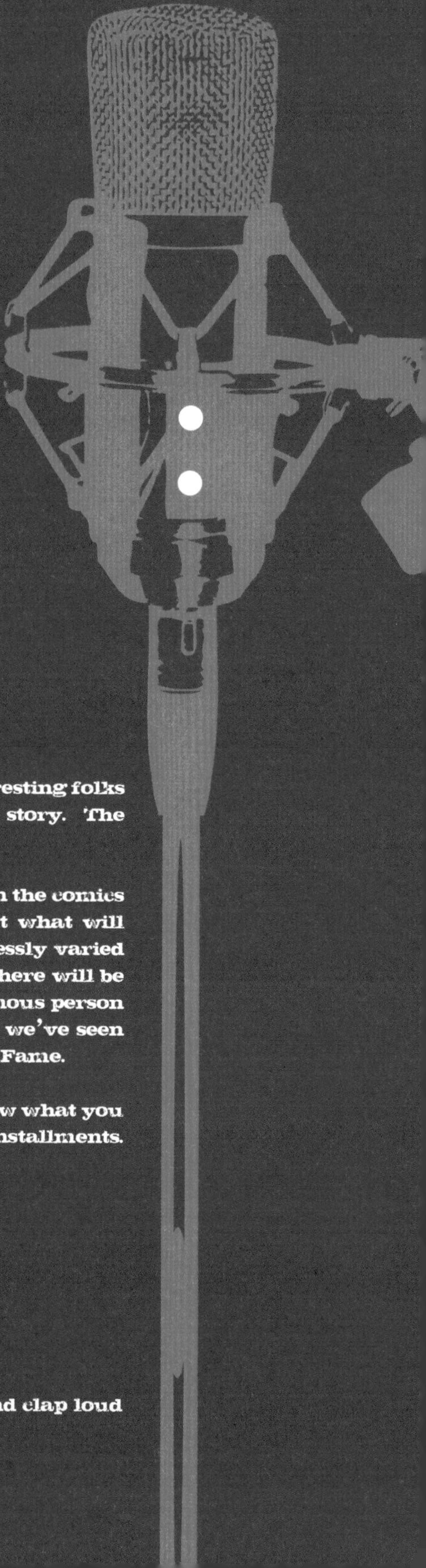

Discussions about Second Set started relatively early into First Set's run, after it was clear that the title had struck a chord (ha!) with readers. While the ending of First Set was fairly conclusive, I had some ideas about where the story might go. I knew from the beginning that I needed to get away from the 27 Club concept, because there were only so many things to be said about that idea, and I felt I'd said most of them in First Set. It wasn't until I hit upon the one-hit wonder idea that everything really began to gel. One-hit wonders are almost as potent a part of rock and roll history as the 27 Club guys. Their individual legacies might not be as important as the big names, but if you look at them as a group, hell, those are some catchy tunes.

Plus, one-hit wonders are tragic! To rise so high and then never be heard from again...there's drama in that arc, and it led naturally to the idea of using a one-hit wonder as the villain of the story. Valerie Hayes is pretty unsympathetic, but you can understand why she makes most of the choices she does.

So, I had my villain, but from there it became about figuring out the next leg of Garland's story. I decided that if 27: First Set was all about creativity, then Second Set would be about fame – what people do to get it, what they do to keep it, and how far they'll go to get it back if they lose it. Garland makes a huge stand at the end of First Set where he flatly states that creativity for its own sake is all you need. Garland, however, is a pretty flawed human being, and he doesn't always learn his lessons as well as he thinks he does. Writing the best songs in the world isn't enough for him if only a hundred people ever hear them.

You know where it goes from there, unless you're one of those interesting folks who reads the materials in the back of a trade before the actual story. The bigger question, perhaps, is where do we go from here?

I'll say this: 27 is being published at a time of incredible transition in the comics industry. It's nearly impossible to make any assumptions about what will happen next. Stories can be told in many different ways for endlessly varied audiences – if you can find them. But, if we play our cards right, there will be more 27 to come. After all, exploring Garland's life as the most famous person in the world seems like it could be plenty interesting. And I doubt we've seen the last of Lucien, the son Valerie Hayes traded away to the God of Fame.

The entire creative team for 27 is on Twitter – find us and let us know what you think of the series so far and what you might want to see in future installments. Here's the list:

Charles Soule (writer): @charlessoule
Renzo Podesta (interior art): @renzopodesta
Scott Forbes (covers): @scottforbes
Shawn DePasquale (letters): @shawnwrites
Shadowline: @shadowlinecomic
Image: @imagecomics

27 is offstage for the moment, but you know how it works: cheer and clap loud enough, and we'll be right back out to finish the show.

Charles Soule
February 2012

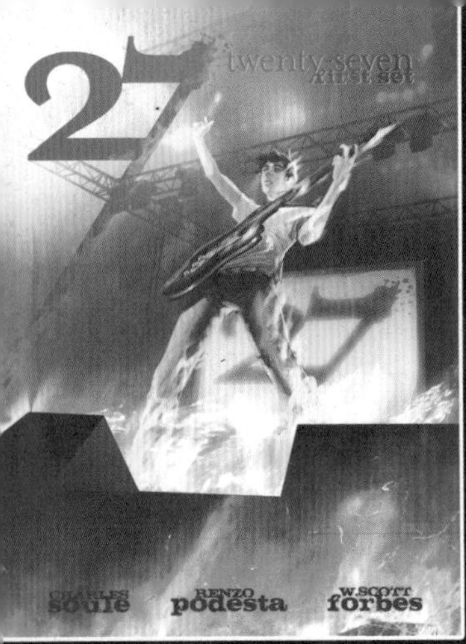
27
twenty-seven
podesta
forbes
SOULE/PODESTA/FORBES

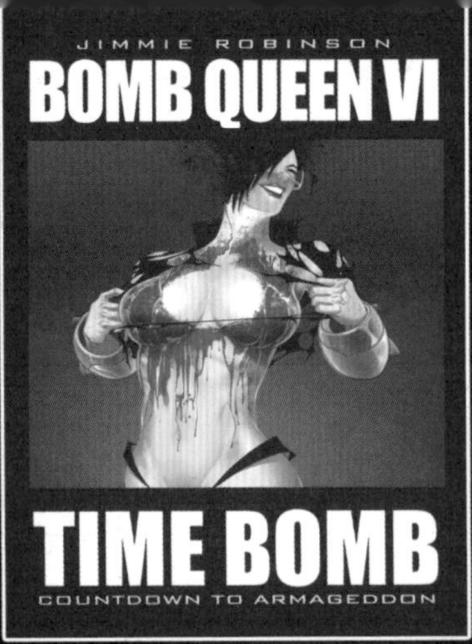
JIMMIE ROBINSON
BOMB QUEEN VI
TIME BOMB
COUNTDOWN TO ARMAGEDDON
JIMMIE ROBINSON

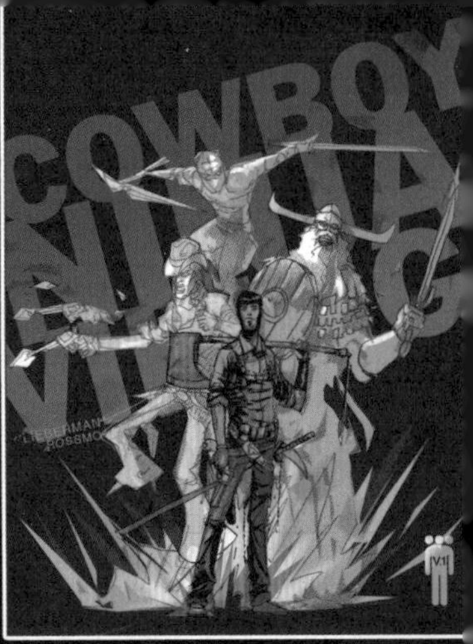
COWBOY
LIEBERMAN/ROSSMO

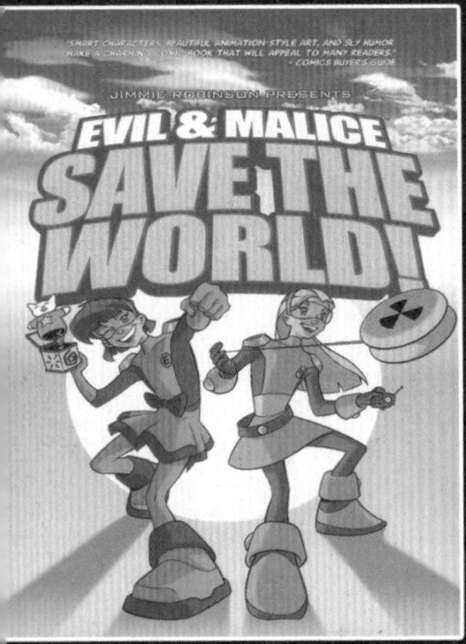
JIMMIE ROBINSON PRESENTS
EVIL & MALICE
SAVE THE WORLD!
JIMMIE ROBINSON

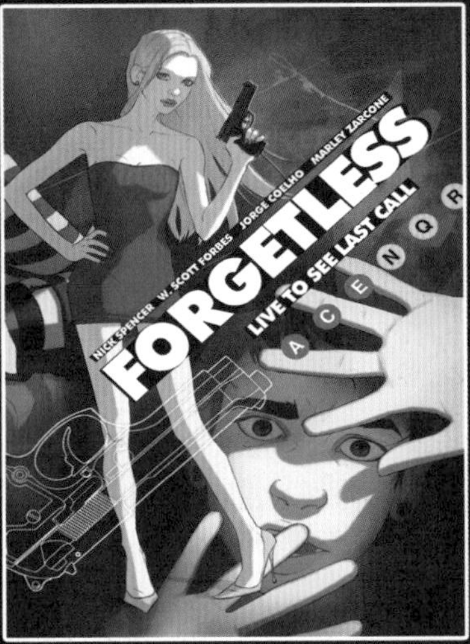
NICK SPENCER W. SCOTT FORBES JORGE COELHO MARLEY ZARCONE
FORGETLESS
LIVE TO SEE LAST CALL
SPENCER/FORBES/ COELHO

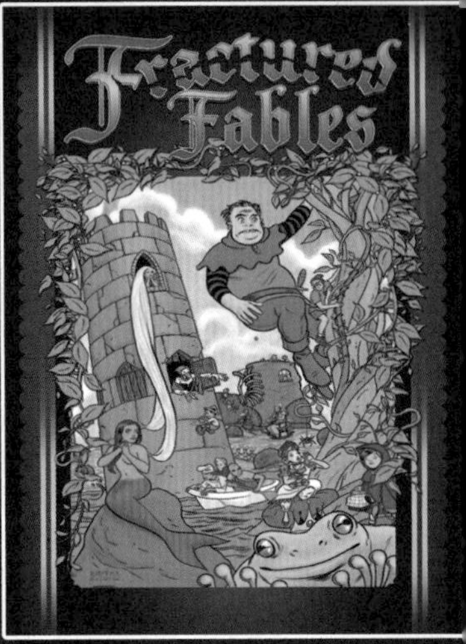
Fractured Fables
VARIOUS ARTISTS

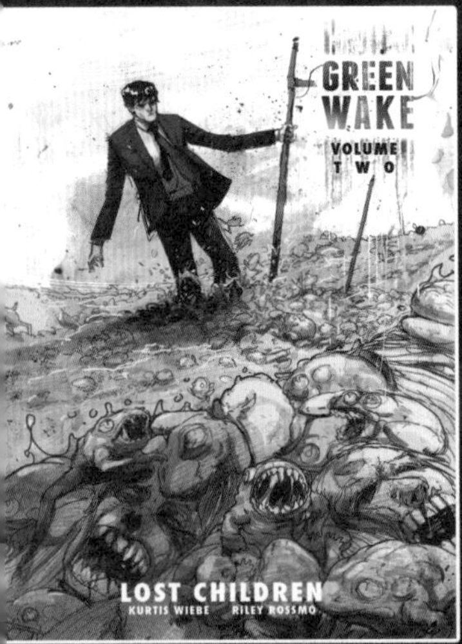
GREEN WAKE
VOLUME TWO
LOST CHILDREN
KURTIS WIEBE RILEY ROSSMO
WIEBE/ROSSMO

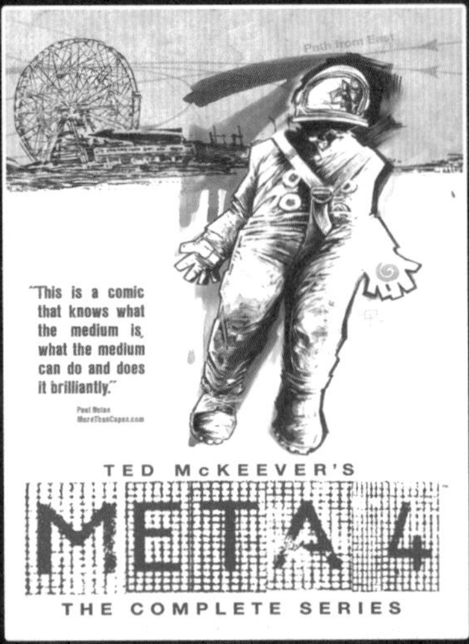
"This is a comic that knows what the medium is, what the medium can do and does it brilliantly."
TED McKEEVER'S
META 4
THE COMPLETE SERIES
TED McKEEVER

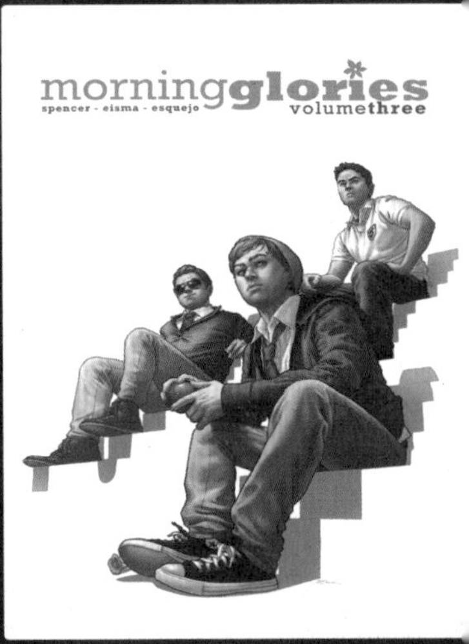
morningglories
spencer - eisma - esquejo
volumethree
SPENCER/EISMA/ESQUEJO

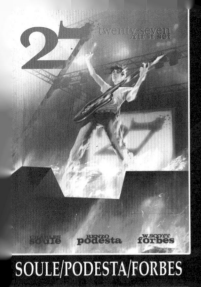